# THE BIBLE AND THE UNIVERSITY

## SOCIETY OF BIBLICAL LITERATURE
## BIBLICAL SCHOLARSHIP IN NORTH AMERICA

Kent Harold Richards, Editor

# The Bible and the University

## The Messianic Vision of
## William Rainey Harper

*by*

JAMES P. WIND

Scholars Press
Atlanta, Georgia

LD
925
1891
·W56
1987

# SOCIETY OF BIBLICAL LITERATURE
# CENTENNIAL PUBLICATIONS

## Editorial Board

The Society of Biblical Literature gratefully acknowledges a grant from the National Endowment for the Humanities to underwrite certain editorial and research expenses of the Centennial Publications Series. Published results and interpretations do not necessarily represent the view of the Endowment.

**Library of Congress Cataloging in Publication Data**

Wind, James P., 1948
  The Bible and the university

  (Biblical scholarship in North America / Society of Biblical Literature ; no. 16)
  Revision of thesis (Ph. D.)—University of Chicago, 1983.
    Bibliography: p.   1856
    1. Harper, William Rainey, 1956-1906.  2. College presidents—Illinois—Biography. 3. Church and college—United States. I. Title. II. Series: Biblical scholarship in North America ; no. 16.
  LD925 1891.W56 1986  378'.111 [B]    87-9485
  ISBN 1-55540-129-5 (alk. paper)
  ISBN 1-55540-130-9 (pbk. : alk. paper)

To Kathleen,
spouse and partner

# ACKNOWLEDGEMENTS

My family, friends and teachers have made more contributions to the scholarship behind this volume than I can ever properly acknowledge. As professor, friend, and dissertation advisor, Martin E. Marty has been both a master teacher of the history of Christianity and a winsome exemplar of the art of telling a story well. My interest in the modern American part of the religious story is only one of many debts I owe him.

Jerald C. Brauer and Neil Harris strengthened the earlier dissertation version of this manuscript by pressing critical and often unexpected questions. I hope that advisor and readers can recognize their contributions in the pages that follow. Robert W. Lynn of the Lilly Endowment, Inc., is the person who first suggested that I "look at Harper." I am grateful for his early advice and subsequent interest.

Ralph W. Loew of the Chautauqua Institution provided entry to Chautauqua's Archives and a comfortable week's lodging at its Hall of Missions. The cordial staff of the Special Collections Department of Joseph Regenstein Library of The University of Chicago carted numerous boxes of papers and pointed out additional sources of information. Linda-Marie Delloff of *The Christian Century* made many helpful editorial suggestions, as did Harry M. Orlinsky of Hebrew Union College. Kent Harold Richards of the Society of Biblical Literature has been a kind and supportive series editor. Toby Resnick and Kathleen Cahalan proved to be exceptional typists in the face of pressing deadlines and heavily edited copy. Finally, I must thank my wife, Kathleen, who has lived with this book and its author as spouse, critic, and encourager. In many ways it is her accomplishment, too. The best way to express my gratitude to each of these people is to bring the project to completion so that others may benefit from their contributions.

# TABLE OF CONTENTS

# INTRODUCTION

The visitor to the Cathedral Church of Saint Peter and Saint Paul in Washington, D.C., cannot wander in the church's nave for long without discovering in one of its south bays the crypt of Woodrow Wilson, twenty-seventh president of the United States, formerly professor and president of Princeton University. The carved stone and its impressive location in the midst of stained glass and soaring arches testify that President Wilson has not been forgotten. As generations of pilgrims take their turns around the sanctuary, they are reminded that this individual was unusual, that what he did and did not do earned him a place in the collective consciousness of a nation.

The same visitor could roam the interior of Rockefeller Chapel at the University of Chicago and never know that within its walls rest the remains of another of America's most significant university presidents, a man who, according to some, might have become the nation's president.[1] If, by accident, the tourist wandered behind the elaborate wood and stone reredos of the Chapel chancel and followed the perambulatory, she would find a solitary spotlight illuminating a section of bare cinder block wall. Above the folding chairs the explorer's eye might linger over several metal plates and words carved into stone: "HIC IACET PRAESIDUM SUORUMQUE CINERES." The ashes of four university presidents and their wives are interred in this obscure resting place. Ten feet up the wall, set off by a stone border and given a little more prominence than the others, is a plaque inscribed in memory of William Rainey Harper, the university's first president.

The prominent spot in the obscure location is illustrative of the "prominent obscurity" which surrounds the name of William Rainey Harper. Important enough to have streets, libraries, high schools and junior colleges bear his name, Harper nonetheless remains hidden in the back corridors of American intellectual, religious and institutional history. The source of

---

[1] The Reverend Philip A. Nordell, Pastor of First Baptist Church, New London, Connecticut, attempted to dissuade Harper from accepting the presidency of the University of Chicago in an April 28, 1888 personal letter. One of his arguments was, "I would not be surprised to hear you mentioned as a candidate for the Presidency of the United States this fall." The letter is a part of the Joseph L. Regenstein Library Collection of the Personal Papers of William Rainey Harper (hereafter Personal Papers), Box I, Folder 5.

much amusing lore, invoked whenever his university wants to touch its roots, Chicago's first president remains a hazy eminence within the quadrangles of the institution he designed and built.

During the years of his presidency, William Rainey Harper was a figure of national, even international, importance. Conductors stopped trains for him; newspapers reported his speeches, and, near the end of his life, carried bulletins about his health. His advice was sought by numerous university and national leaders. Articles under his byline appeared in popular and scholarly publications throughout the land. People wrote to him about their religious problems and filled lecture halls across the country when he came to speak. Colleagues in his Baptist denomination regarded him as their national representative. Scholars in the emerging profession of Old Testament Studies looked to Harper as their dean. At the time of his premature death from cancer in 1906, tributes came from leaders in education, scholars of biblical literature, students, captains of industry such as Andrew Carnegie and John D. Rockefeller, diplomats and national leaders, all of whom viewed Harper as a shining star on the horizon of American intellectual life.

Eighty years after his death, Harper holds no such prominent place. Once a leader of liberal Protestantism, he is barely mentioned in standard histories of American religion.[2] His role as a pioneer of Semitic Studies and professional analysis of the Old Testament remains unappreciated.[3] One of

---

[2] Harper is not mentioned in Paul A. Carter's *The Spiritual Crisis of the Gilded Age* (DeKalb, Ill.: Northern Illinois University Press, 1971), Robert T. Handy's *A Christian America: Protestant Hopes and Historical Realities* (New York: Oxford University Press, 1971), William R. Hutchison's *The Modernist Impulse in American Protestantism* (Cambridge: Harvard University Press, 1976), or Martin E. Marty's *Righteous Empire: The Protestant Experience in America* (New York: The Dial Press, 1970). He receives scant notice in Sydney E. Ahlstrom's *A Religious History of the American People*, 2 vols. (Garden City, N.Y.: Image Books, 1975) and Winthrop S. Hudson's *Religion in America*, 3d ed. (New York: Charles Scribner's Sons, 1981).

[3] This is partly due to the fact that there is no adequate history of American biblical scholarship. Jerry Wayne Brown covers antebellum New England in *The Rise of Biblical Criticism in America, 1800-1870: The New England Scholars* (Middletown, Conn.: Wesleyan University Press, 1969), but the work stands almost alone in an unexplored field. Ira V. Brown assessed the latter part of the century and noted Harper's role as "organizer" of the critical studies movement in "The Higher Criticism Comes to America, 1880–1900," *Journal of the Presbyterian Historical Society* 38 (December 1960):193–212. In "The Watershed of the American Biblical Tradition: The Chicago School, First Phase, 1892–1920" (Journal of Biblical Literature 95 [March 1976]), Robert Funk suggested that Harper founded one of "two dynasties" of biblical scholarship at his university. Funk believed that Harper's colleague, Ernest DeWitt Burton founded a more dominant tradition which was less "orthodox" than Harper's approach (pp. 4–22). Funk's argument is discussed below, pp. 131ff. More recently Thomas H. Olbricht, Charles R. Kniker, and Grant Wacker advanced the study of late nineteenth century biblical criticism in individual essays on the subject. Olbricht's "Intellectual Ferment and Instruction in the Scripture: The Bible in Higher Education" and Kniker's "New Attitudes and New Curricula: The Changing Role of the Bible in Protestant Education, 1880–1920," both appear in *The Bible*

a generation of great university presidents, Harper has received only slight attention from historians of higher education in America.[4]

A few attempts have been made to keep Harper visible on the modern horizon. Harper's friend and long-time colleague, Thomas Wakefield Goodspeed, authored an admiring biography twenty years after the president's death.[5] The only other attempt at anything more than the briefest of biographical sketches was Milton Mayer's *Young Man in a Hurry*, written in 1957.[6] Both works succumb to the mystique which surrounds Harper's amazing energy and talent and do little to assess the lasting significance of their focal figure.

Several monographs concentrate on specific facets of Harper's work, but no attempt has been made to grasp his fundamental ideas or vision. Gale W. Engle, for example, analyzed Harper's academic design from a structural functional perspective, but paid no attention to the religious underpinnings of the plan.[7] Kenneth Nathaniel Beck explored the history of the American Institute of Sacred Literature, a favored Harper enterprise, but restricted his attention to one part of the Harper picture.[8] Lars Hoffman gave special

---

in *American Education: From Source Book to Textbook* (Philadelphia: Fortress Press, 1982), ed. David L. Barr and Nicholas Piediscalzi. Wacker's "The Demise of Biblical Civilization" appears in Nathan O. Hatch and Mark A. Noll, eds., *The Bible in America: Essays in Cultural History* (New York: Oxford University Press, 1982). A synthetic work which can integrate the subplots of the complicated biblical critical story in America is still needed.

[4] An exception is Laurence R. Veysey, who treats Harper as exemplar of "the tendency to blend and reconcile" in later nineteenth century America. Because he views Harper as representative of the second generation of American university presidents who are important for their administrative innovations and not for their larger visions, he overlooks much of Harper's significance. Veysey is representative of a pervasive tendency to see religion primarily as a negative element in the university story. Because of that perspective, the religious character of Harper's effort remains unnoticed. *The Emergence of the American University* (Chicago: University of Chicago Press, 1962), pp. 360–80, viii, 21–56. President Harper is cited only in passing in other standard histories. For example, see Frederick Rudolph, *The American College and University* (New York: Vintage Books, 1962), pp. 349–52. Harper is named only twice in Burton J. Bledstein, *The Culture of Professionalism: The Middle Class and the Development of Higher Education in America* (New York: W.W. Norton & Company, Inc., 1976) and Christopher Jencks and David Reisman, *The Academic Revolution* (Chicago: University of Chicago Press, 1968). Merle Curti does not mention him in *The Social Ideas of American Educators* (Totowa, N.J.: Littlefield, Adams Co., 1978).

[5] Thomas Wakefield Goodspeed, *William Rainey Harper: First President of the University of Chicago* (Chicago: University of Chicago Press, 1928).

[6] Milton Mayer, *Young Man in a Hurry: The Story of William Rainey Harper, First President of the University of Chicago* (Chicago: University of Chicago, Alumni Association, 1957).

[7] Gale W. Engle, "William Rainey Harper's Conceptions of the Structuring of the Functions Performed by Educational Institutions" (Ph.D. dissertation, Stanford University, 1954).

[8] Kenneth Nathaniel Beck, "The American Institute of Sacred Literature: A Historical

attention to the relationship between Harper and his Baptist colleagues, highlighting political constraints which the denomination placed upon the president.[9] Harper's view of science was the subject of a dissertation by Lincoln C. Blake.[10] The story of Harper's greatest creation, the University of Chicago, has emerged in an admiring history by Goodspeed and a more recent and critical work by Richard J. Storr.[11] Each of these scholars examined a facet of Harper's legacy; none made a coherent whole out of his story.

William Rainey Harper will not receive his appropriate place in American religious and intellectual history until the integrating vision that supported his varied activities and enterprises is discovered and evaluated. Interrupted by death in mid-career, Harper failed to leave a cohesive statement of his vision. To find it, we will examine his career in a manner which Harper would have approved. By gathering the facts of his life and work and searching the data for fundamental ideas, we can inductively discover the overarching canopy—a sacred one—which integrated fragments of the person and his work.

In the Hebrew Scriptures Harper found the raw material that provided the ground of his personal beliefs, the field of his professional competence and the paradigm for reshaping education in America. Within those cherished texts, Harper discerned a God at work in history lifting humanity toward a still to be realized "higher life."[12] The most fundamental idea of all for him was that God moves some to suffer vicariously for others.[13] Israel suffered for the scattered nations; Jesus suffered for a fallen humanity; the biblical scholar struggled to provide new meaning for suffering moderns; and the university, in its grappling with the great problems of the ages, was called to suffer for society in order that all its members might ascend to higher life. Ultimately Harper's vision was messianic. He traced the messianic idea from its prophetic origins up to its application in his day; indeed he

---

Analysis of An Adult Education Institution" (Ph.D. dissertation, University of Chicago, 1968).

[9] Lars Hoffman, "William Rainey Harper and the Chicago Fellowship" (Ph.D. dissertation, University of Iowa, 1978).

[10] Lincoln C. Blake, "The Concept and Development of Science at The University of Chicago 1890–1905" (Ph.D. dissertation, University of Chicago, 1966).

[11] Thomas Wakefield Goodspeed, *A History of The University of Chicago: The First Quarter Century* (Chicago: University of Chicago Press, 1972), and Richard J. Storr, *Harper's University: The Beginnings* (Chicago: University of Chicago Press, 1966).

[12] The "higher life" lured Harper. He, in turn, frequently dangled that notion before his contemporaries. See, for example, his collected essays in *Religion and the Higher Life* (Chicago: University of Chicago Press, 1904).

[13] William Rainey Harper, "The Prophetic Element in the Old Testament as Related to Christianity," manuscript of unpublished lectures (Personal Papers, Box 16, Folder 9), pp. 48–50.

could claim without batting an exegetical eye—that the university was "Messiah."[14]

While he never claimed that role for himself, Harper lived by the messianic vision. He drove himself relentlessly. Often up and at his desk by 4:00 a.m., he extended his working day until 10:30 or 11:00 at night. Vacations were spent running summer schools in Chicago and commuting to New York's Chautauqua, where he directed the most prominent of America's late nineteenth-century ventures into popular education. Personal correspondence reveals that while many thought him a super-human dynamo, the reality was more grim. Continually beset by "La Grippe," Harper would be confined to bed one day only to race through his hectic schedule the next. Even cancer could not break his commitment to push himself to the limits.  On one occasion he mentioned to the president of the Board of Trustees of the University of Chicago that he had suffered for twenty years before his doctor discovered his malady.[15] After the "sentence of execution" had been spoken in 1905,[16] Harper went back to work completing a commentary on Amos and Hosea for the International Critical Commentary Series while administering the university. Still corresponding in the last week of his life, Harper planned his funeral service down to such details as cots for the honor guard who would keep the night watch over his casket.[17]

This fundamental vision of divinely led vicarious suffering integrated all of Harper's activities. He shuttled between Chautauqua and the University of Chicago because he perceived the popular work of the one to be in a vital  world-transforming relationship with the research of the other. It made sense to him to run the University of Chicago out of one room in Haskell Hall on the campus and to administer the American Institute of Sacred Literature out of the office next door. During the week President Harper taught Hebrew in the university's Semitics Department; on Sundays he supervised the Sunday School of Hyde Park Baptist Church. He planned the Yerkes Observatory, figured out during office hours how to fund it, and then retired to his study at night to edit articles for the *Biblical World*. All of these efforts, though taking their toll on him, he understood as for the nation's sake.

More than simply deciding to found and edit publications dealing with biblical subjects, Harper discovered and lived in a biblical world. By means of inductive and scientific study of the Scriptures, he found a way to reappropriate their message for his age. His lifework, although conducted in

---

[14] William Rainey Harper, "The University and Democracy," *The Trend in Higher Education in America* (Chicago: University of Chicago Press, 1905), p. 12.

[15] William Rainey Harper to Martin A. Ryerson, March 26, 1904, Personal Papers, Box 16, Folder 13.

[16] The phrase is contained in a letter from Harper to Mrs. J.C. Johnson, February 17, 1905, Personal Papers, Box 1, Folder 20.

[17] "Arrangements for the Funeral of President Harper," p. 7, Personal Papers, Box 16, Folder 13.

many different arenas and enterprises, was devoted to offering a vision for America that was fundamentally biblical, without being archaic. At the beginning of his career he announced the creation of a Hebrew "movement," an attempt to revitalize Old Testament studies.[18] As his horizons expanded beyond teaching Semitics to include administering Chautauqua and creating a new university for what was then the West, Harper never wavered from his first fundamental commitment. The construction of the University of Chicago cannot be understood as an effort in addition to, along side of, or separate from his attempt to revitalize biblical study in America. On the contrary, he built this university because of a commitment to a higher life for the nation, rooted in a Bible critically studied and believed.

As Harper's career moved from seminary to university classroom to president's office, the task remained fundamentally the same: to move the Bible from the periphery of academic inquiry into prominence. Thus as a young instructor on the south side of Chicago at Morgan Park Seminary, he called in 1886 for an expanded place for biblical studies. Half the seminary curriculum, he claimed, should be devoted to the Bible, studied in the original languages and in English.[19] Two years later as professor at Yale University he initiated lectures on the English Bible and soon was spearheading a movement to place the study of the Bible in the curricula of state colleges and universities throughout the land.[20] When called to the presidency of the new University of Chicago he placed the study of the Bible in the mainstream of his curriculum. Before the new school opened, its president announced that its first professional school would be Morgan Park Seminary, renamed the Divinity School. To be certain that the Bible would be a document valued by the whole university and not just the private book of divinity scholars, Harper formed an independent Semitics Department which took its place alongside other disciplines in the university. Sundays on the university calendar were given to religious questions, guest lectures and worship. Student attendance at weekday chapel in those early days was mandatory, in keeping with the prevailing American collegiate pattern. But Harper's vision always stretched further. Three years before his death, he launched one last integrative effort. The Religious Education Association was created to promote biblical studies for American people from infancy to adulthood, with specialized programs for every educational and interest level.

In this book I intend to trace the development of Harper's vision from smalltown beginnings to culmination in a revisioned religion for the American public. Chapter 1 sketches the social, educational and religious contexts

---

[18] Harper first used the word "movement" to describe his activities in an editorial in *The Old Testament Student* 5, no. 1 (September 1885):37.

[19] Harper "Editorial," *Old Testament Student* 5, no. 8 (April 1886):321ff.

[20] Herbert Lockwood Willett, "The Corridor of Years," unpublished autobiography, The Archives of *The Christian Century*, Chicago, Illinois, pp. 91–96.

in which Harper created and subsequently fought for his vision. Chapter 2 follows Harper and the development of his ideas from his birthplace at New Concord, Ohio, to his emergence as spokesman for biblical studies in America. The specific content of his vision is the subject of Chapter 3. Chapter 4 examines Harper's critical reformation of his generation's forms of religious education. The incarnation of his biblical vision in the University of Chicago, and the expansion of that vision to embrace all Americans, is the subject of Chapter 5. Chapter 6 ponders the fate of Harper's vision, and attempts to account for its now obscure place in American memory.

Much of what Harper attempted did not become a permanent part of American religious and educational life. Daily chapel has disappeared from the official schedule of the University of Chicago. The American Institute of Sacred Literature ended its existence in 1948. Hyde Park Baptist Church is no longer an advanced center for Sunday School teaching. The Religious  Education Association carries on as the organization of professional religious educators but has abandoned pretensions to responsibility for all religious education in America. The Hebrew movement, so dear to Harper's heart, has ceased to be a popular passion though Hebrew has found its niche among all the other specialized disciplines in American higher education. The critically studied Scriptures have not become the great integrator of society which Harper believed they could be.

Yet a distinguished university stands, and the professional study of Semitic languages takes place in the university context, ample warrants for according Harper a prominent place in American educational history. His significance, however, goes beyond these contributions to intellectual and institutional history. He is important because he acted decisively at the zenith of a period in American history when many believed that a new American culture was in the making. In his era it was possible to build a university from scratch, to start a journal with the money in one's own pocket, to create a profession in one's own image. Harper is one of those representative individuals who epitomize the tenor of a period. He was the quintessential nineteenth century American evangelical liberal: optimistic, progressive, biblical and open to the unfolding of his own culture. Harper's labors were congruent with the dominant character of an era of American Protestantism which H. Richard Niebuhr identified in his classic study, *The Kingdom of God in America*.[21] In the lifting of a culture to the higher life Harper sought to transform it into something more like the "coming" kingdom proclaimed in the sacred Scriptures. He lived during the last moments when Americans were able to believe, without second thoughts, that their nation could be the messianic deliverer of the world. A decade

---

[21] H. Richard Niebuhr, *The Kingdom of God in America* (New York: Harper Torchbooks, 1959), pp. 127ff.

after his death, Americans would find themselves entangled in a brutal war, one that crushed the spirit which Harper embodied.

American self-perceptions in the turbulent decades since the Great War have become darker and less confident, a phenomenon which may help to explain why Harper, and Wilson too, are so distant. They seem to belong in out-of-the-way places, one more prominent than the other, because their visions appear naive in the face of the world conditions we now encounter. Yet, both our pluralistic nation and its evermore specialized worlds of learning present needs for integration which are as pressing now as they were the day of Harper's death. While late twentieth century readers may not be capable of the optimism of that bygone era, they cannot escape a similar pressure to bring coherence to a fragmented world. For those who believe that coherence can devolve from a religious construction of reality, and for those who contend for a biblically grounded world view, there are yet more reasons for a serious reappraisal of Harper and his vision.

# CHAPTER 1
## AMERICA IN TRANSITION

On Saturday, October 1, 1892, the University of Chicago unceremoniously opened its doors with a day of classes, a chapel service and a faculty meeting. "We were anxious to have the opening day so planned in advance that everything would move as if the University had been in session ten years," Harry Pratt Judson, then Head Dean of the Colleges and eventually Harper's successor as president, later reminisced.[1] The appearance of routine and normalcy could not mask newness, however. Judson recalled watching students pass under scaffolding and listening to the sounds of workmen in the halls on opening day. From its inception, the school was "bran [sic] splinter new"[2] and everyone knew it.

At the first meeting of the university faculty, President Harper presented a problem to his new colleagues: "The question before us is how to become one in spirit, not necessarily in opinion."[3] Concern for oneness in the face of increasing diversity was more than an academic matter for a new faculty. It was the burden of a nation searching for oneness in the midst of unparalleled change and increasing diversity. To understand Harper's solution for the question he posed on opening day, it is necessary to survey the social, educational and religious terrains where he labored.

### A New America

The new university, rooted in the vision of its thirty-six-year-old president, burst into life in an age dazzled by the new. The closing decade of the nineteenth century capped a half century during which America had been remade. Within fifty years the nation had divided into North and South, fought a bitter war and reunited. The West was the lure of the period. People trekked to the edge of the frontier and carried with them the American

---

[1] Harry Pratt Judson, as quoted in Goodspeed's *A History of the University of Chicago*, p. 244.

[2] The phrase is contained in a September 22, 1890 letter from Harper to H.L. Morehouse (Frederick T. Gates Papers), and is quoted in Robert Rosenthal, ed., *One in Spirit* (Chicago: University of Chicago Press, 1973), p. 19.

[3] Harper's question is recorded in "Minutes of the First Faculty Meeting, October 1, 1892" (Marion Talbot Papers), and quoted ibid., p. 25.

burden of incorporating new reality into old ways of thought. One year after the opening of the University of Chicago, Frederick Jackson Turner articulated the dominant role of the frontier in shaping American thought and action; ironically, he also noted its passing as the nation encountered geographic limits. Turner wondered what the closing of the frontier would mean for an America that had depended on it to fire its imagination and serve as safety valve for its conflicts.[4]

With railroad lines, barbed wire, Winchester rifles, balloon frame houses, windmills and John Deere plows, Americans domesticated their land and began to turn the North American wilderness into a great agricultural garden. As the West was tamed, citizens also began to flock to a new habitat which for many became a different kind of wilderness: the city. Arthur Meier Schlesinger, Sr., in his magisterial *The Rise of the City 1878-98*, traced the contours of this momentous reshaping of American life. The historian provided descriptions of startling possibilities and problems for urban newcomers like Harper. For example, in 1890 one-fourth of the people of Philadelphia, one-third of the inhabitants of Boston, and fully four-fifths of those in greater New York City were either foreigners or children of foreign-born parents. This meant that old-stock Americans like Harper, whose ancestors had ventured to the New World in 1795, confronted an unprecedented variety of languages and customs. Nervous, sometimes violent outbursts of nativism often followed such encounters. The new reality represented by these and other troubling indicators led Schlesinger to a conclusion: America was experiencing a "clash of two cultures," urban and rural. The nation was "trembling between two worlds, one rural and agricultural, the other urban and industrial." A fateful transition had occurred: "traditional America gave way to a new America."[5]

The impact of the arrival of 14,061,192 immigrants within the four decades that closed the nineteenth century threatened cherished self-understandings.[6] But if pressures felt as a result of new types of immigrants and new styles of urban living seemed to break apart the America of the founding fathers and mothers, other dynamics appeared to weave together the unraveling threads of the republic and provide circumstances that evoked and nurtured Harper's dream. The amazing inventiveness of Americans forged what Daniel J. Boorstin has named "the republic of technology" out of scattering tribes and individuals.[7] One symbol of the new technolog-

---

[4] Frederick Jackson Turner, "The Significance of the Frontier in American History," *The Frontier in American History* (New York: Holt, Rinehart and Winston, 1920), pp. 1–38.

[5] Arthur Meier Schlesinger, *The Rise of the City 1878-1898* (New York: New Viewpoints, 1975), pp. 1, 76, 72–73, 355, 350, xii.

[6] Sydney E. Ahlstrom provides a helpful summary of immigrant population statistics in *A Religious History of the American People*, 2 vols. (Garden City, N.Y.: Image Books, 1975), 2: 208–9.

[7] Daniel T. Boorstin coined the phrase in a much more celebrative sense when

ical linkage was the coupling of Union Pacific and Central Pacific railroad tracks on May 10, 1869, at Promontory Point, Utah. Other inventions like Thomas Alva Edison's "talking machine," incandescent lamp, electric generator, and motion picture reshaped American habits and perceptions. The booming growth in daily newspapers which increased in number from 971 in 1880 to 2226 by 1900, introduced people to worlds which were unknown decades before.[8]

Along with the growth of the city and the great leaps in technology witnessed during the last half of the nineteenth century, there came two new economic institutions which aided in reshaping America: the personal fortune and the corporation. Both provided raw materials for Harper's achievements. In 1870 John D. Rockefeller organized his oil holdings into the Standard Oil Company of Ohio and began to consolidate a fortune that would make him the richest man in America—the nation's first billionaire—and prepare him for his role as founder of Harper's university. Banking and railroad tycoon John Pierpont Morgan restructured American economic reality in 1901 with the creation of the first billion-dollar corporation—U.S. Steel. With these great financial empires came new developments like organized philanthropy (the Rockefeller Foundation), the problems of monopoly, and the standardization of finance and industry. In addition, people like the Mellons and the Vanderbilts became arbiters of taste and custodians of culture as they built museums, libraries, and universities.[9]

If, as Hansfried Kellner and Brigitte and Peter Berger assert, the primary carriers of modernity are technological production and the bureaucratic state,[10] then modernity had largely arrived. The demands of the city and a rapidly technologizing and industrializing nation called for new and more complex institutional responses to human needs. Robert H. Wiebe has labeled the period of transition from independent antebellum America to the emergent interdependence of modernity a "search for order."[11]

---

describing the future of America in *The Republic of Technology: Reflections on Our Future Community* (New York: Harper & Row, 1978).

[8] Schlesinger, *Rise of the City*, p. 185.

[9] Helen Lefkowitz Horowitz traces the history of wealthy philanthropists and their attempts to provide culture for the city of Chicago in *Culture and the City: Cultural Philanthropy in Chicago from 1880s to 1917* (Lexington: University Press of Kentucky, 1976). Harper's relations to several of the Chicago cultural elite and their institutions are given considerable attention, pp. 157ff. Oscar and Mary Handlin have tracked the seismic shift in wealth in America in *The Wealth of the American People* (New York: McGraw-Hill Book Company, 1975). They found that prior to the Civil War $100,000 was a "substantial fortune." By their count twenty-five New Yorkers and nine Philadelphians comprised the super-rich category of ante-bellum millionaires. By 1890 the number of millionaires had increased to 3000 and a great fortune was "one of a hundred million dollars" (p. 162).

[10] Peter Berger, Brigitte Berger and Hansfried Kellner, *The Homeless Mind: Modernization and Consciousness* (New York: Vintage Books, 1974), p. 103.

[11] Robert H. Wiebe, *The Search for Order, 1877-1920* (New York: Hill and Wang, 1967).

Perplexed by a variety of social problems, Americans lined up behind reformers who offered new solutions such as a civil service approach to government, regulations for child employment, a standardized work week and antitrust legislation. Political bosses became specialized manipulators of the bewildering machinery of urban politics. Powerless in the face of huge concentrations of wealth and impersonal machines, factory workers banded together to form organizations like the Noble and Holy Order of the Knights of Labor and the Federation of Organized Trades and Labor Unions.

Important changes also occurred in racial and sexual patterns. Blacks like Booker T. Washington left behind plantation slavery to struggle for economic and social equality. Although legally free, they encountered a "color line" so entrenched as to move articulate representatives like W.E.B. DuBois to offer radical criticism of the social order.[12]

While black Americans sought new social spaces, American women took their places in the work force in larger numbers. Two and one-half million women out of a national population of 50,155,783 labored outside their homes in 1880. By 1900 there were 75,994,575 Americans and the number of employed women had more than doubled.[13] The women's suffrage movement, along with the temperance cause, provided era-long evidence that women were assuming new roles in politics as well. With these changes came others of a more painful nature. For example, divorces tripled between 1878 and 1898; and by 1890 there was one divorce granted for every sixteen marriages performed.[14]

Within fifty years the daily lives of many American citizens had been transformed. Immigrants adrift in the sea of faces at Ellis Island and small-town parents watching children follow the lure of the city experienced different, though equally intense varieties of social dislocation.

But the turmoil of the age was only part of the story. In the midst of confusion and uncertainty Americans seized opportunities to reshape the nation. Symphony orchestras were born, a distinctively American architecture appeared, and American literature blossomed. Like William Rainey Harper, Theodore Thomas, Frank Lloyd Wright, Mark Twain and Francis Willard were representatives of the effervescence of American creativity fostered in these decades of transition. While there is ample warrant for Paul Carter to title his history of the period *The Spiritual Crisis of the Gilded Age*,

[12] Booker T. Washington recounted his version of the transit from slavery to freedom in *Up From Slavery*, introduced by Louis Lomax (New York: Dell Publishing Company, 1965). The agony of encounter with the "color line" received powerful articulation in W.E. Burghardt DuBois, *The Souls of Black Folk*, introduced by Saunders Redding (Greenwich, Conn.: Fawcett Publications, Inc., 1961).

[13] *The Cosmopolitan World Atlas* (Chicago: Rand McNally & Co., 1978) summarizes U.S. Census data on page 153. The statistics about employed women are from Schlesinger, *Rise of the City*, p. 142.

[14] Ibid., p. 154.

there is also reason for William G. McLoughlin to describe the era as "America's Third Great Awakening."[15] The age can be understood only if trauma and revitalization are held in tension. Old ways of life came undone, but visions which would have been dismissed as impossible only a century earlier were realized. In no phase of American life was this dynamism more evident than in the world of education.

## THE REVOLUTION IN HIGHER EDUCATION

From its beginning with the founding of Harvard College in 1636, American higher education had been sylvan and clerically dominated. Gardens for the cultivation of gentlemen in the American wilderness, early colleges were clerical preserves dedicated to training young males to carry on a way of life. Harvard set the pattern. The college's first commencement program proclaimed its purpose: "to advance *Learning* and perpetuate it to Posterity." Beneath the noble commitment to learning lay a deeper concern. The founders were afraid "to leave an illiterate Ministery [sic] to the Churches, when our present Ministers shall lie in the Dust."[16]

Harvard's Henry Dunster was the first in a long succession of American college presidents who were clergymen. Along with a clerically dominated board of overseers, Dunster and all succeeding clergy presidents of American colleges had the responsibility of leading young pupils through the rigors of a "mental discipline" which produced people of good character. [17] The primary motive for the early colleges like Harvard, William and Mary, Yale, and the College of New Jersey, was preparation of ministers for America's fledgling churches. Although the schools soon opened their doors wide to include other than budding churchmen, the clerical pattern prevailed. Students were pushed through a curriculum dominated by the study of Greek and Latin. In the last year of undergraduate work, these students crowned their education with a course in "Moral Philosophy," usually taught by the college president.

Despite attempts to remove learning from clerical auspices by Enlightenment advocates like Benjamin Franklin in Philadelphia, Thomas Jefferson at the University of Virginia and Thomas Cooper at the University of South Carolina, the pattern held until after the Civil War. For more than two centuries, citizens of American hamlets continued to build small colleges which served as citadels for the clerically shepherded values of the community.

[15] Carter, *The Spiritual Crisis of the Gilded Age* and William G. McLoughlin, *Revivals, Awakenings, and Reform* (Chicago: University of Chicago Press, 1978), pp. 141–78.

[16] The Harvard Commencement Program is quoted in Perry Miller, *The New England Mind: The Seventeenth Century* (Boston: Beacon Press, 1961), p. 75.

[17] The clerical pattern for American higher education is described in detail in Veysey, *The Emergence of the American University*, pp. 9ff.

Within a decade of the Treaty at Appomattox it was clear that the old pattern was fading. In his inaugural address delivered on October 11, 1871, Yale's new president, the Rev. Noah Porter, expressed the concern of many. America's institutions of higher education were "convulsed by a revolution." Porter reported sharp criticism of "old methods and studies" and strong demand "for sweeping and fundamental changes."[18]

Not every student of the period accepts Porter's labeling of nineteenth century changes in higher education as a "revolution," but there is little resemblance between the small college pattern of antebellum America and the complex universities constructed by people like Harper. Statistics tell part of the story. In 1870 approximately 52,300 undergraduates matriculated in American institutions. Twenty years later the student population had almost tripled. And a new type of student emerged during these years. Harper was part of a new generation of *graduate* students that signaled the passing of the old college model. Between 1870 and 1900 total graduate enrollments increased from 50 to almost 6,000. Professional education (also championed by Harper) came of age during the period. The legal profession, for example, mustered only 150 students in 1833; but by the beginning of the first World War there were 140 schools preparing almost 20,000 students for legal careers.[19]

In 1861 Yale University awarded the first American Ph.D. degree. It was not the first American post-baccalaureate degree, but it was the first for specialized study. Previously American colleges had followed a pattern begun in 1692 when Harvard awarded its president, the Rev. Increase Mather, an S.T.D., an honorary degree.[20] At first the Ph.D. was awarded both for specialized study and to bestow honor on an individual. The academic nature of the degree became more secure in 1900 when Harper led in organizing the Association of American Universities to protect the degree's dignity.[21]

The Ph.D. sat at the apex of the new edifice of learning which Harper and other university builders constructed. In order to grasp the significance of this new structure for Harper and his colleagues it is necessary to recall its German origins and the earliest American experiences with it. The modern German university was given its institutional shape by Wilhelm von Humboldt who carried the ideas of his mentor, Friedrich August Wolf, into the new structure of learning he erected at Berlin as Minister of Education. At the core of Humboldt's model was Professor Wolf's revolutionary posing

[18] Porter's address is quoted ibid., p. 1.

[19] C. Wright Mills, *Sociology and Pragmatism: The Higher Learning in America* (New York: Oxford University Press, 1966), p. 51.

[20] George Hunston Williams, *Wilderness and Paradise in Christian Thought* (New York: Harper & Brothers, 1962), p. 152.

[21] William Rainey Harper to Martin Ryerson, March 30, 1900, Personal Papers, Box 5, Folder 15.

in 1795 of the Homeric question as his life's work. Wolf invented the pattern for "professional" scholarship by devoting his career to one question, that of the authorship of the Homeric epics.[22] Under Humboldt's leadership, the German university rapidly became an institution filled with such specialists. These specialists gathered clusters of advanced students into seminars, and research became the new enterprise of education. The badge of competence in this specialized world of learning was the Ph.D. To Americans this new system of education was as foreign as the language of its advocates.

But the lure of the research ideal was eventually to triumph over American provincialism. In 1928 Charles F. Thwing estimated that nearly ten thousand eager Americans pursued the holy grail of German scholarship to its native source. Subsequent research has revised the number of Americans studying in Germany between 1820 and 1920 down to nine thousand, still a remarkable figure in an age when sea travel remained arduous.[23] These wayfarers encountered ideas and institutions, as well as individuals, which overwhelmed inherited patterns of teaching and learning.

Letters home from first-generation American innocents abroad indicate the trauma of clashes between new German scholarship and old American ways. Joseph Stevens Buckminster wrote his father of his despair of "attaining . . . to those views which you deem essential."[24] Prior to becoming the first American to win the coveted German Ph.D. in 1817, Edward Everett reported that something else had happened to him. If no one troubled him he would not upset the faith of people, he claimed. But if anyone questioned him too closely, "I will do what has never yet been done,—exhibit those views of the subject of Christianity which the modern historical and critical enquiries fully establish . . . ."[25] Everett was quite certain that the new German scholarship allowed "no defence" for traditional ways of thinking. George Bancroft, another Harvard-trained pilgrim and eventually the author of the first national history of the United States, also described his German experience. He wrote to Harvard's President Kirkland that the theologians he encountered were quite different from the pious divines of New England. They had no religious feeling, Bancroft complained, and their lectures were filled with a "vulgarity" which was more appropriate to a "jailyard" or a "fishmarket." It bothered him that biblical "narratives are laughed at as an

[22] Carl Diehl, *American and German Scholarship, 1770-1870* (New Haven, Conn.: Yale University Press, 1978), pp. 47–48.

[23] Charles F. Thwing, *The American and the German University* (New York: The Macmillan Company, 1928), p. 40, as quoted in Jurgen Herbst, *The German Historical School in American Scholarship: A Study in the Transfer of Culture* (Port Washington, N.Y.: Kennikat Press, 1965), p. 2 n. 1.

[24] Buckminster is quoted in Jerry Wayne Brown, *The Rise of Biblical Criticism in America, 1800-1870: The New England Scholars* (Middletown, Conn.: Wesleyan University Press, 1969), p. 18.

[25] Everett is quoted ibid., 41.

old wife's tale, fit to be believed in the nursery." There was, the young scholar believed, more religion in a few lines of Xenophon than in a whole course of Eichorn.[26]

The agony of these and other early American explorers of the German university world was primarily religious. One way to account for their difficulty is to point to the radical ideas of some of the German biblical scholars. More was involved than new religious ideas, however. Critical questioning of the Bible had occurred in America from the days when America's quintessential Enlightenment figure, Thomas Jefferson, spent his White House leisure time editing the New Testament and freeing it from "amphibologisms." While students were undergoing crisis abroad, many proper New Englanders who stayed home were viewing the dawn of a Unitarianism that also challenged traditional Puritan notions.

Carl Diehl, in his examination of *Americans and German Scholarship 1770-1890,* has argued persuasively that Americans in Germany encountered much more than a few new ideas, however forcefully those ideas may have been advocated. Rather, Americans also confronted a major cultural movement, *Neuhumanismus,* which flourished in the new university institutions. The Germans, following the lead of philologist Wolf, turned to a new paradigm for facing their emergence as a Prussian nation. They rediscovered the classical period and, through linguistic and historical study, shaped a new view of the world. What traumatized the Americans, Diehl claimed, was this larger cultural movement, still in robust days of a new scholarship for a new Germany.[27]

The Americans' quandary was that they could neither completely accept nor reject what the Germans were doing. The German professors excelled at scholarship; but they also represented a culture that Americans could not assimilate. Bancroft described the tension:

> Though I may not love the land of the learned, I certainly wonder at them, and tho' I cannot value them very highly for moral feeling, they still have very vigorous understandings, and tho' the style of most German books is tedious, and void of beauty, still the matter contained in them is wonderfully deep. A spirit of learning pervades everything. Their works teem with citation, and have at least the merit for the most part of being written by men who are masters of their subject.[28]

Because he was of a later generation and because his graduate education took place at American Yale rather than on the Continent, Harper was spared the traumatic collision of cultures felt by these pioneers in the world of specialized learning.

The Americans who went abroad to study in pre-war days and returned

---

[26] Bancroft is quoted ibid., p. 34.
[27] Diehl, *Americans and Germans,* pp. 11ff.
[28] Bancroft is quoted ibid., pp. 88–89.

with their Ph.D.s did not find professions waiting for them. Everett and Bancroft created careers in statecraft and history-writing, leaving their academic studies behind. The significance of their career paths is that despite trauma in Germany, they were exemplars of a kind of learning that Americans both desired and did not know how to use.

As late as 1870, William Graham Sumner remarked that "there is no such thing yet at Yale as an academical *career*."[29] American colleges still had no room for specialized study. Daniel Coit Gilman, founding president of Johns Hopkins, the first university in America which fully incorporated the advanced German model, remembered days at Yale when he served as librarian and professor of political and physical geography. He left Yale tired of lighting the fire in the library every morning and not being allowed to hire an assistant to help with his varied duties. If Yale, one of America's premier colleges, demanded such generalism of its professors, then the idea of specialization must have seemed most foreign to smaller colleges with fewer resources.

As the legions of German-trained scholars returned to the U.S., they found that America was gradually becoming more hospitable to specialization than it had been in the days of Everett and Bancroft. Transitions in the larger society were reshaping the American academic environment until what John Higham has termed a "matrix of specialization" emerged.[30] In 1869 the American Philological Association, founded by Harper's Yale mentor, William Dwight Whitney, inaugurated a professional pattern of organization soon to be followed by historians, mathematicians, and psychologists. A nation that had known only three professions—medicine, law, and ministry—soon saw new ones coming into existence at a bewildering rate. Beneath much of the professional explosion was the drive by academics to create a new career in America: that of the professor. Previously teachers had most often been on the way to or from the ministry. But they were now being replaced with individuals who had special competence in one field, whether economics or Sanskrit.

With the opening of the Johns Hopkins University in 1876, the modern American university became established. Hopkins' President Gilman and his mostly Quaker board of trustees adopted much of the German model and made it possible for true academic careers to develop. Indeed, Johns Hopkins was the first American institution designed to be a graduate school; and with that pivotal decision, the school's founders participated in what

---

[29] Sumner is quoted in Veysey, *Emergence of the American University*, p. 6.

[30] John Higham, "The Matrix of Specialization," *The Organization of Knowledge in Modern America, 1860-1920*, Alexandra Oleson and John Voss, eds. (Baltimore: Johns Hopkins University, 1979), p. 3.

Edward Shils has termed "perhaps the single most decisive event in the history of learning in the Western Hemisphere."[31]

The seminar, which was to become another key component in Harper's model of learning, was introduced to America at the University of Michigan by Charles Kendall Adams in 1869, but it did not emerge into prominence until specialists like Herbert Baxter Adams and others of the Johns Hopkins faculty enshrined it in their new institution.[32] The seminar method implied new assumptions about teaching and learning, and about knowledge itself. Colonial notions of passing on a way of life and a received tradition fell before the belief that research was a never-ending task. There were no final solutions to intellectual questions; truth was continually discovered, not deposited once and for all in time-proof tomes. At the base of the seminar approach was a desire to do scientific study—an important part of the German tradition. Hopkins' Professor Adams was not at all reluctant to move his history seminars into an old biological laboratory since the environment there helped to "cultivate more and more the laboratory method of work." Students began to treat books as "material for laboratory use." Old dissection tables were planed, then converted into "desks for the dissection of government documents and other materials for American institutional history." The seminar was evolving "from a nursery of dogma into a laboratory of scientific truth."[33]

Even Boston Brahmin Charles Eliot, president of Harvard, had to admit the growing influence of this educational model. Graduate study at his own university "did not thrive" until "the example of Johns Hopkins forced our Faculty to put their strength into the development of our institution for graduates."[34] Specialization of knowledge and education was especially evident in the founding of Clark University in Worcester, Massachusetts. Opening in 1889 as a "purely graduate institution," it offered one degree: the Ph.D. Between its opening and the first World War, the small school awarded 192 of the degrees.[35]

The influence of German academic ideals on American education was apparent in the career of Clark's first president, G.S. Hall, who seemed to make a religion out of specialized study. About Hall William James once remarked that a "mystification of some kind seems never far distant from everything he does." For Hall, the researcher was a "knight of the Holy Spirit of truth" caught up in a "holy fervor of investigation." One entered this spiritual state through a "kind of logical and psychic conversion," and from

---

[31] Edward Shils, "The Order of Learning in the United States: The Ascendancy of the University," ibid., p. 28.

[32] Herbst, *German Historical School*, pp. 35–36.

[33] Adams is quoted ibid.

[34] Eliot is quoted in Frederick Rudolph, *The American College and University: A History* (New York: Vintage Books, 1962), p. 336.

[35] Mills, *Sociology and Pragmatism*, p. 68.

then on was a "member of the great body corporate of science, having his own function in the church militant yet invisible."[36] Toward the end of his life, Hall went even further. Research, he claimed, was

> the very highest vocation of man. We felt that we belonged to the larger university not made by hands, eternal in the world of science and learning; that we were not so much an institution as a state of mind and that wherever and to what extent the ideals that inspired us reigned we were at home; that research is nothing less than a religion; that every advance in knowledge today may set free energies that benefit the whole race tomorrow. [37]

By 1923, when Hall was rhapsodizing about his new religion, American higher education had been reshaped with Johns Hopkins setting the pattern. Special schools like Pennsylvania's Wharton School of Finance became virtual kingdoms unto themselves. Students no longer were perceived as part of a class which graduated at the end of a prescribed period of time. To Gilman it did not matter whether a student's academic career lasted one year or ten, as long as research was accomplished. The homogeneous small-town character of the American college gave way before the diversity and size of the universities that were assuming more dominant places on the American landscape. Professors spoke a variety of technical languages, represented different religious traditions and taught out of a variety of academic and personal backgrounds. Women assumed more prominent roles in the higher education story as the large schools became co-educational. Blacks followed the path opened by W.E.B. DuBois, who studied at Harvard in the 1890s, as they became a small but growing part of the student populations. And in the most subtle change within academic life, students ceased to be the "end" of the educational process. Under the impact of the German notion of research, they became means to the higher end of knowledge.

Lawrence A. Cremin, in his *Traditions of American Education*, has argued that to understand education in America one must look not only at educational institutions and at individuals, but at the whole constellation or "configuration" of the nation's educational structure. Informal means of education such as newspapers, religious and social organizations and familial teaching all contributed to the general "gestalt" or educational shape of any given period. Cremin further suggested that the nation's educational configuration has assumed three successive major and distinct shapes: colonial, national, and metropolitan.[38] Harper's era was the period of transition from the national to the metropolitan configuration. As we shall see in the chapters that follow, Harper had his own plan for a complete configuration for the new epoch in American education.

---

[36] James and Hall are quoted in Veysey, *Emergence of the American University*, p. 151.

[37] Hall is quoted in Herbst, *German Historical School*, p. 31.

[38] Lawrence A. Cremin, *Traditions of American Education* (New York: Basic Books, Inc., 1977), pp. 142, 91ff.

SHAKING FOUNDATIONS

In 1891 Louis Sullivan altered the midwestern terrain with the construction of the Wainright building in St. Louis, Missouri. One of the nation's first "skyscrapers," Sullivan's creation represented much more than a change in architectural styles. His famous dictum—"form follows function"—indicated that needs of the new American environment were overwhelming traditional forms. Stately church steeples began to lose their prominence on American skylines; they became dwarfed by citadels of commerce and industry. The coming of the skyscraper was a clue to an important shift in the consciousness of a people. As the steeple lost its dominant place on the horizon, so too religion in America seemed to lose its prior status. Old beliefs and customs appeared flimsy in the face of the ambiguous urban environment. As Americans struggled with the agony of religious dislocation and relocation, they responded in a variety of ways: 1) surrender of cherished religious beliefs to the new thoughts of the age; 2) strident reassertion of a faith that ignored whatever was causing dissonance; 3) invention of new religions tailored to new needs; or 4) attempts to find ways to adapt old-time religion to new ideas or circumstances. Harper's response to the religious flux of his age was an example of the fourth option; and his choice is best understood when viewed in the context of the other alternatives.

Many of the new breed of academics who made the transit from small American colleges to the new university world were traumatized by the collapse of old religious foundations. Like Harper, they were reared in homogeneous and, in most cases, overtly Protestant communities. These talented individuals made their way from intact small-town worlds into the whirl of modernity. New ideas greeted them at an astonishing pace and often left the young scholars, whether in Germany or in America, feeling adrift, lost. A classic example of a scholar who lost his moorings in the flood of new ideas in the late nineteenth century was William Graham Sumner, for many years the most popular teacher at Yale University. Sumner set out from Paterson, New Jersey, to become an Episcopal clergyman. After a few years as rector in Morristown, Connecticut, he was appointed professor of political and social science at Yale in 1872.

Sumner became known as a champion of a social form of Charles Darwin's notion of the "survival of the fittest." In the course of his academic career, religion, once his main interest, faded away. He claimed he had put his beliefs in a drawer, locked it with the key, only to discover some time later upon opening the drawer that it was empty.[39] Sumner's experience was remarkably similar to that of the great naturalist whose theory he had adapted: Charles Darwin had abandoned ministerial preparation to embrace

---

[39] Richard Hofstadter locates Sumner as a key figure in the plot of *Social Darwinism in American Thought* (Boston: Beacon Press, 1955), pp. 52–53. See also Carter, *The Spiritual Crisis in the Gilded Age*, p. 3.

new ideas obtained in the Galapagos Islands and from a reading of Thomas Malthus. The once colorful world of religion had turned gray for him. In his *Autobiography*, written a few years after Sumner assumed his Yale chair, Darwin admitted that he too had experienced the slipping away of old beliefs. "I gradually came to disbelieve in Christianity as a divine revelation." The loss came at a "very slow rate, but was at last complete." Darwin felt "colour-blind," unable to see supernatural colorings in the natural order.[40]

Darwin's discoveries, although first published in England in 1859, did not make a public impact in America until after the Civil War. For many during the post-War period, the ideas encountered in their initial biological form or in the subsequent sociological reinterpretation made by Herbert Spencer, proved to be the first great tremor that shook the religious foundations.

At almost the same time that Darwin shocked America, James Freeman Clarke relativized American Christianity with publication in 1871 of *Ten Great Religions*. Americans were being increasingly confronted with an evermore complicated variety of religious truths. The problem in this case was not Darwin's grayness; in fact, the variety of religious coloration overwhelmed sensibilities accustomed to the limited palette of Protestant hues. The World's Parliament of Religions held in Chicago in 1893 underscored the evidence of pluralism in religion with its dazzling display of saffron robes from India on the same platform alongside the bright red of a cardinal's regalia and the business suits of Protestant leaders like Harper.[41]

The scientific offensive against traditional notions of human origins and discoveries in the emerging field of comparative religion joined with the rise of biblical criticism to create a formidable array of forces working against accepted religious beliefs. Although individuals had been questioning certain biblical accounts for centuries, American popular beliefs remained relatively untroubled by the findings of even so important a critic as Thomas Jefferson. Critical ideas largely remained the private preserve of elites who had the resources to develop them. Everett and Bancroft, for example, pondered such notions but caused little trouble to others. With the rise of the new university in America, however, it became possible for biblical critics like Harper to find an institutional home that allowed for full time pursuit and dissemination of these unsettling perspectives.

These three developments in the intellectual world of the nineteenth century, together with the host of new social problems that came as a result of America's new urban, immigrant and technological realities, pushed

---

[40] Charles Darwin, *The Autobiography*, Nora Barlow, ed. (London: Collins, 1958), pp. 86–87, 91.
[41] Kent Dreyvesteyn, "The World's Parliament of Religions" (Ph.D. dissertation, University of Chicago, 1976).

American believers into what Arthur M. Schlesinger has called "A Critical Period in American Religion."[42] More recently, Sydney Ahlstrom characterized the complexity and turmoil of this period: "No aspect of American church history is more in need of summary and yet so difficult to summarize as the movements of dissent and reaction that occurred between the Civil War and World War I." The "era lacked the spiritual foundation" which had been present in other times in America's religious history.[43]

The experience of William Graham Sumner is representative of many in the Gilded Age whose beliefs slipped away or caved in. But there were other responses. Dwight L. Moody looked at the chaos of his age and saw a "wrecked vessel." "God has given me a lifeboat and said to me, 'Moody, save all you can.'"[44] The shoe-salesman-turned-revivalist led the fight, along with later crusaders like William Jennings Bryan, to shore up the old ways. Moody invented "gap-men," individuals especially equipped with a portable, simple message with which to minister to citizens of the urban environment. To reaffirm the core message of his faith, he stretched a string of evangelical institutions across the country. His Bible Institute at Chicago and the Northfield Academy in Massachusetts sought to respond with simplicity to the complexity of modern religious thought. In the face of urban sophistication and pluralism, Moody counseled his many followers to keep their revivals lively and their sermons short. Not quite as untouched by the spirit of his age as he presented himself, Moody wedded a simple theology with new techniques of the business world; in so doing, he created a dramatic response to the change experienced by many in the urban environment.[45] The complex Gordian knot of modernity could be sliced through with one simple act—filling out the decision card for the old time message.

It is a mistake to caricature American religion of the time as if all was collapsing and only dramatic reaction could spare a few from trauma. Edwin Scott Gaustad's analysis of American denominational growth patterns reveals that all of the major church bodies experienced sustained and, in some cases, phenomenal growth during this period.[46] Many religious groups were booming, especially those whose ethnicity provided some shelter from changes sweeping the larger culture. Thanks to waves of immigrants, Catholics in America increased from 1,606,000 in 1850 to more than 12,000,000 in 1900. A small band of German Lutheran exiles prospered in

[42] Arthur Meier Schlesinger, Sr., *A Critical Period in American Religion 1875-1900* (Philadelphia: Fortress Press, 1967).

[43] Ahlstrom, *Religious History*, 2:296–97.

[44] Moody is quoted in McLoughlin, *Revivals*, p. 144.

[45] George C. Bedell, Leo Sandon, Jr., and Charles T. Wellborn note the business style of Moody's revivalism in *Religion in America* (New York: Macmillan Publishing Co., Inc., 1975), pp. 169ff.

[46] Edwin Scott Gaustad, *Historical Atlas of Religion in America*, rev. ed. (New York: Harper & Row, 1976), pp. 52–53.

the Midwest, increasing from 700 to 725,000 during the same years. Ironically, as each new group built a particular way of life upon its traditional understanding of the Scriptures, the sacred book became increasingly unable to provide a common foundation for the many varieties of believers who claimed it.

Social dislocation and pluralism of ways of life stimulated a variety of new religious movements that managed to aid some people in their struggles with modernity, while adding to the religious bewilderment of others. In 1872 Charles Taze Russell reinterpreted conventional teaching about the Second Coming and began the Jehovah's Witness movement. Mary Baker Eddy fashioned an amalgam of scientific language, biblical ideas, and the teaching of sometime mesmerist-healer Phineas Parkhurst Quimby, which in 1875 she named Christian Science. Madame Helena Petrovna Blavatsky and Annie Wood Besant organized their Theosophical Society in New York in the same decade and offered a syncretistic solution to the problem of religious pluralism.

Responses of surrender, retrenchment and innovation were not the only ways in which Americans coped with the "clash of cultures" taking place in their nation. Many leaders of established religious communities tried to mediate between their received traditions and the tempestuous changes in the American climate of opinion. Rabbi Isaac Mayer Wise led his Jewish followers into a reformed type of Judaism that allowed believers to be modern and Jewish at the same time. Cardinal James Gibbons helped American Catholics transcend their ethnic heritages, affirm the American experiment and hold on to traditional beliefs.

Within Protestantism, during those years still the majority faith, a number of gifted leaders labored at the task of transforming the "Righteous Empire" of agrarian America into a modern version of the Kingdom of God. One clergyman especially sensitive to the tensions of being both faithful and modern was Henry Ward Beecher, pastor of Plymouth Church in Brooklyn, New York. Beecher had supported the Union cause in the Civil War because Southerners, while affirming the primacy of the Scriptures, were "infidel on the question of its contents."[47] Through the pages of his *Christian Union* which reached a circulation of almost 100,000, he advocated a synthesis of Christianity and the troublesome teaching of England's lapsed divinity student. Terming himself a "cordial Christian evolutionist," Beecher found comfort in the fact that "design by wholesale is grander than design by retail," a felicitous phrase that managed to join Darwin, American business and piety into a curious, but, for many Americans, comfortable mix.[48]

[47] Beecher's remarks about the Civil War are from the sermon "The Battle Set in Array," *God's New Israel: Religious Interpretations of American Destiny*, Conrad Cherry, ed. (Englewood Cliffs, N.J.: Prentice-Hall, Inc. 1971), p. 170.
[48] Beecher's self-designation is quoted in Hofstadter, *Social Darwinism*, p. 29.

If Beecher found a path between the old faith and the new science, advocates of the "social Gospel"—people such as Walter Rauschenbusch and Washington Gladden—sought to find ways to bring together the problems of the city and the solutions of the Christian tradition. Not content with Moody's life-boat approach, these reformers wanted to transform urban wildernesses like New York's Hells Kitchen into the "kingdom of God." Academics like Richard Ely pioneered a synthesis of American Protestantism and the new economics; Albion Small did the same in the field of sociology, seeking ways to solve the serious new social problems of the day.

One of the principal areas in which creative efforts were made to bridge the widening gap between inherited religious understanding and modernity was the emerging field of biblical studies. While some attempted to protect the Bible from modern scholarship by building institutions like Nyack Missionary College, founded in New York City in 1882, others perceived the critical study of the Scriptures to be the vehicle for making the book accessible to moderns. Far from having the negative experiences of a Bancroft or an Everett, Charles Briggs believed that biblical criticism, as he experienced it at the University of Berlin, opened wide the Scriptures. "I cannot doubt but what I have been blessed with a new—divine light," he wrote home sounding like someone fresh from a religious revival. "I feel a different man from what I was five months ago. The Bible is lit up with a new light."[49] Briggs returned to America to fill the Edward Robinson Chair of Biblical Theology at Union Theological Seminary in 1890. In his letter of acceptance he indicated that the new approach to the Bible, which yielded something novel called "Biblical Theology," provided "the vantage ground for the solution of these important problems in religion, doctrine, and morals that are compelling the attention of the men of our times."[50] With a theology that could provide a fresh foundation for faith in a land troubled by modern knowledge, pluralism and flux, Briggs was one of a cohort of biblical scholars who attempted to reestablish the Bible as the foundation book for the culture. His approach called for revision of many traditional notions about the Scriptures. A heresy trial together with subsequent removal from his denomination's ministerial roster revealed an unexpected irony: Briggs' efforts to establish a strong biblical foundation for American Christians simply caused the wobbly bases of many of his Presbyterian colleagues to shake even more.

William Rainey Harper was part of this generation of exegetical reformers who sought to establish solid biblical ground for life amid modern circumstances. With his platoon of critically trained colleagues, he labored to

---

[49] Briggs is quoted in Max Gray Rogers, "Charles Augustus Briggs Heresy at Union," *American Religious Heretics: Formal* and *Informal Trials*, George H. Shriver, ed. (Nashville: Abingdon Press, 1966), p. 90.

[50] Ibid., p. 97.

mediate between the village faith of pre-Civil War America and a remade nation of peoples seeking an identity adequate for very different experiences. Against the backdrop of tremendous social, educational, and religious effervescence and disturbance, and employing a vision which he believed could save America, Harper opened his university on that October 1892 day.

# CHAPTER 2
# THE DEVELOPING VISION

William Rainey Harper's life journey took him from a small Ohio town
to what Rudyard Kipling called the "splendid chaos" of Chicago, one of
nineteenth century America's booming cities.[1] Like many other Americans
in this period, he began life in a stable village environment, but came of age,
achieved prominence and died in the flux of a large city. Along with other
members of this generation of urban newcomers, Harper was unable to leave
his small town origins entirely behind, however. Although separated from
his birthplace by many miles and by a variety of modern experiences,
Harper carried New Concord's values with him, modifing and drawing upon
them as he encountered new ideas and realities. The university he created
eighteen years after leaving New Concord, despite all its heralded innovations, bore imprints of that small Ohio town, and also of Yale University, the
Chautauqua Institution and the Baptist prayer meeting. From impressions
gathered at these influential stations on his journey, Harper fashioned a
vision by which he sought to make all who would participate in his extended
community of learning "one in spirit."

## THE COLLEGE ON THE HILL

Irishborn David Findley founded New Concord, Ohio, in 1828. Beginning with a one room cabin, Findley soon attracted other settlers and sold
them parcels of his 193 acres of land. A town grew: 32 residents in 1830, 75
by 1833, 200 by 1837. In its first decade, the tiny community acquired a
college, a mayor, and thirty-nine houses. Located on the eastern edge of
Muskingum County, New Concord was at first accessible only by Zane's
Trace, a trail named for Ebenezer Zane who cut a footpath back toward the
East from the Muskingum River in 1797. New Concord did not long remain
an isolated hamlet, however. The telegraph wired it to the rest of America in
1846, and the first train chugged into town in 1854. Never larger than a

---

[1] Kipling is quoted in Arthur M. Schlesinger, *The Rise of the City, 1878–1898* (New York:
New Viewpoints, 1975), p. 86.

village, New Concord belonged to a larger, more interdependent world almost from its beginning.[2]

Settled by Scotch and Irish people from Pennsylvania who had followed the promise of open land west of the Alleghenies, New Concord was diverse enough to boast a variety of Protestants—Baptists, Covenanters, Methodists and Presbyterians—but still sufficiently homogeneous to have a generally Anglo-Saxon and Protestant complexion. With one mind it supported the Republican party at the time of the Civil War. Traces of citizen involvement with the underground railroad testify to its pro-Union character.

Samuel Harper, one of the first successful entrepreneurs of the fledgling town, was part of the second generation of Harpers who experienced life on the Ohio frontier. A hamlet-sized prototype of his better-known son, Samuel Harper majored in American enterprise. At various times he ran a cooperage, a sawmill, a grist mill and a distillery, before opening the general store where his precocious son learned early lessons about finance and business.

The Harper family's log cabin homestead still stands on Main Street at the foot of the town's dominant hill. Muskingum College, atop the hill, dominated the village horizon and gave Harper his first vision of "the higher life." The college offered New Concordians a sense of importance, allowing them to feel superior to neighboring villages. The state could not establish a school system until 1850, but the Presbyterians of Muskingum County found a way to support their liberal arts college from its opening on March 18, 1837. Unfettered by established customs or traditions, the college admitted women in 1854, long before more pedigreed institutions opened their doors to female students.

The small town, with its academic status symbol, was twenty-eight years old when Samuel Harper made a July 24, 1856, entry into his diary: "I attended store and we had a babe born about 11–1/2 o'clock A.M."[3] The name William Rainey Harper added one more to the town's 1850 census total of 334.[4] From his strategic location on Main Street, Samuel Harper had opportunity to hold community offices, serve as elder of his Presbyterian church, and be a trustee and treasurer of the college, thus assuring that Willie Harper's childhood would be permeated with religious, commercial, educational and social activity.

Little information remains about Harper's New Concord days. Thomas Wakefield Goodspeed, author of the earliest biography about Harper, provides some clues about this period. According to Goodspeed, Harper was baptized on September 11, 1856, and raised in a snug Presbyterian home

---

[2] Lorle Ann Porter and Galen R. Wilson, *A Sesquicentennial History, 1828-1928: New Concord and Norwich, Bloomfield, Rix Mills, Stations on the National Road* (Muskingum, Ohio: Muskingum College Archives, 1978), pp. 3, 12, 14.

[3] Goodspeed, *William Rainey Harper*, p. 5.

[4] Porter, *A Sesquicentennial History*, p. 11.

with twice-a-day family worship, Sunday catechism recitations and table blessings. Stories about his childhood stressed his self-confidence and precocity. One anecdote which Goodspeed recorded related how young Willie strolled up to the pulpit while the Reverend Mr. Murch was delivering a Sunday sermon, helped himself to a drink from the preacher's water glass, and then calmly returned to his pew. Five years later, at age eight, a well-read young lad climbed the hill to the college preparatory school where he came under the influence of Dr. David Paul, president of Muskingum College.

In two years William Rainey Harper was a freshman, sitting next to students ten years his senior. Graduation followed four years later when the young salutatorian astounded the audience by delivering his address in Hebrew. Impressive as Harper's collegiate record was, it becomes more understandable when seen in light of criticisms similar to those Harper made two decades later as a reformer of American education. Small colleges in the second half of the nineteenth century lacked systems and standards. Gifted students entered advanced schools without a requisite primary education and experienced little difficulty competing with students twice their age who fumbled with basics like grammar or addition and subtraction problems.

The dimensions of Harper's Hebrew triumph also merit a second glance. Each subject of instruction was represented at the commencement exercises. One-third of the Hebrew class, Harper "won" the honor of speaking at commencement by drawing lots. A reminiscence of Muskingum's Professor Joseph F. Spencer further tarnished the image of the Hebrew prodigy. He had drilled Harper on Hebrew verbs and helped him memorize quotations from Moses and the prophets. But, he admitted, "every linguist will understand that it would have been impossible for a boy of fourteen to have written and delivered a lengthy oration in Hebrew with proper use of nouns and verbs."[5] If the boy-wonder lost some of his luster under the scrutiny of his teacher, it nonetheless remained true that Harper had demonstrated early proficiency and passion for the subject which became his life's work. He knew more Hebrew at age fourteen than Moses Stuart did when the latter assumed the Chair of Sacred Literature at Andover Seminary in 1810.[6]

Harper's parents and President Paul faced a perplexing problem on June 23, 1870. Samuel Harper pondered matters in his diary entry for the day:

[5] Goodspeed, *William Rainey Harper*, pp. 13–14.

[6] Jerry Wayne Brown quotes Stuart's admission of lack of Hebrew preparation for his exegetical post in *The Rise of Biblical Criticism in America, 1800-1870: The New England Scholars*, p. 47.

> I attended store and commencement. Willie graduated. It was a very
> solemn matter to me. Think of having a son to graduate before he was
> 14 years old.[7]

As a result, Harper spent the next three years at home, clerking his father's
store, teaching music lessons, and studying languages with Professor O.H.
Roberts, a new faculty member at the college. His father's diary alluded to a
serious illness in 1871: "I fear he will not be long with us." Willie was
"unwell," suffering from "bad spells" throughout the summer, autumn and
winter of 1871.[8] But as he would do frequently in his adult years, Harper
emerged from the sick room to begin a new project. The New Concord Silver
Cornet Band, under the direction of W.R. Harper, transformed Main Street
into a parade route as it marched and played on special occasions. Its band
leader also managed to play the piano with Ella Paul, daughter of the
president of the college (who four years later would become Mrs. William
Rainey Harper). Throughout these interim years Harper's proficiency in
Hebrew continued to become more obvious. At age sixteen he taught his first
college class, guiding three students through Introductory Hebrew.

### THE NEW WORLD OF SCHOLARSHIP

Finally the senior Harpers, President Paul, and William agreed the time
had come for the young scholar to journey to New Haven, Connecticut. He
arrived just as "Yale was passing through the transition from a college to a
university." The college, with its 1,000 students, had a larger population
than the town of New Concord. Fifty-five graduate students competed with
undergraduates for the time of seventy-five faculty members.[9] Many years
later a fellow student, L.A. Sherman, recalled, perhaps with a tinge of
jealousy, the initial impression Harper made. At age seventeen he was "a
somewhat unsophisticated country lad . . . not very well prepared for the
work we were doing."[10]

Notwithstanding his rough edges, Harper met the challenge of life at
Yale, demonstrating quickly his proficiency with languages and moving
through the graduate program with customary speed. Working under William Dwight Whitney in philology and Sanskrit, Lewis R. Packard in Greek,
and George E. Day in Hebrew, Harper, not yet nineteen, presented his
dissertation "A Comparative Study of the Prepositions in Latin, Greek,
Sanskrit, and Gothic," in June of 1875.

A lack of material evidence confines most of Harper's student years to
obscurity. Even his Yale dissertation is lost.[11] Goodspeed provides the

---

[7] Samuel Harper is quoted in Goodspeed, *William Rainey Harper*, p. 16.
[8] Ibid., p 18.
[9] Ibid., p 24.
[10] Sherman is quoted ibid.
[11] Suzanne Selinger, Reference Librarian, Yale University Library, in an August 12, 1980,

reminiscences of a few people who encountered Harper along the way, but most of these recollections fall into the category of lore. The outlines of his experience can be discerned in the Goodspeed narrative, however, and they suggest several generalizations.

When Harper boarded the train in New Concord in 1873 and made his first journey to Yale, he traveled beyond the limits of what Peter Berger and others have called a "home world."[12] Experiences of a young Ohio town, a homogeneous and perhaps not too demanding education, an ordinary Presbyterian piety, and the Main Street General Store collided with the more cosmopolitan way of life encountered in New England. New Haven had a more established legacy of education, a learned ministry, and a college with more than 170 years of its own tradition to pass on to entering students. When he began his graduate studies at Yale, Harper exchanged social locations. Instead of a position at the hub of New Concord life, he now assumed a place at the periphery of a more sophisticated world. Perhaps Harper's seldom-broken silence about these early years is an indication of their difficulty for him.

The movement from the center of one world to the periphery of another is a frequently discussed theme in the writings of many psychologists and anthropologists. Erik H. Erikson's notion of the "identity crisis," for example, defines the transition years of adolescence as a time when the old parentally formed identity of an individual breaks apart in the face of internal and external changes in the life trajectory.[13] Anthropologist Victor Turner identified liminal moments in the biological and social life of a person when transitions in self-perception occur. At these moments the individual moves on a pilgrimage away from the integrated life of the past toward a time of crisis and reconstruction. At the end of the process, a reintegrated individual emerges with an experience of "*communitas*," or existential belonging, a new self-understanding and a new paradigm for how to relate to the world of experience.[14]

Harper followed a path somewhat similar to the one these scholars have described. His journey to New England came at the time when he was leaving behind the world of childhood. At the very instant when his social world might have provided a sheltered environment for the time of transi-

---

letter to James P. Wind, stated: "We can report that no copies of the dissertation were found in our two inventories of 1935 and 1974."

[12] Berger, *Homeless Mind: Modernization and Consciousness*, p. 66.

[13] Erik H. Erikson, *Identity, Youth and Crisis* (New York: W.W. Norton & Company, Inc., 1968), pp. 128–35.

[14] Turner developed these themes first in *The Ritual Process: Structure and Anti-Structure* (Ithaca: Cornell Paperbacks, 1969), pp. 94ff, and then together with Edith Turner, in *Image and Pilgrimage in Christian Culture* (New York: Columbia University Press, 1978), pp. 2ff.

tion, he moved away, thus increasing the degree of dislocation. The Yale years were lived on the threshold between the identities of Ohio boy-wonder and the Hebrew specialist who returned home. In a sense, Harper was a "marginal man," a person with each foot in a different world.[15] He did not jettison his past. There was no dramatic repudiation, but there was also no simple return to the same world he had left behind.

The depth of Harper's personal transformation became clear in his later years. He returned home infused with a zeal for scholarship which, while not discontinuous with his early love of books and talent for learning, showed signs of an encounter with new ideals about research and learning. The Hebrew which he had loved as a boy became a "profession." He was now a specialist.

The chief source of Harper's new self-image was his major Yale mentor, William Dwight Whitney. Unlike most of the other creators of the modern American university, Harper did *not* follow the migration patterns of his generation and spend several years at a German university. His contact with the new ideas and methods of German education were mediated to him through this master teacher. The great-great-grandson of Jonathan Edwards, Whitney discovered his profession by an accident that sounds like a New England version of Ignatius Loyola's conversion.

After graduation from Williams College and a brief stint at his father's Northampton bank, Whitney began to prepare for the medical profession by working in a doctor's office. The day after his apprenticeship began, October 2, 1845, he contracted measles and was forced to bed. While convalescing, he picked up a copy of Franz Bopp's Sanskrit *Grammar* and a new interest awakened. The next year Whitney studied at Yale with the only teacher in America who knew anything about the mysterious language, German-trained Edward Elbridge Salisbury. In 1850 Whitney migrated to Germany where for three years he studied at the Universities of Berlin and Tübingen. Whitney assumed a new chair at Yale in 1854: "Professorship of the Sanskrit and its relations to kindred languages, and Sanskrit literature." His career there spanned forty productive years, represented by a bibliography which included more than 360 titles. Whitney helped organize the American Philological Association in 1869 and served as its first president. Essentially a grammarian, he was interested in linguistic facts, carefully arranged and

---

[15] Arthur Mann labeled Fiorella La Guardia a "marginal man" in *La Guardia: A Fighter Against His Times, 1882-1933* (Chicago: University of Chicago Press, 1969), p. 21. Mann used the concept to describe the variety of ethnic and social groups in which La Guardia participated but to which he did not fully belong. In this case I am using the notion in a different sense. Harper did not straddle a number of ethnic subcultures. Instead he crossed the threshold between small town and urban America, between the old and new configurations of learning.

described. He rejected the trend to make philology into speculative, abstract study, instead opting for the "science" of linguistics.[16]

The German university world that Whitney encountered had changed since the days of Bancroft and Everett's trauma. He did not write home complaining of loneliness or German arrogance. Instead his problem was "the number of American acquaintances I have." There were northern and southern "coteries" which managed to take up all of his time—"none is left to cultivate German acquaintances."[17] Whitney was part of what Carl Diehl has called a "new generation" of American scholars in Germany.[18] These scholars did not have to adapt to the newness of German culture and ideas singlehandedly as had those who pioneered in Germany at the beginning of the century. A network of Americans was present which provided individuals ready to ease the transition and discuss the problems that newcomers encountered.

More significant than the presence of an American community of scholars in many of the German universities were changes within German scholarship. The *Neuhumanismus* that so unsettled the first American migrants had lost some of its vigor. Emphasis was shifting away from the philosophical speculation inspired by Georg Wilhelm Friedrich Hegel and Johann Gottfried Herder toward increasing specialization. The German ideals of scholarship which Whitney mastered and later mediated to Harper did not carry the same heavy ideological freight which Bancroft and Everett carried home. The result was a second generation of scholars which returned from Germany having mastered individual professions and having resisted the troubling world view that had plagued the first wave. Diehl suggested that Whitney did not experience a clash between world views. Rather he meshed the "Protestant work ethic" of his New England heritage with the regimen of the scholar. His journal revealed no crisis, only the daily devotion of a scholar to arduous work.[19]

The premier American linguist of his era, Whitney felt little need to speculate beyond the data of his research. The new breakthroughs of comparative philology that he assimilated while in Germany allowed him to turn "back the vast & complicated body of languages as they at present exist to a few simple principles working among & upon a few simple utterances."[20] Whitney's work contained the paradigm for Harper's study of Hebrew. One looked at all the linguistic data, arranged the findings in neat columns, like any banker's or general store owner's son might, and then, "inductively," to use Harper's word, found the general principles contained in the data. To Whitney and Harper, this was *scientific* study, unencumbered

[16] "William Dwight Whitney," *Dictionary of American Biography*, Dumas Malone, ed. (New York: Charles Scribner's Sons, 1936), 20:166–69.
[17] Diehl, *Americans and German Scholarship, 1770-1870*, pp. 129–30.
[18] Ibid., p. 115.
[19] Ibid., pp. 125ff.
[20] Ibid., p. 123.

by any taint of German idealism which others thought went hand in hand with critical linguistic study. Scientific study did not retain this attitude of self-evident objectivity forever. Harper, however, never seemed to question the Whitney approach.

Harper went home from Yale, not yet twenty years of age, with Ph.D. in hand and a scholarly ideal in mind. He aimed to be a scholar, a specialist in the study of Hebrew. Like his German predecessors in the study of languages, he found in an ancient language and culture the basic insights with which to interpret the world. Harper, however, selected a different language and culture from most of his contemporaries. Instead of following the lead of Wolf and the other great scholars who lit their torches of learning "at the funeral pyre of ancient Greece,"[21] Harper turned to the Hebrew Scriptures for his basic construction of reality. At Yale he had encountered a paradigm that took him beyond his New Concord horizon: the specialized scholarship learned from Whitney that included the concern to get at all the facts, the desire to make study a life work, and the use of an ancient language as a means for coming to terms with the modern world.

## CHOOSING A BAPTIST WORLD

Harper left Yale to continue the task of forging a world that could include scholarly ideals and smalltown reality. He returned to New Concord long enough to marry Ella Paul. But he then followed the impulses of his new profession and began to migrate through the academic world. After a year as principal of Masonic College in Macon, Tennessee, where he taught Latin and mathematics, organized a band and disciplined students who raided a turnip patch, Harper went in 1876 to Denison University in Granville, Ohio, to become tutor of ancient languages in the university's preparatory school. The move from principal to tutor was down the status ladder but it offered Harper the opportunity to come closer to his goal of being a full-time scholar of languages, even if the language at first was Greek rather than Hebrew. Another strong president, Dr. E. Benjamin Andrews, took Harper under his wing and guided his career. With Andrew's backing and the aid of a colleague, Richard S. Colwell, Harper organized an extra-curricular class for those interested in Hebrew. Soon the twenty-one-

---

[21] The phrase is from George Bancroft's admiring description of the German classical scholarship he encountered at Goettingen in the early nineteenth century. It is quoted ibid., p. 87. Chapters 3 and 4 will demonstrate that Harper attempted to refashion America into a biblical world, made in the image of the Hebrew people whose language he had mastered. Harper's appropriation of Hebrew allowed him to propose a vision for America that was not as discontinuous to its received tradition as the idealism of his German-trained colleagues. The Hebrew Scriptures had never been far from the consciousness of Americans who had interpreted their reality with Old Testament images since the Puritans made their first journey into the wilderness.

year-old teacher counted several faculty members among his Hebrew students.

After a year at Denison Harper became principal of the academy and singlemindedly pursued the study of languages. At that time President Andrews saw in him no indication of interest in theological issues, or even in biblical study. "You would not have picked him out then as likely to head a department in a theological faculty, or to distinguish himself as an organizer of theological work in any branch. His interests were not speculative but concrete." Harper's career seldom wavered from this characteristic propensity for the concrete. More comfortable with fine linguistic points than with abstract theological speculation, Harper also seemed more attentive to details of administration than to development of a full-blown philosophy of education. His ventures into either theology or educational philosophy were occasional, never systematic or sustained.

Harper's skills as a teacher, however, were quite evident. "Teaching was his delight. . . . He looked forward to each class period as a feast. . . . Before his class his mind and his body also were all activity. His thought was instantaneous. Question or correction followed answers like a flash." Andrews was overwhelmed by the young teacher: "It was model teaching. Bright pupils shot forward phenomenally; dull ones made good progress." [22]

Harper's rapid movement to prominence as a gifted teacher during his two and one-half years at Denison accompanied a more private but nonetheless significant event. The son of a stalwart Presbyterian became a Baptist. Toward the end of 1876 Harper rose to testify from a back seat of a Baptist prayer meeting in Granville. His colleague, Professor Charles Chandler, could not believe he was hearing Harper. So stunned that he forgot most of what Harper said, Chandler could remember only one line of his testimonial. "I want to be a Christian. I don't know what it is to be a Christian, but I know I am not a Christian and I want to be one." [23]

Harper never interpreted his conversion. But when he stepped forward at that prayer meeting he entered a denomination which he affirmed and led for the remainder of his life. His silence about the change of denominational homes can tempt one to overestimate or undervalue it. Certainly Harper's future role as leader of the Baptist university on the south side of Chicago could not have developed had he remained in the Presbyterian orbit. But more important was the fact that the move to an open, aggressive and progressive Baptistdom was congenial to Harper's religious needs. In his later career as advocate of biblical criticism he challenged cherished interpretations imposed upon Scripture by inherited traditions. He also called for a constructive spirit on the part of the new biblical student, a spirit based both on what the facts of the biblical material presented and on the

[22] Goodspeed, *William Rainey Harper*, pp. 40–41.
[23] Chandler is quoted ibid., pp. 35–36.

experience of biblical truth.[24] The movement from creedal Presbyterianism to a choice-centered Baptist faith points to the emergence of a piety which was congruent with key themes which the scholar later proclaimed.

Harper's conversion experience further demonstrates that his transit to New Haven had carried him beyond the home world of New Concord. While spared a massive identity crisis, Harper nonetheless experienced enough dislocation or diffusion to require reintegration once back on the home soil of Ohio. Among his new Baptist associates Harper experienced "*communitas*" or belonging.[25] Although later dealings with biblical criticism and the construction of a new edifice of learning occasionally troubled Harper's self understanding, the paradigm of the Baptist scholar forged in Denison held throughout his life.

Harper's conversion makes it problematic to attempt to locate him within conventional liberal/conservative categories. In *The Modernist Impulse in American Protestantism*, William R. Hutchison has identified a "cluster of beliefs" as distinctively "modern." According to Hutchison modernists believed in "adaptation, cultural immanentism, and a religiously-based progressivism."[26] As the succeeding chapters will show, Harper shared those distinctive fundamental convictions. Problems develop, however, when Harper is compared with other aspects of Hutchison's portrait. As he followed the contours of the generation which came into prominence in the 1880s, Hutchison found conversion experiences "notably lacking."[27] Yet Charles A. Briggs' experience of the "new light" in Germany mentioned in Chapter 1, and Walter Rauschenbusch's conversion experience, suggest that such happenings continued to occur to those who came to be thought of as modernists, but that these individuals began to value those experiences differently.[28] Instead of making instances of personal conversion authoritative for the message they proclaimed to others, this new generation of reborn individuals became diffident. Never repudiating their own experiences, they also did not attempt to reproduce them. Instead, they sought to change the hearts and minds of people with a more publicly available knowledge and experience, that of a reinterpreted Bible. The conventional type of conversion was still privately important; in the public sphere, however, where the modernists wished to work, it was not normative.

For individuals like Briggs and Harper the scientific facts of a properly interpreted Bible were available to all people, not just the privileged few. With the availability of a more public form of religious data, conversion

---

[24] See Chapter 3 below, pp. 61ff.

[25] See Chapter 2 above, pp. 31ff.

[26] William R. Hutchison, *The Modernist Impulse in American Protestantism* (Cambridge: Harvard University Press, 1976), p. 2.

[27] Ibid., p. 78.

[28] See above p. 24 and Dores Robinson Sharpe, *Walter Rauschenbusch* (New York: The Macmillan Company, 1942), p. 43.

could be civilized; it was relocated in private zones by people who wanted to reach diverse audiences. Private experiences could not convince those who did not share them. As Americans encountered more numerous varieties of religious experience, no one type could appeal to everyone. Harper and his generation of biblical scholars sought a new basis for public agreement: scientifically established religious facts.

## THE HEBREW PROFESSION

Two years after converting to the Baptist denomination, Harper was nominated by President Andrews to fill the position of instructor of Hebrew at Baptist Union Theological Seminary in Chicago. The Board of Trustees balked at the thought of a twenty-two-year-old faculty member, but Andrews' recommendation persuaded President George W. Northrup to invite the young scholar for an interview. Goodspeed recalled the session:

> I met him in President Northrup's study in Morgan Park, then a suburb, now a part of Chicago. I found a young man, black-haired, stockily built, five feet seven inches tall, smooth-faced, spectacled, youthful in looks, but so astonishingly mature in mind that I immediately forgot that he was not of my own age. He had a singularly winning personality. We both yielded to its charm and from that day forward were his devoted friends and admirers.[29]

As he would repeatedly do in his days as university builder and advocate of a new way to read the Bible, Harper turned doubters into partners. On January 1, 1879, he began his work at Morgan Park Seminary, appointed, at last, instructor of Hebrew at the salary of $1000 a year.

With typical gusto, Harper took the seminary by storm, generating instant interest in Hebrew and earning a Bachelor of Divinity degree within his first year on the faculty.[30] His colleague, later the Dean of the new University of Chicago Divinity School, Dr. Eri B. Hulbert, called him a "young enthusiastic Hebraist," a "boundlessly enthusiastic" Hebrew teacher "with all the excellencies and some of the defects of such a character."[31]

The traditional curriculum could not contain Harper's energies. The minutes of the seminary Board of Trustees indicate that by May of 1881, he had expanded his activities far beyond his colleagues' expectations. In addition to regular classes in Hebrew and Old Testament exegesis, Harper was offering special classes in Chaldee and Sanskrit. Worse yet, Harper lured six students to devote the ten days of their Christmas vacation to

---

[29] Goodspeed, *William Rainey Harper*, p. 43.
[30] Ibid., p. 45.
[31] Hulbert is quoted ibid., p. 45.

spending eight hours a day sight-reading the Hebrew Scriptures.[32] At Commencement time that same year the Examining Committee of visiting pastors and scholars marvelled at the "intense enthusiasm" which immediately struck them when reviewing the work of the Hebrew department. They told the Board that students at the seminary "pursue Hebrew as though their immediate settlement in the pastorate and their final success in the ministry depended upon a knowledge of the entire Hebrew Bible."[33] Students who graduated from the seminary continued their Hebrew studies by belonging to the Morgan Park Hebrew Club. Harper even petitioned for permission to use the seminary building during the summer vacation to conduct a Hebrew summer school (a harbinger of his later introduction of the summer school into his university's academic calendar).

These early signs of enthusiasm for Hebrew were the beginnings of what Harper later called the "Hebrew movement" in America.[34] With a knack that few teachers possess, Harper had the ability to make the drudgery of basic language study come alive. Ira M. Price, one of Harper's Morgan Park students who followed his mentor into the Hebrew profession, described what happened in the classroom:

> At the first meeting in the class-room the contagious enthusiasm of the teacher seized us. It was here, as we met day after day, week after week, that we saw, with increasing delight, the attractiveness and charm and skill of the teacher. The intense earnestness and concentrated energy with which the work of the hour was carried on fairly electrified the class. . . . This inspiration, or goading to thought, was marvellously enhanced by another trait, . . . the ability to state all the arguments on the two sides of a question with fullness and fairness.[35]

Price had spotted what made Harper so appealing. He overwhelmed his students—and later his colleagues, fellow educators, and various philanthropists—with his sheer fervor. There was an almost evangelical quality about his teaching. Students were transformed into followers of a movement and its charismatic figure. At the same time, Harper was also a thoroughly professional scholar. His ability to summarize all opinions and leave the decision to his students drew many to him, even if they did not always agree with or even know of his views.

Twenty-three students attended Harper's first summer school in July 1881; attendance climbed the next summer to 65. Demand for Harper's

[32] Ibid., p. 48.

[33] Ibid., p. 49.

[34] Kenneth Nathaniel Beck's careful probing of the files of the American Institute of Sacred Literature unearthed the earliest reference to the Hebrew movement in Harper's article, "The Hebrew Book Exchange," published by his American Institute of Hebrew from Morgan Park, Illinois, in 1882. It is quoted in Beck's "The American Institute of Sacred Literature: A Historical Analysis of an Adult Education Institution," p. 36.

[35] Price is quoted in Goodspeed, *William Rainey Harper*, p. 47.

teaching led the young professor to branch out. In 1883 he conducted a summer school at Chautauqua in New York. During the decade of the eighties, over thirty of his summer schools followed in New Haven, Connecticut, Worcester, Massachusetts, the University of Virginia, Evanston, Illinois, Philadelphia and Cambridge, Massachusetts. An average of 300 students studied Hebrew under his direction each summer.[36]

Other students, who could not work with Harper at Morgan Park or at one of the summer schools, soon clamored for Hebrew. In response to their interest, Harper created The Correspondence School of Hebrew in 1880 and then sent out on February 14, 1881, the first of thousands of correspondence lessons. In less than two years Harper had launched a national movement. The weight of correspondence required him to move from his private seminary study to a vacant store, where he housed fonts of Hebrew type and a growing staff of assistants. During that amazingly productive time, Harper authored *Elements of Hebrew* and *Hebrew Vocabularies* to aid his expanding network of students. As his students advanced, so did their teacher's list of scholarly publications. His *Lessons of the Intermediate Course* and *Lessons of the Progressive Course* followed in 1882; *A Hebrew Manual* and *Lessons of the Elementary Course* appeared in 1883. In 1885 Harper added *Introductory Hebrew Method and Manual* to the growing collection of resources for the study of Hebrew.[37]

Summer schools and publishing successes notwithstanding, Harper was not through creating. A journal was needed to link together the followers of his movement, so the *Hebrew Student* appeared on April 8, 1882, with Harper as editor. To fund his various enterprises, Harper became an entrepreneur, founding a joint stock company with shares for sale at $100 each. To unite the teachers in his Hebrew movement into an organization, he created the American Institute of Hebrew during that same year.

Although President Andrews may not have seen Harper's leadership qualities during the Denison days, they became apparent at Morgan Park. Harper was an impresario—teaching a full-time load, commuting to summer schools, editing a journal, publishing books to fuel a movement, raising money, nudging people into an organization. Amazingly, he still had time to contribute to Morgan Park Baptist Church. Goodspeed, the church's founding pastor, recalled that Harper served as clerk, deacon, finance committee member, treasurer, and Sunday School superintendent during his seven years at Morgan Park.[38] Yet, even with all of these demands upon his energies Harper could find room on his agenda for responding to opportunities which might take him in different directions. That characteristic openness prompted Harper to accept an invitation from a creative Methodist

[36] Ibid., p. 52.
[37] Ibid., p. 53.
[38] Ibid., p. 50.

educator who would stretch Harper's vision beyond the horizons of his seminary and the study of Hebrew.

## THE CHAUTAUQUA VISION

The Rev. John Heyl Vincent, former Methodist circuit rider and promoter of the "uniform lesson plan" for the Sunday School, had teamed with Lewis W. Miller, inventor of the Buckeye Mower and Reaper, to establish a Normal School for Sunday School teachers at Fair Point on the southwestern shore of eighteen-mile-long Lake Chautauqua in western New York. They opened their camp on August 8, 1874, for a two-week session devoted to aiding Sunday School teachers in their tasks.[39] The following year Vincent prevailed upon old friend Ulysses Simpson Grant to come as guest speaker. President Grant's arrival on August 15, 1875, at the head of a flotilla of eleven steamboats, drew an estimated crowd of 30,000 and assured that, in spite of its modest origins, Chautauqua would make a major impact on American life in the late nineteenth century.

Almost immediately after the president's visit, Vincent and Miller looked beyond the needs of America's Sunday Schools to envision a much larger educational enterprise. By the time they finished dreaming they had created the Chautauqua Literary and Scientific Circle, the Chautauqua Press, the Chautauqua University, and the Chautauqua University Extension Program. To spread their educational program they eventually spawned numerous Chautauquas across the country.[40]

A combination of respect for the reputation of the young Hebrew phenomenon and a desire to nip competition in the bud moved Vincent to arrange a meeting with Professor Harper in 1883. Aware of a rival camp to his own coming into existence across Lake Chautauqua, Vincent confided to his son that "the Baptists will find some bright, aggressive young minister of their denomination, put him in charge over there, and give him a free hand."[41] The Methodist champion of popular Christian education had no hesitancy about cornering a market in order to protect the Chautauqua Gospel. Vincent sent Harper a telegram and the two met somewhere along the train route between St. Louis and Chicago. Of the meeting Harper recalled:

> I shall never forget that first half hour I had the privilege of spending with Dr. Vincent; no day of my life has ever meant so much to me, a

[39] Theodore Morrison, *Chautauqua: A Center for Education, Religion, and the Arts in America* (Chicago: University of Chicago Press, 1974), pp. 18–26.
[40] Joseph E. Gould, *The Chautauqua Movement: An Episode in the Continuing American Revolution* (Fredonia, N.Y.: State University of New York, 1961).
[41] Leon H. Vincent, *John Heyl Vincent: A Biographical Sketch* (New York: The Macmillan Company, 1925), p. 130.

time of the beginning of sympathies and the beginning of work which
I had never before dreamed of.

At Chautauqua Harper developed the "sympathy with the work of popular
education, the interest in the education of the masses which I am sure I
should never have felt but for contact with Chautauqua men and
Chautauqua ideas."[42]

Harper arrived at Chautauqua in 1883 just in time to encounter people
in the grip of a very successful idea. Victorian cottages had replaced the tents
of the original camp meetings; the summer community had a daily newspaper which heralded his arrival. Steamboats made regular stops at the
Chautauqua dock and the Atheneum hotel hosted guests who did not choose
to become permanent residents. Harper roomed at what came to be called
"Knower's Ark," a home for guest bishops and faculty members. Not far from
his lodging lay Palestine Park, a geographic scale model of the Holy Land
showing the Dead Sea and other important places in Bible history.

A passion for Christian culture permeated the atmosphere. People who
aspired to a richer and more meaningful life performed music or discussed
good books on the village's ubiquitous front porches. Distinguished lectur-
ers held forth in the Hall in the Grove; preachers proclaimed a non-sectarian
gospel several times each day. Sessions lengthened from the original fifteen
days of 1874 to forty-three-day-long periods providing more time for people
to equip themselves for living in their modern environment.

Chautauqua served as a pulpit for people with worthy ideas or causes.
Frances Willard came with her message of temperance; Anthony Comstock
sought supporters of the Society for the Suppression of Vice. Lyman Abbott
claimed he was converted to evolutionary thought by a lecture given at
Chautauqua by Professor E. Ogden Doremus.

But Vincent was determined to reach beyond those who attended the
annual summer assemblies. On August 10, 1878, he announced the formation of the Chautauqua Literary and Scientific Circle, a home reading plan,
the first in a series of educational innovations. In 1879 Vincent created a
School of Languages, another organizational step beyond concern for immediate needs of Sunday School teachers. The next year he went even further,
inviting teachers from secular schools to a Teacher's Retreat that studied
pedagogical approaches. The National Education Association came that year
for a national convention. Vincent continued to expand his horizon, adding
musical theory to his curriculum. In 1881 Chautauqua announced the
opening of its own School of Theology, chartered by the State of New York
to train candidates for the ministry. This school was designed for those who
did not have access to seminary education, and it included provision for
correspondence study, something almost unheard of in America. At least one
other experiment with correspondence study was underway when Vincent

---

[42] "Dr. Harper Banqueted," *Chautauqua Assembly Herald* 20, no. 4 (July 25, 1891):4.

began this new program—Harper's program had begun less than a year earlier.

At the same moment that Harper arrived to begin his Hebrew teaching, the State of New York chartered the Chautauqua University, an institution with authority to grant academic degrees. The Sunday School camp remained a university until Harper opened his new institution in Chicago, which would be complete with many of the features he encountered and with which he experimented in rural western New York.[43]

Vincent's talents as organizer and promoter served a vision. Remembering a background that had offered no luxuries like higher education, the clergyman sought ways to provide learning for all. He saw no gap between the world of learning and the message he was ordained to proclaim. Education and the Christian message went hand in hand. In 1886 Vincent described *The Chautauqua Movement* and readily admitted his presuppositions. He saw "the whole of life" as "a school" that worked "from the earliest moment to the day of death." The "basis of education" was religious and for the believer "all knowledge, religious or secular, is sacred." One studied to "become like God, according to the divinely appointed processes for building character." Vincent singled out the adult years for special attention partly because many, like him, had experienced "early lack of culture." Vincent, however, turned this apparent deficiency into a motive for his movement. Cultural impoverishment "begets a certain exaltation of its value and desirability, and a craving for its possession." For these reasons America's great Sunday School teacher labored so that "the influence of the best teachers may be brought to bear upon [the mature mind] by frequent correspondence, including questions, answers, praxes, theses, and final written examinations of the most exhaustive and crucial character."[44]

Vincent was infatuated with college education, an experience he had missed in his Alabama youth, but which he now offered to anyone who would sign up for courses. He romanticized about its advantages:

> The action by which a youth becomes a college student—the simple going-forth, leaving one set of circumstances, and voluntarily entering another, with a specific purpose—is an action which has educating influence in it.

The process was a "new birth" in the life of all who left one world for another. As students participated together in this process of environmental exchange, a new association, a "fellowship" was formed. "They have left the same world; they now together enter another world." This preacher who saw all human experience as a school thought that "college life is the whole of life packed into a brief period, with the elements that make life, magnified

---

[43] Morrison, *Chautauqua*, pp. 41–48.

[44] John H. Vincent, *The Chautauqua Movement* (Boston: Chautauqua Press, 1886), pp. 12–15.

and intensified, so that test of character may easily be made." College was a "laboratory of experiment" where students experienced life's "natural laws and conditions" in a compressed period.[45]

The creation of Chautauqua University was the organizational capstone of the vision which began in Vincent's attempts to reform Sunday School instruction. Every innovation that he attempted served the goal of redemptive education. Thus the Chautauqua Literary and Scientific Circle was "John the Baptist, preparing the way for seminary and university." With his own university, Vincent created "a college for one's own home," offering college life to those who could not savor delights offered at traditional institutions.[46] He sought to aid people who

> believe that into the closely woven texture of every-day home and business life, there may be drawn threads of scarlet, crimson, blue and gold, until their homespun walls become radiant with form and color worthy to decorate the royal chamber—the chamber of their King, God, the Father of earnest souls.[47]

Such an expansive view precluded denominational exclusivism. For example, in 1880 Vincent invited Rabbi Nathan Noah of New York to teach Hebrew in the School of Languages. From its start the School of Theology carefully stepped around the thorny issues of denominational traditions with regular printed announcements of its guiding perspective:

> The various schools of the Church, ecclesiastical and doctrinal, are reported to all students of the Chautauqua School of Theology by their respective representatives. The Calvinist defines Calvinism; the Armenian [sic], Armenianism; a Baptist gives the distinctive views of his branch of the Church; and thus the Chautauqua School of Theology is strictly denominational, in that it guarantees to each member not only a course of doctrinal studies prepared by men authorized to speak for his Church, but it enables him to test the soundness of such statements by a careful reading of the positions taken by other or rival schools. There is a sense in which this may be called "union" but it is in the highest and best sense denominational.[48]

In Vincent's plans Harper found an exalted and expansive vision that incorporated all of his concerns and transcended many of them. Vincent emphasized learning fused with an evangelical version of Christianity. From him Harper acquired a passion to include those who were cut off from normal avenues of education. At Chautauqua Harper was shown a way around the barriers of denominationalism—not repudiation, but creation of a community of scholarship.

[45] Ibid., pp. 169–74.
[46] Ibid., pp. 178, 15.
[47] Ibid.
[48] Ibid., p. 198.

To be able to include so many different types of Christians seeking culture, Vincent and his colleagues took pains to keep some distance between themselves and traditional notions of evangelical piety. "Chautauqua is not a camp meeting," proclaimed advance publicity for the seventeenth season, "although it is controlled by those who believe in the Evangelical Protestant Empire." Run "on a broad, liberal, undenominational basis," the summer program was "free from any of the eccentricities and extravagances which have prejudiced many people against the so-called camp-meeting."[49]

Concern to avoid guilt by association with the popular forms of revivalism which people met at camp meetings did not completely mask the fact that Chautauqua was participating in a much larger revival than the kind which made Vincent nervous. People who came to Chautauqua participated in "that unique and remarkable movement now known all over the world; one in consecration to a splendid work—the promotion of symmetrical culture among the people everywhere."[50] It was a revival based on the Bible but concerned with much more than denominational boundaries and traditions. "The leaders of this educational movement are believers in Revelation and lovers of 'whatsoever things are true' in art, in literature, and in science. Their faith is so firm that they are confident of perfect harmony between the 'Word' and the 'Works' when both are rightly interpreted."[51] The Hall in the Grove, site of popular lectures on a variety of secular subjects, stood adjacent to St. Paul's Grove on the side of the hill by Lake Chautauqua, symbol of the synthetic Christian culture that was revitalizing many in the American evangelical world.

There was ample room for Harper's ambition and energy within John Vincent's expansive vision. The twenty-seven-year-old professor began his Hebrew magic at Chautauqua in 1883. Four years later Vincent appointed him principal of the College of Liberal Arts, stimulating Harper's first impulse to venture beyond the realm of Hebrew study. Harper became the star of Chautauqua, reorganizing its existing curriculum and adding new course offerings under Vincent's benevolent eye, until the latter moved on to become the Methodist's bishop in Topeka, Kansas, in 1888.[52]

When leaders of the University of Chicago attempted to convince Harper to sever his connections with Chautauqua in favor of full-time efforts on behalf of their new institution, Harper demonstrated his commitment to

[49] "Chautauqua Seventeenth Season (1890) Preliminary Announcement," *Chautauqua University and Chautauqua College of Liberal Arts: Circulars, Announcements, Specimen Lesson Sheets, Specimen Syllabuses, Letter Heads, Volume I, 1884-1892* (Chautauqua Archives), p. 47.

[50] Vincent, "The Chautauqua University," ibid., p. 2.

[51] Vincent, "Chautauqua: A Popular University," ibid., p. 733.

[52] Jesse Lyman Hurlbut, *The Story of Chautauqua* (New York: G.P. Putnam's Sons, 1921), p. 272.

Vincent's vision by accepting the responsibility of serving as principal of the entire Chautauqua System of Education in 1892. By that time Harper's administrative chores were staggering. He reorganized the Chautauqua System, dropped the name "university," and assumed the duties of "securing fifteen department heads and one hundred or more teachers, preparing sections for over two thousand students, planning a curriculum to include language and literature, mathematics and science, music, art, physical culture and practical art." In addition he edited the catalogue, planned the publicity, and arranged nearly 300 "events" for each session.[53]

Harper's rise from teaching to taking responsibility for an entire educational institution began at the biblical base of Vincent's vision. Harper was an expert on the subject which remained the core of the Chautauqua program: the Scriptures. That expertise, when joined with his impressive organizational ability, carried him via the Chautauqua path into national prominence and a much wider educational world. As he scheduled classes, lectures, sermons and events for Chautauqua's wide audience, Harper encountered the leaders of scholarship, political life and Protestantism. Richard T. Ely, Herbert Baxter Adams, Woodrow Wilson, Francis G. Peabody, Moses Coit Tyler, Frederick Jackson Turner, William Graham Sumner, Edward Everett Hale, Theodore Roosevelt, Josiah Strong, Frances Willard, Henry Drummond, Alonzo Stagg, Lyman Abbott, Washington Gladden, John Henry Barrows, Booker T. Washington and G. Stanley Hall each contributed to some phase of the total educational program run by Harper. Vincent's efforts to make evangelical education available to popular audiences which hungered for it provided Harper a route to the apex of the nation's religious and educational life.

Harper's own scholarly scope widened under the influence of the Chautauqua experience. In 1888 he opened a School of the English Bible to make available the results of biblical scholarship to Chautauquans with no Hebrew or Greek skills. By 1890 this new field required a separate section in the Preliminary Announcements for the Seventeenth Season. At that time Harper supervised a comprehensive structure of "Schools of Sacred Literature." The Christian Endeavor School of the English Bible, the College Student's School of the English Bible, the School of the English Bible, the School of Hebrew and the Old Testament, the School of New Testament Greek and the School of Semitic Languages and Ancient Versions indicate the breadth of the field which Harper sought to embrace.[54]

It is important to remember that Chautauqua, although formative for Harper, did not have the same effect on everyone who experienced it. After a July week there in 1896 William James admitted that he had learned "a lot"

[53] Morrison, *Chautauqua*, p. 76.
[54] "Chautauqua Seventeenth Season (1890) Preliminary Announcement No. 2," *Circulars, Announcements*, p. 64.

from the endless round of lectures, demonstrations and performances. But the basic goodness of the place troubled him. He looked forward to something "less blameless. . . . The flash of a pistol, a dagger, or a devilish eye, anything to break the unlovely level of 10,000 good people—a crime, murder, rape, elopement, anything would do."[55] Harper, on the other hand, experienced anything but boredom. Chautauqua provided both the vocational means to move beyond the professional world of seminary teaching, and the chance to widen his horizon to include a national range of problems and people that would be woven into the scriptural fabric of his new university.

### THE YALE PROFESSOR

While Harper climbed in esteem as teacher and administrator in his moonlighting efforts at Chautauqua, he also moved into prominence in his full-time profession as he become recognized as *the* teacher of Hebrew and Old Testament in the nation. Morgan Park, his vocational home for seven years, could not hold him. Even an offer to head the financially moribund old University of Chicago could not compete with a chance to return to Yale, this time as acknowledged leader of a scholarly profession. As a thirty-year-old, Harper returned to his alma mater in 1886 as professor of Semitic Languages in the Graduate Department and instructor in the Divinity School. A letter to his mentor Whitney revealed personal doubts about his abilities: "I am diffident in undertaking the work because I feel how poorly I am prepared as compared with many others, who hold chairs in Yale College; but I am sure that I shall do my best to build up the Department." Three weeks after this confession Harper accepted Whitney's suggestion "to take as much of the coming year as possible for study." He even promised not to open any new Hebrew Schools during the coming year.[56]

A promise to ease up on his schedule was relative, of course, to Harper's characteristic speed and energy. He built his department rapidly. Arriving with an entire professional apparatus, Harper needed the whole summer of 1886 to move his Hebrew enterprise into New Haven, renting a three-story building to house it. His correspondence programs, summer schools and Chautauqua enterprises made Harper on many days a larger user of the U.S. Post Office than all the rest of Yale University combined.[57]

A survey of Yale catalogues during Harper's tenure there reveals how his professional purview expanded. In his first year at his new post, Harper confined his efforts to teaching Hebrew, Arabic, Assyrian, and Aramaic. The

[55] Morrison, *Chautauqua*, p. 83.
[56] William Rainey Harper personal letters to William Dwight Whitney, June 12, 1886, and July 2, 1886 (William Dwight Whitney Collection, Yale University Archives, New Haven, Conn.).
[57] Mayer, *Young Man in a Hurry*, pp. 26–27.

next year, however, Harper's brother, Robert, whose scholarly biography in many ways paralleled William's, joined the department of Semitic Studies, bringing Ethiopic and Babylonian studies into Harper's field of vision. By the 1888–89 academic year the department included three other Harper proteges.

Harper's responsibilities included biblical subjects alongside the linguistic program. In 1890 Harper added the Woolsey Professorship of Biblical Literature to his other responsibilities. The Hebrew enthusiast's labors quickly dwarfed those of his mentor. In the 1890–91 university catalogue, Whitney's courses took up only a quarter of a page—his usual amount of space—while Harper's sprawled over three pages. Also that year he assumed an additional title: University Professor of the Semitic Languages.[58]

In his new setting, Harper again conducted a revival in the midst of a seemingly dry subject. Frank Knight Sanders, a long-time assistant to Harper and later Woolsey Professor of Biblical Literature and Dean of the Yale Divinity School, recalled Harper's impact: "He threw himself with stirring enthusiasm into his work, making himself almost at a bound the center of a group of earnest students. . . . To us all his methods and his ambitions were a revelation." In his first year at Yale Harper taught fifty theological students and, for the first time, seven graduate students.[59]

The Chautauqua experience had demonstrated Harper's ability to translate his scholarly work into a popular idiom. At Yale Harper made another move against the stream of specialization by introducing the study of the English Bible into the institution's curriculum. In the College he gave a series of lectures on Old Testament wisdom literature and soon found himself assigned by President Timothy Dwight to teach Bible regularly to undergraduates. From these beginnings Harper developed a national movement to open the college curriculum to the study of the English scriptures.[60]

At Yale Harper achieved an extraordinary degree of scholarly prominence. He held simultaneous professorships in the Divinity School and the departments of Semitic studies and biblical literature. President Dwight and others saw no limit to what he might achieve; his name was even mentioned as a likely future president of this most respected American college, recently turned university.

At the height of his prominence Harper turned away from all that Yale offered. Summoned by the Baptist leaders of Morgan Park Seminary and by the money of John D. Rockefeller, Harper took what seemed to be a discontinuous step into the perilous world of university administration. His years as leader of the Hebrew and Chautauqua movements had certainly

[58] *The Catalogue of Yale University* (New Haven: Yale University Press, 1886–87), pp. 40–41, 100, 115; (1887–88), pp. 40, 101, 116; (1888–89), pp. 43, 106–7, 122; (1889–90), pp. 43, 47, 119, 139–40.
[59] Sanders is quoted in Goodspeed, *William Rainey Harper*, p. 75.
[60] Ibid., pp. 75–78. The movement is discussed below, pp. 102–103.

prepared him for administration. More important than this administrative experience, however, was the basic vision which Harper carried with him to his new position in Chicago. He went there to construct a great community of learning, grounded on a biblical perspective which he had been fashioning for decades. Like other progressives of this period, Harper carried many of the core values of smalltown America with him as he approached his new environment.[61] But the mature vision which he brought to Chicago also contained elements from the other stops on his journey. He carried images of the professional scholar from his days under Whitney, a style of Baptist piety that made room for a variety of individual beliefs, and the concern he developed at Chautauqua for educating all Americans in a Christian culture. From these distinct worlds Harper fashioned his own unique and compelling vision. Constructive biblical scholarship, scientifically done, unfettered by the weight of tradition, carried out in the right spirit, became the means by which he sought to remake his troublesome American environment into a modern version of the biblical world.

[61] For a discussion of progressives and small town values see Jean B. Quandt, *From the Small Town to the Great Community: The Social Thought of Progressive Intellectuals* (New Brunswick, N.J.: Rutgers University Press, 1970).

# CHAPTER 3
## SHAPING A NEW BIBLICAL WORLD

In 1889, near the end of an article on "Yale Rationalism," Harper made a rare statement about the relationship between his conversion experience and his life's work.

> When converted to a belief in the religion of the Lord Jesus Christ (a conversion *after* school and college life) the writer pledged himself to the work of Bible study and Bible teaching. He has done what he could to build up not only an interest in the study of the Scriptures, but a faith in their divine origin.[1]

Written less than two years before Harper became president of the University of Chicago, Harper's rare self revelation was a cryptic indicator of professional purpose, academic vision and biblical perspective. As his personal notebooks and his many publications reveal, Harper's scholarly days and nights were spent in the promotion and encouragement of a Bible study movement in America. Although the plans for his new university were developed after Harper made his self-disclosure, they reveal that the institution he founded was also shaped in fundamental ways by the commitment he made in 1876 at a Granville, Ohio, Baptist prayer service. Even Harper's inchoate hermeneutic can be glimpsed in his statement's juxtaposition of biblical study and personal conversion.

### JOURNALISTIC BENCHMARKS

One of the primary ways in which Harper fulfilled his sacred pledge was through religious and scholarly journalism. During his career he founded and edited four periodicals aimed at a variety of audiences and interests. His first venture, *The Hebrew Student*, appeared in 1882, less than a year after the young professor began teaching Hebrew at Morgan Park Seminary. Within a year *The Hebrew Student* became *The Old Testament Student*, signalling a shift in interest beyond the limits of the editor's linguistic specialty.

One year later Harper separated scholarly linguistic work from the less

[1] William Rainey Harper, "Yale Rationalism," *The Old and New Testament Student* 9 (July 1889): 54.

technical but equally important task of reviving biblical study in America. The scholarly *Hebraica* appeared in 1884 while *The Student* became Harper's primary medium for reaching a wider public.[2] That Harper's horizon had expanded once again became clear in 1889 when *The Old Testament Student* added "and New" to its title page. Clearly, his experiences with popular audiences at Chautauqua and Yale had produced new journalistic imperatives.

In 1893 *The Old And New Testament Student* became *The Biblical World*, an indication that during the years of transition from professorship to university presidency, Harper's vision and purpose had widened still further.[3] Extrabiblical subjects such as religious education and the comparative study of religion began to appear in his tables of contents. As his scholarly vision matured and his journals grew, Harper developed a perspective which incorporated insights from historical analysis, literary criticism, sociology, psychology, comparative religion and other fields of inquiry into one expansive biblical vision.

## HARPER AND WELLHAUSEN

Harper's initial forays into biblical interpretation seemed quite conservative. The opening issue of *The Hebrew Student* carried a disclaimer informing readers of its editor's "sufficiently conservative" stance.[4] Several times during his publishing career he took the opportunity to reiterate that conservative position. In 1889, for example, when he published a series of articles in *Hebraica* debating Pentateuchal questions with Princeton's Professor Henry Green, Harper cautiously informed readers of the *Student* that he was merely summarizing opinions of more liberal scholars who favored multiple authorship of the first five books of the Bible. "The statements given are made without any reference to the conclusions to which he

[2] Kenneth Nathaniel Beck discussed the history of Harper's journals in "The American Institute of Sacred Literature: A Historical Analysis of an Adult Education Institution" (Ph.D. dissertation, University of Chicago, 1968) pp. 51ff. These journals outlived their founder, but not without considerable redefinition in scope and purpose. Thus *Hebraica* became *The American Journal of Semitic Languages* in 1895 and the *Student*, later *The Biblical World*, merged with *The American Journal of Theology* in 1921 to become *The Journal of Religion*, p. 127.

[3] Harper made two additional forays into religious journalism. *The American Journal of Theology* appeared in 1897 and was from its inception an official publication of the University of Chicago. In 1903 Harper appointed Shailer Mathews Managing Editor of *Christendom*, a shortlived (April 18–August 29, 1903) attempt at producing a popular magazine. Mathews felt the venture failed because it had been undercapitalized and mistakenly launched in the summer when readers were difficult to reach. See Shailer Mathews, *New Faith For Old: An Autobiography* (New York: The Macmillan Company, 1936), pp. 90–92.

[4] See the footnote on the cover page of William Rainey Harper, *The Hebrew Student* 1 (April 1882): 1.

[Harper] himself may have come, which, as a matter of fact, are, in many respects, widely different."[5] Yet a few years after assuming the presidency of his university, Harper unabashedly published articles on the first twelve chapters of Genesis which made it clear that he accepted many of the views which previously he had hedged with reservations.

Lars Hoffman has suggested that Harper experienced a "second conversion" to the ideas of Julius Wellhausen during the later years of the 1880s.[6] In order both to evaluate Hoffman's suggestion and, more importantly, to discern Harper's distinctive contribution to biblical scholarship, it is helpful to consider the impact of Wellhausen upon biblical scholarship as seen through the eyes of several more recent scholars of the field. The purpose of such a review is not to retell the history of biblical studies. Rather, by reviewing portions of that history, Harper's distinctive blending of evangelical belief and critical scholarship becomes more apparent.

Wellhausen's *Prolegomena to the History of Israel* appeared in its original German edition in 1878, three years after Harper had presented his dissertation to William Dwight Whitney and the Yale faculty. While the book is little known to those outside the field of biblical studies, it holds a place in its own discipline analogous to that of Charles Darwin's *Origin of the Species* in biology. Like Darwin, Wellhausen had precursors who had discovered major anomalies in traditional models of thinking. And also like Darwin, Wellhausen differed from his precursors in his ability to present what Rudolph Smend has called a "total view" of his subject which incorporated troublesome historical discoveries into an overarching new perspective.[7]

From the beginning of the 18th century, Old Testament scholars had been pondering the possibility of several narrative sources for the book of Genesis and, by extension, the rest of the Pentateuch. In a review of biblical scholarship in that period Douglas Knight has traced the proposal of "distinguishable sources" back to Henning Bernhard Witter in 1711.[8] During the next century and a half the evidence and speculation steadily accumulated against the traditional notion of Mosaic authorship. In 1753 Jean Astruc, once the physician to Louis XV of France and later a professor at the royal college at Paris, argued that two different narratives could be distinguished in Genesis on the basis of whether the Hebrew word employed for God was Yahweh or Elohim. By 1833 German theologian W.M.L. De Wette had moved attention to the problematic dating of the book of

---

[5] William Rainey Harper, "Editorial," *The Old Testament Student* 8 (February 1889): 205.

[6] Hoffman, "William Rainey Harper and the Chicago Fellowship," p. 68.

[7] Rudolph Smend, "Julius Wellhausen and His *Prolegomena to the History of Israel*," *Semeia* 25 (1982):13.

[8] Douglas A. Knight, "Wellhausen and the Interpretation of Israel's Literature," *Semeia* 25 (1982):21.

Deuteronomy, suggesting that instead of coming from the hand of Moses or from either of the two sources commonly called J and E, Deuteronomy was composed sometime in the 7th century B.C.E. By the time that K.H. Graf suggested, in 1865, that a fourth distinct source, the Priestly document, was the most recent of all the Pentateuchal sources, a tremendous amount of scholarship and evidence had accumulated which challenged conventional explanations.[9]

At age 34, Wellhausen, the son of a high church Lutheran minister, supplied a comprehensive new theory which could accommodate the new knowledge. The breakthrough which led to his complete reconstruction of Old Testament history had happened almost a decade before Wellhausen published his *Prolegomena*. The scholar recalled how:

> Dimly I began to perceive that throughout (the Pentateuch) there was between them (prophetic literature and Law) all the difference that separates two wholly distinct worlds. . . . At last, in the course of a casual visit in Göttingen in the summer of 1867, I learned through Ritschl that Karl Heinrich Graf placed the Law later than the Prophets, and almost without knowing his reasons for the hypothesis, I was prepared to accept it;
>
> I readily acknowledged to myself the possibility of understanding Hebrew antiquity without the book of the Law.[10]

Wellhausen gathered the insights from literary criticism and used them to reconstruct the history of Israel. If the Law attributed to Moses was one of the latest products of that history, then existing explanations of that history needed to be overhauled. Although other scholars would subsequently fault him for his preoccupation with the origins of the Law, that problem became the decisive one for Wellhausen. The "question to be considered is whether that law is the starting point of the history of ancient Israel, or not rather for that of Judaism, *i.e.*, of the religious communion which survived the destruction of the nation by the Assyrians and Chaldeans."[11]

What followed as the solution to this problem was what Patrick D. Miller, Jr., has recently described as Wellhausen's "schema." Wellhausen's history of Israel's religion was organized around three different sources for Israel's relationship to God. Through the centuries, that relationship shifted from an initial orientation to nature, to a subsequent orientation to history and then, finally, to an orientation to Law.[12] Correspondingly, Israel's history could be divided into three distinct phases: the period from the Exodus to

[9] Herbert L. Hahn, *The Old Testament in Modern Research* (Philadelphia: Fortress Press, 1966) pp. 4–5. Smend, "Julius Wellhausen and His *Prolegomena to the History of Israel*," p. 10.

[10] Wellhausen is quoted in Smend, p. 10.

[11] Ibid., p. 12.

[12] Patrick D. Miller, Jr., "Wellhausen and the History of Israel's Religion," *Semeia* 25 (1982), p. 62.

the emergence of Elijah in which God and Israel met in the elemental realm of nature; the prophetic period with its emphasis on God's actions in history; and the postexilic age, which was characterized by emphasis on the legal relations between God and the chosen people.

In Wellhausen's version, the primitive period of early Israelite history was typified by a natural religion lacking anything resembling the monotheism of later Judaism. John H. Hayes has summarized Wellhausen's reconstruction of the early history:

> There is little if any uniqueness to the history of the Israelite ancestors, no desert theocracy, no monotheistic faith, no law set once and for all, no unified experience of all the tribes in Egypt, no covenant theology.[13]

In essence, Wellhausen had jettisoned the patriarchal period, employing what Douglas Knight has called the "principle of historical projection" to deal with the biblical material about Abraham and his people.[14] The only historical knowledge one could gain from such stories was "of the time when the stories about them arose in the Israelite people."[15]

Wellhausen attempted to divorce the history of Israel from theological interpretations. His history was informed by the general principle that "the nearer history is to its origin the more profane it is."[16] But in spite of his efforts to offset theological biases, other prejudices crept into his reconstruction. In many ways a temperamental opposite to Harper, Wellhausen shunned "congresses and conferences, went on no lecture tours, and hardly ever participated in the normal sociability of colleagues" at Halle, Marburg and Göttingen where he held professorships.[17] Knight suggests that such an "anti-institutional posture" made him unsympathetic to "post-exilic intentions" and "drew him to the free spirit which he saw at play in the early period."[18]

If one turns to Harper's scholarly writing in his post-Yale days, it is tempting to accept Hoffman's hypothesis of a "second conversion" to Wellhausen. Harper clearly accepted many of the elements of Wellhausen's program. Like the seminal German thinker, Harper found the literary evidence in favor of the thesis that Genesis was essentially the product of four historically distinct sources to be of major significance in understanding Israel's history. He too was unable to draw a straight historical line from Eden to Jesus. While differing slightly from Wellhausen regarding the figure of Abraham, whom Harper regarded as a "simple superstitious sheik," he

---

[13] John H. Hayes, "Wellhausen as a Historian of Israel," *Semeia* 25 (1982), p. 53.
[14] Knight, p. 28.
[15] Wellhausen is quoted in ibid.
[16] Wellhausen is quoted in ibid., p. 30.
[17] Smend, p. 8.
[18] Knight, p. 33.

concurred with Wellhausen's assessment that the religion of the pre-M ,saic period was primitive and very similar to the tribal religions of other Semitic peoples.[19] Further, Harper agreed with Wellhausen that the view of God attributed to the patriarchal period reflected the beliefs of Judaism in its post-exilic phase. Such a reconceiving of patriarchal history did not, however, lead Harper to disvalue Israel's earliest history. What made the Hebrews special for Harper was their twenty centuries of intermigrating among the civilizations of the ancient Near Eastern world. This "unparalleled" contact with all the great civilizations allowed Israel to absorb the best from each of these contacts.[20]

Harper also concurred with Wellhausen's assessment that Moses did not author the Decalogue, at least in the form it takes in the Pentateuch. Moses was, in Harper's estimation, a "despot" who moved his people ahead from the polytheism of the patriarchal age to henotheism. Harper agreed that Moses did not offer a fully developed monotheism, but felt that he did offer a new conception of God which did not become dominant in Israel for hundreds of years. Study of the prophetic era led Harper to share Wellhausen's opinion that monotheism did not enter the mainstream of Israel's life until after the Babylonian exile.[21]

Like Wellhausen, Harper also found the career of Elijah to be a watershed in Israel's history. The "prophetic revolt" of 933 B.C. was led by this "fanatic" who secured a victory for the "country religion" of Israel over that of its Canaanite neighbors.[22] Harper shared with Wellhausen a preoccupation with the period that lasted from Elijah's time through the career of Jeremiah. John H. Hayes has argued that Wellhausen shared in a general 19th century "rediscovery of prophecy" and that Wellhausen overemphasized the importance of the prophets.[23] Harper also participated in his era's preoccupation with prophecy, which was in his estimation "the central mountain range," the "backbone" of the Old Testament.[24]

While Harper may have been sympathetic to the basic historical reconstructions offered by Wellhausen, he differed with him regarding their

[19] William Rainey Harper, "Editorial," *The Biblical World* 11 (May 1898):291; "Editorial," ibid. 12 (September 1898):148; "The Human Element in the Early Stories of Genesis," ibid. 4 (October 1894):267; "A Theory of the Divine and Human Elements in Genesis I-XI," ibid. 4 (December 1894):410; "Constructive Studies in the Priestly Element in the Old Testament—Part II," ibid. 17 (February 1901):124.

[20] William Rainey Harper, "The Prophetic Element in the Old Testament As Related to Christianity," unpublished lecture, Personal Papers, Box 16, Folder 9, pp. 14, 19.

[21] Ibid, pp. 14, 20–21, 32.

[22] William Rainey Harper, "Constructive Studies in the Prophetic Element. Study VI," *The Biblical World* 24 (October 1904): 292, 299; "Editorial," *The Biblical World* 25 (March 1905):168.

[23] Hayes, pp. 53–54.

[24] William Rainey Harper, "Editorial," *The Biblical World* 20 (August 1902):84, and "Editorial," *The Biblical World* 2 (September 1893):164.

interpretation. Wellhausen explained the history of Israel as a gradual triumph of institutional religion over the free, spontaneous religion of the individual. Harper, on the other hand, read the Old Testament progressively, constantly pointing out evidence of steady development toward higher views of God and the individual. Thus Jeremiah discovered the "doctrine of individualism" during the relatively late period which began with the Deuteronomic revolution (622 B.C.E.) and lasted through the exile (beginning in 586 B.C.E.)[25] Harper agreed that prophecy culminated and died during this period, but unlike Wellhausen he was able to trace the continuance of a development of prophetic beliefs about God to a higher level in Judaism. Post-exilic life developed the "highest" sense of God's transcendence and the most pervasive sense of sin in Israel's history. While Harper was especially drawn to the intermigratory pattern of the pre-exilic forms of Hebrew religion and even incorporated the image into his model of college life, he was able to attach a more positive significance to the more inward-looking, cult-centered religion of Judaism than was Wellhausen.[26]

While a description of several similar historical conclusions shared by Harper and Wellhausen seems to support the "second conversion" argument, it is important not to overlook Harper's public statements about his exegetical position. Those statements reveal that although he accepted many historical findings advanced by Wellhausen and his German colleagues, Harper appropriated those ideas selectively and set them in a framework quite different from Wellhausen's. Rather than merely echo Wellhausen's ideas, Harper incorporated them into his own interpretation of biblical history which, unlike that of the great continental scholar, was both critical and evangelical.

There is little doubt that Harper's public stance regarding the new biblical scholarship developed from caution as a young editor to bold advocacy in the 1890s. But Harper's journals reveal an awareness of critical issues from the start. In the second issue of *The Hebrew Student*, Harper reprinted the views of another distinguished German scholar, Franz Delitzsch, under the title "The New Criticism." Delitzsch had admitted that it was "true that many, and, at least, four hands participated in the codification of the Pentateuchal history and legislation." This more conservative scholar warned, however, that results of biblical criticism "are not as unquestionable as they pretend to be." In contradiction to more famous contemporaries like Wellhausen, Delitzsch stated that he began his study

> from an idea of God, from which the possibility of *miracle* follows, and confessing the resurrection of Christ, it confesses the reality of a

[25] Harper, "The Prophetic Element in the Old Testament As Related to Christianity," p. 43.
[26] Harper, "Constructive Studies in the Priestly Element in the Old Testament. Part IV," *The Biblical World* 17 (May 1901):366ff.

central miracle, to which the miracles of redemption-history refer as
the planets do to the sun.

Delitzsch rejected "*a priori* all results of criticism which abolish the Old
Testament premises of the religion of redemption."[27]

Elsewhere in the same issue the editor commented on "the burning
questions" of the day. Harper declared that what was causing

> so great anxiety to many, is not so much the results of Wellhausen's
> investigations as the irreverent and even frivolous manner, in which
> he has declared almost the whole Mosaic law a product of the exilic
> and post-exilic age, pronouncing the history of the Exodus and of the
> legislation legendary or merely fictitious.

He was more congenial to Delitzsch, on the other hand, who attempted "to
show that it is possible to maintain the union of different records and
codifications in the Pentateuch without denying the essential truth of the
history, and without surrendering the reverence which we owe to the Holy
Scriptures."[28]

When Harper became more outspoken on critical issues in the 1890s his
public position remained much nearer to that of Delitzsch, who received
frequent favorable reviews in Harper's journals, than to that of Wellhausen,
with whom he differed on fundamental grounds. But already in 1882 Harper
rhetorically had asked, "Radical or Conservative, that is the question?" He
wondered whether views which appeared to be radical "from our American
stand-point" were really "conservative when viewed from the German
stand-point." American students should pursue the study of these issues, but
with "great care." A single irresponsible paper could do harm that years of
subsequent labor might not overcome. "Make haste slowly," he suggested,
"should be the ruling principle." Any changes in biblical interpretation that
might occur "must come gradually."[29]

In March of 1886 Harper reviewed Wellhausen's troublesome but
seminal book, *Prolegomena to the History of Israel*. Conceding that the
work came from a "masterhand," Harper nevertheless offered several criticisms reminiscent of Delitzsch's position. He faulted the work for being
"thoroughly rationalistic." It knew "nothing of infallible inspiration, nothing
of supernatural revelation." Further, the tone of the work was "far from
reverent to those who receive the Old Testament as the Word of God."
Harper felt that Wellhausen adjusted the facts to his theory. There was little
doubt that Wellhausen's scholarship was useful in presenting "the many
facts of Scripture . . . in a new light" which necessitated further careful
scientific study. But, he concluded, "the truth will be more fully known; and

[27] Franz Delitzsch, "The New Criticism," *The Hebrew Student* 1 (May 1882):6–7.

[28] William Rainey Harper, "A General Statement," *The Hebrew Student* 1 (May 1882):10
and "Editorial Notes," ibid., p. 11.

[29] William Rainey Harper, "Editorial Notes," *The Hebrew Student* 1 (June, 1882):51.

though received views may be modified, yet God's word will be clarified and will shine more perfectly in the Law, the Prophets and the Scriptures."[30]

Harper's early reticence about expressing his own critical views may have had less to do with a "second conversion" than with another factor Hoffman noticed. Aware of his constituency, Harper made haste slowly. Although urged by journal readers and colleagues like Charles Briggs of Union Seminary to declare himself on sensitive issues of exegesis, Harper resisted. Instead he conducted a symposium through the pages of his journal, asking "Shall the Analyzed Pentateuch Be Published in *The Old Testament Student?*" Many said Yes. Harper declined: "The time has not yet come when even such a journal as *The Student* can take up and present such material with impunity." [31] Harper's editorial discretion—much more than a sudden intellectual conversion—may help account for his reluctant forthrightness. He felt free to advance in an unambiguous way critically informed interpretations only after those who elected him to the presidency at Chicago had vindicated him in the face of Augustus Strong's politically motivated heresy charges.[32]

### THE HARPER HERMENEUTIC

In *Literary Criticism and Biblical Hermeneutics: A Critique of Formalist Approaches*, Lynn M. Poland has recently argued that as a result of the rise of modern historical consciousness "the interpretative relation between text and reader essentially reversed its direction." Instead of trying to fit personal experience into an authoritative biblical world as pre-critical readers did, modern interpreters had to accomodate the biblical material into the new world of science and historical knowledge. Historical criticism, as advanced by Wellhausen and his colleagues, demonstrated and deepened a previously unrecognized "alienation of texts from the interpreter." The result of these new approaches towards the Bible and other ancient texts Poland labelled "the distinctive problematic of modern scriptural hermeneutics." People in Harper's generation had to be "at once an insider and an outsider, negotiating between the critical perspectives of the modern sciences and the recovery of meaning for faith" if their sacred texts were to continue to have "abiding religious significance."[33]

Poland's description of the modern hermeneutical problem provides an important clue to much of the religious turmoil of Harper's age. Shifting

[30] William Rainey Harper, "Wellhausen's History of Israel," *The Old Testament Student* 5 (March 1886):319.

[31] "A Symposium: Shall the Analyzed Pentateuch Be Published in *The Old Testament Student*" 7 (June, 1888):312–19 and "Editorial" ibid., p. 306.

[32] The accusation of heresy against Harper by Augustus H. Strong is discussed below, pp. 107ff.

[33] Lynn M. Poland, *Literary Criticism and Biblical Hermeneutics: A Critique of Formalistic Approaches* (Chico, California: Scholars Press, 1985), p. 33, 24.

relationships between modern readers of Scripture and their sacred book were apparent in the ferment of 19th century biblical scholarship and in the dramatic surge of popular interest in biblical subjects to which Harper's career attests.

Both Harper's scholarly career and his university presidency must be set within the context of the fracturing of traditional relationships between Protestants and their primary source of authority, the Bible. In the face of such trauma, Harper attempted to construct a new scientific hermeneutic, based on facts established by "reverent criticism." In essence, he attempted to carry out a critical reformation of a relationship at the center of America's religious life.

Some of Harper's sharpest words were reserved for conventional notions of biblical interpretation which prevailed in 19th-century America. Years of preparation and study led him to label traditional approaches to Scripture as "artificial and monstrous." Harper first concluded that the Bible had in fact been "misrepresented," and then embarked upon a vocation of "clearing away the rubbish" that separated modern readers from the sacred book. From his perspective the "babbling" of traditional interpreters was more dangerous to modern readers than were "the sneers of an Ingersoll," the quintessential infidel of the era. Looking backward he discerned that literal and artificial methods of interpretation had blinded first century Jews, locking them into a way of believing that kept them from recognizing Jesus as Messiah. Faulty interpretation also blinded modern readers to the true message of the Scriptures in the 19th century.[34]

For Harper the evangelical faith was at "the parting of the ways" regarding Bible study. He divided American attitudes toward the Bible into three categories. While many fell into the "sin" of bibliolatry, others gathered at the opposite end of the spectrum, filled with skepticism. A third group remained indifferent to scriptural claims. But all three groups misread their sacred texts.[35] Of those who bothered to read the Bible fully three quarters seemed to allegorize or spiritualize its contents. Noting that systematic theologians were speaking with a "less confident tone," Harper's journal proclaimed that popular evangelical theology was "docetic" and "gnostic." An *a priorist* approach to the Scriptures made Jesus into "an extra-legal interruption into history" rather than a fully historical, and therefore believable figure. Popular readers placed the Bible outside history—separate from

[34] William Rainey Harper, "A Theory of the Divine and Human Elements in Genesis I-XI," *The Biblical World* 4 (December 1894):418; "Editorial," *The Old and New Testament Student* 15 (July/August 1892):4–5; "Editorial," ibid. 10 (February 1890):71–72; "Outline Topics in the History of Old Testament Prophecy: Study 11," *The Biblical World* 7 (February 1896):129.

[35] William Rainey Harper, "The Parting of the Ways," *The Biblical World* 20 (July 1902):3ff; "Some General Considerations Relating to Genesis I-XI," ibid. 4 (September 1894):189–91.

it—and did not view its various books as responses to the historical events and beliefs of a people.[36]

Harper refused to "degrade" God as the *a priorists* did by making divine activity fit into the mold of literal understandings. Instead he offered a "reasonable view" that allowed no bifurcation between devotional and intellectual approaches to the Scriptures. The Bible was not two books, he claimed, but one. No longer did the Bible occupy the "supreme position" it once held. Indeed, the misuse of the book had relegated it to a "secondary" place.

For these reasons, Harper's journals took on a missionary hue as they relentlessly advocated a new approach to the Scriptures. Proper study would carry one past the threshold of doubt as the old understandings (rubbish) slipped away. If students followed Harper's approach, the end of the process was a new "home." The "critical question" for his era was how to carry the student through the transition period from the embrace of one perspective to adoption of another. One had to endure the painful stage of "passage from an unthinking to a rational faith."[37]

Harper's most complete statement about issues of interpretation was a lecture, "The Rational and The Rationalistic Higher Criticism," given at Chautauqua on August 2, 1892. Assuming that the Bible held a "place fundamental in all thought and life," Harper observed that conflict raged about the book "on every side." Unfortunately, to the general public the word "criticism" conveyed an "unpleasant idea," but to Harper the word simply meant "inquiry." In that sense "every real student of the Sacred Word is a higher critic." The higher critic sought

> to discover the date of the book, its authorship, the particular circum-
> stances under which it had its origin, the various characteristics of
> style which it presents; the occasion of the book; the purpose which
> in the mind of its author it was intended to subserve.[38]

Working with this understanding of criticism Harper had been able on an earlier occasion to hold up as an example of higher criticism his conservative counterpart in the Pentateuchal debates which had gone on in *Hebraica*. Thus Princeton's Professor Henry Green, who opposed the critical opinions of Wellhausen and other "radical critics," had received an unsolicited

[36] William Rainey Harper, "Editorial," *The Biblical World* 2 (August 1893):83; "Editorial," ibid. 9 (February 1897):81; "Editorial," ibid. 16 (August 1900):84.

[37] William Rainey Harper, "A Theory of the Divine and Human Elements in Genesis I-XI," *The Biblical World* 4 (December 1894):419; "Editorial," *The Old and New Testament Student* 13 (November 1891):258; "Editorial," *The Biblical World* 2 (July 1893):4; "Editorial," ibid. 2 (August 1893):81; "Editorial," *The Old and New Testament Student* 12 (January 1891):3; "Editorial," *The Biblical World* 13 (February 1899):65.

[38] William Rainey Harper, "The Rational and the Rationalistic Higher Criticism," *Chautauqua Assembly Herald* 17 (August 4, 1892):2–3, 6–7.

compliment which may not have helped an already confused public grasp a complex issue.[39]

Harper urged his Chautauqua listeners to join "in an effort to distinguish the true criticism from the false, a rational criticism from a rationalistic." These two types of criticism did not differ primarily in purpose, principles or material. The difference between the two was "in the method of work and in the spirit" with which the work was conducted. The rationalistic critic gave "undue prominence to the authority of reason." Two groups were subclasses of this type. One class enthroned reason as sole authority, "denying the authority of the scriptures, and the supernatural origin of Christianity." The other group did not sense its affinities with the explicitly rationalistic viewpoint. These interpreters magnified the authority of Scripture, but unconsciously placed reason "still higher." This group's argument proceeded, "God being so and so, therefore . . . ; Jesus Christ being so and so, therefore. . . ." Although their premises were opposite, one class denying supernatural revelation and the other affirming it, the groups really operated with "two parallel formulas." The "great multitude of critics" belonged to one or the other of the subclasses.[40]

Yet "here and there," Harper claimed, one might find a "disciple of another school," one "hardly yet organized." This was the "rational school," and although Harper did not say so, he was its champion. The first characteristic of a rational critic was a "scientific" spirit that moved through a three-step process: induction, reasoning and verification. Rational critics first observed, then formulated conclusions and finally sought to "find a theory which shall include all the facts." To be truly scientific, the critic held conclusions "subject to modifications or verification from other similar work."[41]

Both traditional interpreters and "materialistic" ones operated under the guise of science. But Harper cautioned that their approaches were "scientistic not scientific." One way of distinguishing between rational and rationalistic stances was to discern whether interpreters were "broad and open" or "narrow and dogmatic." In making such a determination, Harper risked a judgment of his own profession. Specialists were "of necessity" narrow individuals, who often had "an inability to generalize." Rational critics, however, based their conclusions "upon all the facts and upon those facts arranged in their proper relations." Wellhausen and other representatives of "those who deny the supernatural origin" of the Bible, were guilty of just such a "narrowness beyond belief," which led to "a dogmatism of the most arrogant type."[42]

[39] William Rainey Harper, "Editorial," *The Old Testament Student* 6 (October 1886):36.
[40] Harper, "Rational and Rationalistic," p. 3.
[41] Ibid.
[42] Ibid., pp. 3–4.

Another mark of the rational spirit was its "constructive" character. Scholars had to search for the foundations of phenomena, but care was required so that untrained minds were not "led to give up old positions before new positions have been formulated." Harper spotted many "theological and religious wrecks" on his horizon and concluded that the "*work* of destruction must be distinguished from the *spirit* of destruction." At times it was necessary to challenge cherished beliefs, but the motive and manner of this destructive work was crucial. People animated by the destructive spirit "seem possessed by the evil one himself, so malignant is their feeling, so malicious is their purpose."[43]

The final mark of rational criticism was reverence. The reverent critic did not see God as "some far distant power" but rather as "a father" interested in all the activities of the creation. A rational critic believed "in a divine revelation culminating in the incarnation of the deity himself and in the life on earth and death and resurrection of that incarnate Word." Such revelation was gradual, "coming little by little through the centuries." For Harper the most telling difference between rational and rationalistic critics was whether the motivating spirit was one of reverence or blasphemy.[44] Elsewhere Harper asserted that the key ingredient in biblical criticism was a "believing point of view."[45]

In a very preliminary and undeveloped way, Harper anticipated the distinction between the hermeneutics of belief and the hermeneutics of suspicion which Paul Ricoeur developed decades later in his significant work on the interpretation of Scripture.[46] Like Ricoeur, Harper found it necessary to move beyond both implicit faith and critical inquiry. The true biblical scholar still expected the text to address him after the critical process had occurred. Unlike Ricoeur and others of his generation, Harper gave his major effort to the critical uncovering of the history behind the text, rather than to the text as a distinct entity.

At other times Harper assigned different labels to his method of studying the Scriptures. Seven years prior to the presentation of his Chautauqua lecture on the subject, Harper had commented in the *Old Testament Student* about three schools of interpretation: the rationalistic, the allegorizing and the historico-grammatical, "*the* school of our century."[47] In 1896 and again in 1904 he distinguished among three schools of the interpretation of

[43] Ibid., p. 6.
[44] Ibid., p. 7.
[45] William Rainey Harper, "Editorial," *The Old Testament Student* 8 (October 1888):44.
[46] Ricoeur developed the idea of a "conflict of interpretations" or "war of hermeneutics" in *Freud and Philosophy: An Essay on Interpretation*, trans. Denis Savage (New Haven: Yale University Press, 1970), pp. 54–56. He names the two schools in the conflict "the school of suspicion" and "the school of reminiscence" (p. 32).
[47] William Rainey Harper, "The Age of Common Sense in Interpretation," *The Old Testament Student* 5 (October 1885):88.

prophecy: rationalistic, predictive and historical. Those within the last group of interpreters could be classified either as "conditional" or "idealistic" interpreters.[48] Locating himself among the "idealistic" interpreters who recognized the gradual realizations of ideals throughout Israel's history, Harper fashioned a *via media* between the supernatural claims of evangelical faith and the fresh discoveries of historical investigation. As he plumbed for the "fundamental ideas" of biblical material, Harper avoided choosing either of two unpalatable alternatives: he did not ignore the results of modern knowledge, but neither did he renounce the divine factor in history.

### THE SCIENTIFIC STUDY OF THE SCRIPTURES

Like many Americans of his era, Harper was enamored of science. Scientific vocabulary colored his writing, and he urged his students to be scientific in their manner. In a dissertation on the development of scientific study at the University of Chicago, however, Lincoln C. Blake has suggested that while Harper may have believed that he shared in the scientific spirit of his age, in reality his understanding of the natural sciences was more superficial. Harper's decisions when hiring two professors for his nascent science departments revealed to Blake that although he was a professional in his own field, Harper was only a layman in the realms of natural and physical science.[49]

Recalling Harper's undergraduate and graduate education and his limited exposure to German notions of *Wissenschaft* except as mediated through filtering agents like Professor Whitney of Yale, it is likely that his scientific method was a descendant of the common-sense philosophy of Scotland's Thomas Reid. In *The Enlightenment in America*, Henry F. May demonstrated that this common-sense approach "reigned supreme" in American education throughout the greater part of the 19th century.[50] For most American scientists, gathering all the facts, arranging them in categories, and inducing a hypothesis equalled "science." Evidence, for these investigators, seemed rather unambiguous; their problem was simply the incompleteness of knowledge. Echoes of this common-sense version of science can be observed in Harper's statements about his science.

In the March 1888 *Old Testament Student*, for example, Harper defined scientific Bible study as

[48] William Rainey Harper, "Outline Topics in the History of Old Testament Prophecy: Study III," *The Biblical World* 7 (March 1896):199; "Constructive Studies in the Prophetic Element in the Old Testament," ibid. 23 (January 1904):57.
[49] Lincoln C. Blake, "The Concept and Development of Science at The University of Chicago 1890–1905" (Ph.D. dissertation, University of Chicago, 1966).
[50] Henry F. May, *The Enlightenment in America* (New York: Oxford University Press, 1976), p. 348.

> study in the process of which (1) scientific methods are employed; (2) adherence is maintained to the laws of human speech; (3) allowance is made for all the factors which enter into the problem under consideration; (4) the truth is sought, regardless of previous preconceptions.

It was not

> study in the process of which (1) methods belonging to the dark ages are used; (2) the simplest laws of language are violated; (3) only facts favorable to the theory are considered, the others wrested or ignored; (4) a theory must be established, whether by fair or foul means.[51]

Harper admitted that he was not too "rigid" in his employment of an inductive approach. There was a danger, he felt, of induction from one set of facts to the exclusion of others. Thus, while encouraging the reading of the Bible as a piece of great literature, he warned against the inherent danger of reading it as "mere literature." The "supernatural element" would be lost if only literary facts were admitted to the inquiry. One must "find a theory which shall include all the facts." For him a "nonreligious study of the Bible" was every bit as "unscientific" as a non-historical variety.[52]

If the scholar participated in a scientific viewing of "the wonderful facts" of the scriptural record, according to Harper, he or she would be led to "no other explanation but that of God." Following his inductive method to its ultimate conclusion, Harper posited the "hypothesis of the divine factor" in Israel's history. How else, he argued, could one account for this people's peculiar monotheism in the midst of Arabian polytheism? Historical investigation led him to affirm the "supreme facts of Revealed religion . . . God, Christ, Sin, Eternal life, retribution." As a scientific student of the Bible, Harper defended the truthfulness of its writers, even while accepting critical challenges to their literal or historical accuracy. Consideration of their exalted faith led him to argue that it was "psychologically impossible" for prophets to "palm off" false narratives on unsuspecting readers.[53]

Imitating the language of a scientist in his laboratory, Harper wrote that after all the human elements in the biblical material had been analyzed there remained a "divine element" which was the "residuum which cannot be attributed to man." Since the divine was discernible if one was properly scientific in method, it was possible for the faith of modern believers to share a scientific character and certainty. Faith could be constructed on a scientific

---

[51] Harper, "Editorial," *The Old Testament Student* 7 (March 1888):211.

[52] William Rainey Harper, "Editorial," *The Old and New Testament Student* 9 (August 1889):65, 68–70; "Rational and Rationalistic," p. 3; "Editorial," *The Biblical World* 10 (November 1897):322.

[53] William Rainey Harper, "Editorial," *The Old and New Testament Student* 9 (October 1889):196; "The Divine Element in the Early Stories of Genesis," *The Biblical World* 4 (November 1894):356; "Editorial," *The Old and New Testament Student* 12 (March 1891):131; "Editorial," ibid. 12 (June 1891):324.

basis; belief equalled accepting the evidence. One cultivated belief by analyzing the evidence and arranging life according to it.[54]

Harper's scientific approach to faith allowed him to bridge, at least in his own eyes, the epistemological gap between reason and reception of revelation. It followed then that the apostle Paul had been mistaken when he pitted the foolishness of God against the wisdom of humans. God's activity was natural; there was an "essential harmony" between nature's laws and the working of the Kingdom of God. Harper could see the "same Divine methods in human life everywhere." Searching for truth was equivalent to "searching for God." The "grandest fact" was that God did not speak one word in nature and another in revelation; there was one Word of God in both. The child and the savage found supernatural evidence only in the startling, exceptional events of history. The "instructed mind," on the other hand, saw God in the world of natural law and order.[55]

Having established an essential continuity between the Bible and the world of historical and scientific truth, Harper was not troubled by various facts which threatened believers adhering to more traditional perspectives. The existence of 150,000 different scribal renderings in a host of New Testament manuscripts did not weaken his scientifically established faith. Neither did the fact that the Pentateuch had four authors rather than the one of tradition. It was "pseudo-science" to claim that there was nothing historical in the Bible. To claim that every jot and tittle of it was historically accurate was "pseudo-orthodoxy." What Harper advocated was "biblical science," an awareness that the Bible was a historical product but that it contained very little history, as moderns defined the term. It was a "sacrilege" to make the Bible into a scientific treatise.[56]

To such a scientist, the world became a laboratory. His popular journal, *The Biblical World,* called for making both church and university into laboratories where religious truth could be discovered and applied. So compatible were science and the Bible that in one editorial the Holy Land of Palestine was transformed into God's great laboratory, devoted to the solution of a single problem: how to live. In this reading, the Old Testament became a scientific notebook kept by a host of "laboratory assistants" who labored in different periods of experimentation.[57]

[54] Harper, "Editorial," *The Old and New Testament Student* 8 (January 1889):162; "Editorial," *The Biblical World* 1 (June 1893):403.

[55] Harper, "Editorial," *The Old and New Testament Student* 10 (May 1890):263; "Editorial," *The Old Testament Student* 8 (October 1888):41.

[56] Harper, "Editorial," *The Biblical World* 3 (March 1894):163–64; "Paradise and the First Sin: Genesis III," ibid., p. 176; "Editorial," *The Old and New Testament Student* 14 (February 1892):65; "The First Hebrew Story of Creation" *The Biblical World* 3 (January 1894):16.

[57] Harper, "Editorial," *The Biblical World* 24 (December 1904):407; "Editorial," ibid. 9 (March 1897):161ff.

"All the facts" included evidence of development. Harper was aware of the significance of evolutionary theory, even if he refrained from comment upon its implications for Old Testament creation accounts. His recasting of Israel's history, his understanding of the subsequent history of Christianity and his notions of progressive revelation depended upon a developmental model of history. For him the human story was "one great stream," which flowed gradually upward. The history of the Hebrews, for example, passed through three progressive stages: Semitic, Israelite, and Judaistic. In each age or stage or religious development, new and higher knowledge of the "divine method or work" emerged.[58] The advent of Jesus did not end the developmental process. Instead Christianity steadily matured until it arrived at its current "transition stage" moving gradually from a lower ritualistic level toward what Harper believed would be a higher, more spiritual plane.

The Scriptures provided the primary raw material for Harper's progressive views. The Bible could be viewed as "a theistic interpretation" of social evolution. In it one found the "literary remains" of every stage of life of the Hebrew people.[59] In a personal letter to Augustus Strong, who accused him of false doctrine during the critical days of John D. Rockefeller's deliberations about the future location of the proposed Baptist university, Harper revealed that he followed a method which he called "the typical interpretation." He affirmed that "the whole Pentateuch," including its history, institutions, and any miscellaneous material "pointed directly and definitely to Christ." He objected, however, to "the old interpretation" which found "a definite statement concerning the historic Christ in every chapter or verse." All the "so-called Messianic passages," even the cherished Protoevangelium in Genesis 3:15, had their "final fulfillment in the Christ." But Harper insisted—"as today all Old Testament exegetes insist"—upon the typological interpretation.[60]

In his explanation to Strong, Harper quoted from a lecture he had delivered at Vassar College:

> God is unchangeable in that he always acts with certain eternal, unchangeable principles. He is unchangeable in so far as he is continually presenting to us everywhere enlarging manifestations of himself and of his plans. His movement in history is a spiral; all motion in one ring of the spiral is a prophecy of a higher and larger ring. The type is the lower ring of the spiral of which the antitype is the higher or highest ring . . . ; type is a historical person, thing or fact

[58] Harper, "Editorial," *The Biblical World* 11 (May 1898):289ff; "Editorial," ibid. 9 (May 1897):327; "Editorial," ibid. 1 (April, 1893):247.
[59] Harper, "Editorial," *The Biblical World* 17 (February 1901):84; "Editorial," ibid. (March 1901):163.
[60] William Rainey Harper to [Augustus H. Strong], January 4, 1889, Personal Papers, Box 1, Folder 8.

definitely intended to prefigure some corresponding person, thing or
fact in the future.[61]

Revelation spiralled in widening circles, ever upward. It was dynamic; it
could be outgrown. The folktale preceded the Law in Israel's history in the
same fashion as the Law preceded Christ. Each lower stage was "school-
master" to the higher. Old Testament and New were two dispensations from
the same source. They were related as preparation to fulfillment, fragment to
unity, transition to permanence.[62]

Harper steadfastly refused to separate religious and secular history. The
"laws of life" controlled the religious spirit in the same way that they
influenced developments in other areas of human experience. There were
"strata" in religious developments just as there were in other phases of life.
The problem with the old theology was that it "had not grasped the idea of
law, or an organic development in the history of revelation."[63]

COMPARATIVE RELIGION

"All the facts" also included insights from the new academic discipline
of comparative religion. Harper's writings contain frequent references to
new discoveries about ancient religions of the near East and other civilizations. Just as he embraced the supposedly troublesome world of modern
science, so Harper welcomed this emerging discipline, which was often a
stumbling block to those who argued for Christian uniqueness.[64] In a lecture
titled "The Bible and the Monuments" Harper characteristically reviewed
the latest findings of scholarly research and then converted the data into

[61] Ibid.

[62] Harper, "Editorial," *The Biblical World* 17 (March 1901):165; "Editorial," ibid. 3 (May
1894):321–25.

[63] Harper, "The University and Religious Education," *The Biblical World* 24 (November 1904):326–27; "Editorial," *The Old and New Testament Student* 13 (December 1891):
322.

[64] The study of comparative religion was introduced to America by James Freeman Clarke
in 1867. How compelling the subject became for Harper can be seen in his active support
for the new field. Beginning in 1893 *The Biblical World* devoted a special section to the
young discipline. One year earlier the University of Chicago had appointed Professor
George Stephen Goodspeed to head its new Department of Comparative Religion in the
Divinity School, the first such department in America. Professor Joseph M. Kitagawa has
traced the history of the discipline in his essay "The History of Religions in America," *The
History of Religions: Essays in Methodology*, Mircea Eliade and Joseph M. Kitagawa, eds.
(Chicago: University of Chicago Press, 1959), pp. 2, 17. According to Kitagawa the "key to
the scientific investigation of religions was philology" for early figures in the discipline like
Max Muller. Harper's interest in comparative philology had begun during his doctoral
program at Yale. He was thus prepared to be congenial to the new philological discoveries
when they were reported.

evidence which could support an argument for the inspiration of the Christian Scriptures.[65]

According to his survey, there were 50,000 recently unearthed ancient Near Eastern clay tablets in museums around the world, of which a mere 2000 had been read. Among the startling discoveries which Harper shared with his listeners were new findings about the origins of many of Israel's religious practices and beliefs. For example, "the 'Sabbath,' the day of rest, was Accadian." The sacred number seven had "descended to the Semites from their Accadian predecessors." Distinctions between clean and unclean food "were as clearly marked among Babylonians and Assyrians as among the Israelites." Even the interpretation of so pivotal a figure in Israel's history as Moses was affected by the new discoveries. The biblical account of Moses' childhood sounded very similar to an Accadian legend which claimed that one thousand years before Moses, Sargon of Accad "was born in concealment; placed by his mother in a basket of rushes, launched on a river, rescued, and brought up by a stranger, after which he became king." Harper wondered if he should "accept that interpretation of the word *Moses*, which makes it not Egyptian, but *Masu* (Accadian or Semitic) with the meaning *Hero*, a most common Semitic appelation from the earliest times?"[66]

The similarities between Israel and its neighbors did not end with names of ancient leaders. Hebrew poetry borrowed its distinctive and characteristic "parallelism" from the Accadian people. Accadian penitential psalms antedated those of the Hebrew Psalter by "a thousand or more years."[67]

Ranging across sources as disparate as those in Sanskrit and Polynesian languages, Harper compared the primordial history of Israel with accounts of other religions. There were extra-biblical accounts of rainbows and deluges that shared a similarity of "essential facts" with the Genesis material. Other religions related a "fall" from a state of innocence and told of mythical trees of life. Such evidence, Harper concluded, led to an unsettling realization: the Hebrew accounts of the origins of the world and human life were not original. Rather, the different religious accounts were "sister stories," all descendants from a common source—"an objective historical fact which impressed itself upon the minds of many nations."[68]

Discoveries by students of archaelogy and comparative religion, which brought others to spiritual crisis in the Gilded Age, did not overwhelm

[65] William Rainey Harper, "The Bible and the Monuments," Unpublished Lecture, Personal Papers, Box 16, Folder 1.

[66] Ibid., pp. 18, 49–52.

[67] Ibid., p. 54.

[68] William Rainey Harper, "The Deluge in Other Literatures and History," *The Biblical World* 4 (August 1894):115; "The Hebrew Stories of the Deluge, Genesis VI-IX," ibid. 4 (July 1894):30; "Paradise and the First Sin, Genesis III," ibid. 3 (March 1894):185; "The Human Element in the Early Stories of Genesis," ibid. 4 (October 1894):277–78.

Harper. Instead he marvelled at the "wonderful resemblances" between Christianity and other religions. He also noted decisive differences. When he compared Hebrew creation accounts with those of other Near Eastern religions he found those of Israel's neighbors to be

> polytheistic in the extreme, even pantheistic; confusing, confounding; characterized by imperfections and weaknesses of every kind; remarkably similar in tone and spirit to the mythological productions of Greece and Rome.

In short, these stories were "debasing." Israel's accounts, on the other hand, were

> monotheistic, ethical; clear, and distinct; unhesitating. Well nigh perfect in form and utterance, sublime in tone and spirit; as unlike Greek and Roman myths as the sun is unlike the moon.

In a word, they were "elevating."[69]

The particular genius of the Israelites was their ability to demythologize the religious stories of their sister peoples. The story of the *nephilim* in Genesis 6, for example, showed how the Hebrew prophets transformed stories grounded in "exuberant polytheism" and the elaborate mythology of popular legends into vehicles bearing monotheistic meaning. Only in Genesis did the heavenly consorts lose their godlike status. The *nephilim* became angels only in the "purified" legend in Genesis which was used to "subvert" the superstition of the age.[70]

For Harper the comparative approach did not undermine the importance of the sacred Scriptures. On the contrary, careful comparative work underscored the uniqueness and superiority of the biblical message. Harper found an "essential difference between the profane and sacred accounts" of the ancient world, and he approvingly quoted Professor Charles Rufus Brown concerning the "infinite gap between the Hebrew and his brother Semite."

> The thing which every Bible scholar is most concerned for, is that root-element which distinguishes the Hebrew people from all the ancient peoples, and the Hebrew writings from all other ancient literature. The one great distinctive feature of the literary monuments of the Hebrews is that they were informed by a *spirit* to which the inscriptions of Nineveh and Babylon are utter strangers. There is a truth of spiritual conception, a loftiness of spiritual tone, a conviction of unseen realities, a confident reliance upon an invisible and all-controlling power, a humble worship in the presence of the supreme

[69] Harper, "Editorial," *The Old and New Testament Student* 16 (September/October 1892):91; "The Bible and the Monuments," p. 59.
[70] William Rainey Harper, "The Sons of God and the Daughters of Men. Genesis VI," *The Biblical World* 3 (June 1894):446–47; "The Fratricide: The Canaanite Civilization. Genesis IV," ibid. (April 1894):270.

> majesty, a peace in union and communion with the one and only God,
> and the vigorous germs of an ethics reflecting his will . . . .[71]

Nor did the distinctiveness of the Bible require repudiation of other religious traditions. Harper simply absorbed the new data as one more source of light shed on the fundamental elements of religious life.

## A New Argument for the Inspiration of Scriptures

The more Harper surveyed the findings of scientifically studied religion, the more convinced he became that the Bible was divine, inspired. When he compared various accounts of events, or psalms, or poetry, he found in the Scriptures "a something which seizes hold of us; moves us powerfully; inspires us." He looked for that same element in other religious sources, but it was "wholly lacking." Instead he discovered in the others "a dullness, a flatness, an insipidity which disappoints and at times almost disgusts." Why, he asked, when the same subject, story or experience was treated in various texts, "*why* is not the spirit the same?" There was one suitable answer. The one set of writings was "*only* human." The other set, the Hebrew Scriptures, was "human, to be sure, but *also* divine." By surveying and comparing the various texts of the ancient religions, Harper felt he could find "*direct*" evidence which was "absolutely conclusive and must be convincing." With a new scientific version of Christian triumphalism, Harper announced the discovery of a new "fact," one "capable of scientific demonstration, that the Old Testament, the Bible *is*, and that too when considered from an Assyrian point of view, *God-given.*"[72]

Harper's conviction about the superiority of the Bible led him to an almost mystical sense of the uniqueness of Hebrew history. In a series of unpublished lectures on prophecy he subtly inverted the traditional argument for inspiration. Inerrantists usually argued from the divine character of their perfect book to the historical certainty that events happened the way the book described them. Harper changed direction.

> The historical situation is the divine, the prophecy is the human
> interpretation of the situation by a man who is himself included in the
> situation and is therefore divinely guided.

All of Israel's history was "supernatural history." To speak of various miracles in the Scriptures was to lose sight of the fact that the "whole history of the chosen nation is one stupendous miracle." God "moved in Israelitish history as in no other." [73]

---

[71] Harper, "The Bible and the Monuments," pp. 61–62.
[72] Ibid., pp. 65–68.
[73] William Rainey Harper, "General Questions About Prophecy: Lecture VII," unpublished lecture, Personal Papers, Box 16, Folder 8, pp. 3fb, 4fa, 13fa.

Thus history, not the divine book, was the primary inspired medium. For Harper historical knowledge became "fundamental." Scientific study enabled scholars to draw nearer to the primary locus of inspiration. It was important to remember that "in every case the record followed the transaction." Harper went to the heart of the Christian message with his claim.

> Give me the one great event in the history of the Christian church, the resurrection of Jesus Christ, and I care nothing for the record of that. It is the fact upon which Christianity is based.

Rather than wage war for a hermetically sealed book, Harper set out to do battle for the history behind it. This "wonderfully moulded history," the "one great miracle" of the "inspiration of the history of the chosen people," was the one thing for which "we shall today make our fight." If people granted the inspiration of Hebrew history "first of all," Harper was certain that "all the rest will follow."[74]

The prophets had been the great interpreters of inspired history. By making the subject of "prophecy" the central emphasis in his Old Testament studies, Harper placed himself in the prophetic stream, reinterpreting history for moderns who needed to encounter the presence of God in history, not merely within written traditions.

In a private letter to Mrs. J.B. Stewart, a Bible student from Butte County, California, Harper offered one more argument for the inspiration of the Bible certain to unnerve advocates of a dictation theory of inspiration. He repeated the assertion that the Bible was the "human record of a process of divine teaching." But one determined whether or not it was inspired by testing with the question, "Does it inspire?" Harper asked that question of the Scriptures and answered that "no other literature in the world has ever inspired men to such attainments in high and holy living."[75]

Rather than beginning with prior assumptions about the Bible, Harper's "inductive" theory of inspiration encouraged readers to examine the evidence of the Scriptures, comparative religions, history, and human experience with the book and then to define a position. The "question of questions" in his age was that of the inspiration of Scripture. Old theories of interpretation might be shaken, but for Harper the fact of inspiration remained. The human scaffolding surrounding Scripture may have crumbled, but for him the "temple of truth" stood firm. A "valiant service for the cause of truth" would be done when the "verbal theory" of inspiration was "forever silenced."[76]

---

[74] Ibid., p. 16fb.

[75] William Rainey Harper to Mrs. J.B. Stewart, April 11, 1903, Personal Papers, Box 6, Folder 25.

[76] Harper, "Editorial," *The Old Testament Student* 4 (February 1885):284; "Editorial," *The Old and New Testament Student* 11 (November 1890):260–61; "Editorial," *The Biblical World* 2 (August 1893):84–85; "Editorial," *The Old and New Testament Student*

## THE INVISIBLE ROLE OF RELIGIOUS EXPERIENCE

A hidden element in both Harper's reconstruction of biblical history and his assertion of its uniqueness and importance was his personal religious experience. Throughout his career he took the relationship of that experience to his hermeneutic for granted, never pausing to examine it. Just as he traced his lifework to the conversion experienced during his early teaching days in Ohio, so his confidence in the message of the Scriptures seems to have been authenticated by private religious experience, alongside publicly discussed scientific evidence. Editorials in the *Biblical World* occasionally argued for the necessity of religious experience for true biblical interpretation. There was apparently "higher evidence" than even the most carefully collected scientific data.[77]

The problem with the prevailing understanding of the Old Testament was that it "kept many men from putting themselves into an attitude where they might receive the experience necessary to salvation." No theology "ever saved any man from his sins." Theology was "only a human philosophical interpretation" of certain parts of religious experience and "it must always be the experience that brings salvation." Harper hoped that the New Theology being built on the results of scientific study of the Scriptures would create a "hospitable attitude toward the fundamental truths and experiences of Christianity."[78]

The result of Harper's reconstruction of the biblical materials was a modern form of Christianity built upon two foundations—the scientific study of the Scriptures, and personal religious experience. Harper never worked out the exact relationship between the two. The possibility that all his scientific certainty might be erected upon an experiential foundation available only to certain individuals with histories or temperaments like his did not seem to trouble him. The problem of relating specific interpretations to pre-understandings or beliefs which became so pressing for students of hermeneutics from the time of Friedrich D. E. Schleiermacher on through contemporary scholars like Paul Ricouer did not seem to concern him.[79]

11 (September 1890):129; "Editorial," *The Biblical World* 1 (April 1893):246; "Editorial," *The Old and New Testament Student* 14 (February 1892):69.

[77] Harper, "Editorial," *The Biblical World* 25 (April 1905):245; William Rainey Harper and George S. Goodspeed, "The Gospel of John. Study I," *The Old and New Testament Student* 12 (January 1891):52.

[78] William Rainey Harper to Rev. G.D. Edwards, February 11, 1905, Personal Papers, Box 8, Folder 19.

[79] For an overview of the history of hermeneutic theory see Kurt Mueller-Vollmer's "Introduction: Language, Mind and Artifact: An Outline of Hermeneutic Theory Since the Enlightenment," in Kurt Mueller-Vollmer, ed., *Texts of the German Tradition from the Enlightenment to the Present* (New York: Continuum, 1985), pp. 1–53. An example of Paul Ricouer's response to this problem is *Essays on Biblical Interpretation*, Lewis S. Mudge, ed. (Philadelphia: Fortress Press, 1980), p. 58.

Instead Harper focused his attention on reshaping the American religious environment in the image of his reconstructed biblical world. The reinterpretation of the Scriptures provided the impetus for his critical reformation. Biblical criticism became the starting point for attempting a reconstruction of the Christian faith and church. In order to foster his reformation of biblical understanding Harper sought to transform the basic educational configuration of the late 19th century.

## HARPER'S PLACE WITHIN THE WORLD OF BIBLICAL SCHOLARSHIP

The portrait of Harper advanced in this chapter is that of a cautious scholar-editor who, while being open to insights from German scholarship, was free to value those insights in his own characteristic manner. Clearly Harper was not a seminal scholar; there are no major new paradigms announced or offered in his work. But what was distinctive about him was his openness to knowledge from many sources and his ability to "blend and reconcile" perspectives and knowledge which many felt were incompatible.[80] That distinctiveness becomes apparent when Harper is examined in relation first to the history of the Divinity School he created at the University of Chicago, and subsequently to other major developments within the field of biblical scholarship.

The difficulty of relating Harper to the history of the Divinity School readily is apparent in the ongoing debate about the existence of a distinct "Chicago School," with its own unique scholarly methods and assumptions. Among those who agree that such a school exists or existed, there is further debate about the membership of the School and the nature of its project. William J. Hynes, one of those who has attempted to reconstruct the history of the Chicago School, identified at least three different definitions which have been advanced in various scholars' efforts to organize an ambiguous period in the Divinity School's history:

> in various contexts, the Chicago School is spoken of as either (a) a school of New Testament interpretation, for example, by E.C. Colwell and Robert Funk, (b) a school of theology, for example, by [A.C.] McGiffert and [Bernard] Meland, or (c) as a school of church history by Sidney Ahlstrom who sees a "disproportionate number" of this century's American church historians as being from the Chicago School.[81]

Harvey Arnold has dated the origins of "the Chicago School of Theol-

[80] Harper's ability to "blend and reconcile" various academic models was first noticed by Lawrence Veysey in *The Emergence of the American University* (Chicago: The University of Chicago Press, 1965) pp. 367–80. Veysey's characterization is discussed below, pp. 171–173.

[81] William J. Hynes, *Shirley Jackson Case and the Chicago School: The Socio-Historical Method* (Chico, California: Scholars Press, 1981), p. 13.

B.E. MELAND

ogy" from 1906, the year of Harper's death. In Arnold's version, Harper set the stage for the development of an important approach to the study of Christianity, its Scriptures and religion in general. By building the university, making the Divinity School an organic part of it, and recruiting the school's faculty, Harper provided the context in which a distinctive way of thinking could emerge. But Harper, according to this telling, had little to do with the intellectual thrust of the "school." That thrust would be the result of efforts during the post-Harper era, when second-generation Divinity School faculty members such as George Burman Foster, Shailer Mathews and Shirley Jackson Case came into prominence.[82]

In a different version of the early history of the Divinity School, Robert Funk has described two "dynasties" which vied for prominence in the field of biblical studies. The first such dynasty, Harper's, was characterized by a philological and historical approach to the Scriptures. The second, which came to be identified as the socio-historical method, turned away from Harper's preoccupation with the scriptural text. Its progenitor, according to Funk, was Ernest DeWitt Burton, professor of New Testament at the Divinity School from its founding in 1892 and eventually the third president of the university. In essence, Funk claimed, the Divinity School shifted instruments in its attempts to understand the importance of the biblical message for modern Americans. Emphasis on the scriptural text gave way to concerns for the social history that surrounded that text; to pursuit of the events and experiences that lay behind it; and to assessment of the various interpretations given over centuries of transmission.

Funk advanced several explanations for the shift in methods and dynasties. The first Divinity School faculty had been transplanted from a Baptist seminary in Morgan Park, Illinois. Its members were not university-oriented; many of them did not have graduate degrees. The second generation, on the other hand (people like Mathews and Case), came with new models of scholarship drawn from university-based graduate programs. Those who followed and developed the socio-historical line were responding to different issues than those of textual interpretation which so vexed American believers in the days when Harper rose to prominence.

> In place of the philological expertise of the first generation, or in addition to it, they had to meet the full thrust of the physical and social sciences. This accounts for their heavy concentration in history, sociology, and psychology. By these means they hoped to overcome the scholarly limitations of traditional divinity, without sacrificing the prestige that still attached to philological competence.[83]

[82] Charles Harvey Arnold, *Near the Edge of Battle: A Short History of the Divinity School and the "Chicago School of Theology," 1866-1966* (Chicago: The Divinity School Association, 1966), pp. 10–16, 23–60.

[83] Robert Funk, "The Watershed of the American Biblical Tradition: The Chicago School, First Phase, 1892–1920," *Journal of Biblical Literature* 95 (March 1976), p. 25.

Scholars like Case and Mathews "were headed toward open university, i.e. secular, ground" with their programs. The evangelical lay audience which had been so central in Harper's consciousness, faded into the background of the second generation's concerns. This shift, according to Funk, was not so much an indication of scholarly abandonment of the popular mind as it was a sign of a shift in the common consciousness.

> The lineage that runs from Burton through Mathews, Case, Foster and Smith into the Wieman school has proved to be a better index to the common consciousness (than the Harper lineage), in my opinion, since it strikes me as evident that the biblical basis of faith was effectively eroded away before the era of the Scopes trial, precisely in that lay mind Harper and his colleagues were trying so desperately to reach.[84]

More than a tinge of irony is present in Funk's juxtaposition of the defeat of the Harper dynasty at the Divinity School he founded beside an unnoticed triumph of the Harper approach across the country in the seminaries of various denominations. According to Funk's reading of 20th century developments in American biblical scholarship, philological and historical-critical concerns prevailed in biblical studies departments of the very seminaries which Harper had criticized so vocally for their outmoded curricula.[85] But Harper's attempt to locate biblical studies at the core of his own university quickly became a minority movement there.

Perhaps the most significant representative of the Chicago School, or the socio-historical approach to the study of religion, was Shirley Jackson Case, who during his Chicago tenure (1908–1938) was in turn Professor of New Testament Literature, Professor of Early Church History and Dean of the Divinity School. William J. Hynes has found in Case's career ample evidence to support the thesis of a shift in the basic stance of the Divinity School faculty in the post-Harper era. Dating the life of the "Chicago School" from 1914–1938, and restricting its identity to the period when the socio-historical method reigned, Hynes suggested,

> there was not only a shift from the philological to the historical within the biblical field, but also within the macrocosm of the Chicago School there was a further shift from biblical studies to church history and historical theology. All of these shifts were represented in the rise of the socio-historical method. The socio-historical method seemed to develop initially within the biblical field and then to follow Case into church history and historical theology.[86]

In spite of their differences in scope and definition, when the efforts of Arnold, Funk and Hynes are considered together they suggest that a significant shift occurred in the generation of scholars that followed William

---

[84] Funk, p. 6.
[85] Harper's criticisms are discussed at length below, pp. 86–96.
[86] Hynes, p. 22.

Rainey Harper. The text which Harper cherished and labored so strenuously to reinterpet and advance into prominence lost its pre-eminent place at the school he had created.

Yet in light of the portrait of Harper advanced in the preceding pages, the sharp cleavage suggested by these scholars between Harper and his successors must be questioned. Harper's decision in 1891 to locate his Old Testament and Semitic Studies Department in the university rather than in the Divinity School suggests that he had headed for the "open ground" of the university long before Mathews and Case began their efforts. Recalling that decision helps explain why Harper's biblical perspective was never fully entrenched within the Divinity School. The move toward the open university was consistent with Harper's fundamental mission to make the Bible a useful public book.

But Harper's move away from the Divinity School may also have prevented the formation of a school that could perpetuate the type of critical reverence he had advocated. There can be little disputing the assertion of a relative diminishment of biblical studies and an accompanying rise of church history during the post-Harper years at the Divinity School. Yet the characterization of Harper as a mere philologist is inadequate. His embrace of data from comparative religion, historical, sociological and psychological disciplines together with his advocacy on behalf of new disciplines to improve the seminary curricula of his day point to thin lines of continuity between Harper's era and that of Case and his colleagues.[87]

Thus the "factorial profile" which Hynes has distilled from Case's publications reveals more continuity with Harper's scholarship than many students of the Chicago School have seemed aware of. In viewing Case's work as a whole, Hynes identified nine factors which gave his scholarship its distinctive character. Case's socio-historical approach was: 1) historical; 2) scientific-empirical; 3) didactic (meaning that the past should be plundered for its present utility); 4) social; 5) developmental/evolutionary; 6) vitalistic (Case was interested in the "persistent vitality which is seen to be 'the real secret of Christianity's life.' "); 7) functional; 8) genetic; and 9) enhancing human activism.[88]

When Harper's writings on biblical subjects are reviewed in conjunction with Hynes' profile, it becomes apparent that the difference between Harper and Chicago School figures like Case is more one of nuance than of substance. Clearly Harper looked beyond the disciplinary focus of philology to probe the history which shaped the texts he studied. Like Case he embraced science and set out in pursuit of "all the facts." Case's evolutionary dynamism can be paralleled with similar understandings both in Harp-

[87] See below, pp. 93–95.
[88] Hynes, pp. 79–84.

er's reconstruction of biblical history and in his perceptions of his own era.[89]

As his proposals for institutional reform reveal, Harper's biblical scholarship served didactic, functional and activistic purposes. Harper took what he learned from the Scriptures and tried to reshape modern understandings and institutions on that basis. Where Harper was distinctively different from those identified as members of the Chicago School was in his text-centeredness. While Harper did not contend for a "Bible alone" approach to the intellectual, social and religious problems of his age, he certainly advocated a "Bible and" stance. One book stood at the core of Harper's scholarly and administrative concerns. An entire career revolved around the biblical center which Harper had reappropriated through his scholarhip. What set him apart from his colleagues and successors at Chicago was the diversity and number of relationships he forged between the biblical message, modern scholarship and his society's needs.

When placed within the broad horizon of the field of Old Testament studies, Harper's ability to weave together a variety of scholarly approaches with his evangelical heritage becomes more apparent. His openness to new types of knowledge made it possible for him to anticipate in preliminary ways several developments which eventually became distinct subspecialties within an increasingly complex field. Within that field, Herbert F. Hahn has isolated seven distinct approaches to the Old Testament which have appeared during the past two centuries. The first, the critical approach, was the new paradigm during the years when Harper reached scholarly maturity. Wellhausen stands as the representative figure for this strand of biblical scholarship. Clearly the bulk of Harper's writing was in response to this new (especially for Americans) way of reading the Scriptures. In the post-Wellhausen decades, according to Hahn's survey, anthropological, religio-historical, form-critical, sociological, archaeological and theological approaches were advanced as supplements or alternatives to the critical approach adopted by Wellhausen and his successors.[90] A brief overview of the history of those new developments in Old Testament scholarship makes it possible to see several points of convergence between these approaches and Harper's own attempts to re-read the Scriptures in a tradition-free manner.

One finds for example that there are striking similarities between Harper's efforts to understand the world of the Semitic peoples and the anthropological approach of his contemporary, William Robertson Smith. Smith, whom Hahn has identified as the first to apply the anthropological approach to the Old Testament, studied the ritual institutions of Israel in order to discern the people's fundamental beliefs. His writings on sacrifice

[89] Harper's progressive reading of his own era is discussed below, pp. 141ff.
[90] Herbert F. Hahn, *The Old Testament in Modern Research* (Philadelphia: Fortress Press, 1966).

traced an evolutionary development which resonated with the position that Harper worked out in his research. Smith found in his study of the human behavior that shaped the texts of Israel a "consistent unity of scheme" which developed throughout Israel's history and beyond it into Judaism and Christianity. Harper's interpretation of Israel's history shared a developmental continuity which was much closer to Smith's position than to Wellhausen's (which viewed Judaism less as an evolutionary outgrowth of Israel's earlier beliefs than as the triumph of institutional religion over the free spirit of individuals).[91]

In Harper's day, scholars of the religio-historical school were also turning to ancient near Eastern sources for "influences" on Israel's religion; this trait can also be glimpsed in Harper's writing. Followers of this school moved beyond Wellhausen's tendency to isolate Israel's history from external influences of surrounding cultures. Their efforts paralleled those Harper made to relate Hebrew history to that of near Eastern neighbors and other religions beyond the Fertile Crescent. One of the most illustrious representatives of this school, for example, was Hermann Gunkel, who advanced a theory about the relationship of Israel's beliefs to those of neighboring cultures quite similar to Harper's.

> Gunkel pointed out that, although partial imitations and even direct borrowings did take place, the new context into which the derivative elements were transplanted quite often infused them with a different conceptual content and transformed them into vehicles for distinctive beliefs; as when the creation and deluge stories were adapted in such a way that the polytheistic elements were eliminated and a monotheistic emphasis was introduced.[92]

While some within the religio-historical school, like Paul Volz, used the results of comparative study to buttress a non-evolutionary reading of Israel's history, Harper, like Rudolph Kittel and Ernst Sellin (who were part of a later generation of scholars), adopted a mediating position that allowed comparative insights to illumine a complicated process of development.[93]

Although not a form critic in the sense of a Gunkel or a Sigmund Mowinckel—in that he did not attempt to break down major literary sections of the Scriptures into smaller separate literary units—Harper clearly attempted to discern the life situation that provided the context for the texts he studied. While there may have been a methodological gap between Harper and the form critical school, nonetheless he anticipated what Hahn called "the most important development in biblical criticism of the last two decades." Hahn's evaluation is now almost two decades old so some caution needs to surround the use made of it. But the significance for subsequent

[91] Ibid., pp. 47–53.
[92] Ibid., pp. 87–9, 96.
[93] Ibid., pp. 97, 103–9.

scholarhip which Hahn attached to the form critics' "recognition of the religious motivation of Hebrew historiography" points to a discovery which Harper would have celebrated and corroborated.[94]

Neither was Harper also any sort of sociologist, yet the themes Max Weber developed when he wrote about Hebrew prophecy could harmonize with Harper's earlier constructions. Weber, too, had determined that Israel's prophetic element was absent from other religions. And Harper certainly had been aware of the determinative collision of nomadic and more urban ways of life which Weber had claimed was key to understanding the history of Israel. Other sociologists of religion like Adolphe Lods and Antonin Causse viewed the prophets either as reactionaries who opposed the civilized ways of life in the Palestinian cities, or as people who were introducing new conceptions of religion.[95] Harper's portrait of Elijah as a fanatic, or his description of Jeremiah as the discoverer of individualism, show an openness to factors upon which sociologists placed great value.

In the 1940s the distinguished biblical archaeologist William F. Albright presented an argument quite similar to the one made by Harper at the turn of the century. Albright and other students of Semitic archaeology reiterated the comparative distinctiveness of the Old Testament's basic viewpoints. Unlike Harper, Albright explicitly rejected a developmental explanation for the Hebrew conception of God, claiming that the teaching of Moses was a "living tradition . . . which did not change in fundamentals from the time of Moses until the time of Christ." But Harper's use of archaelogical data anticipated the later dominant figure in biblical archaelogy, long before the field boomed in the period between the two World Wars.[96]

Although Harper eschewed efforts at premature theological reconstruction of Old Testament history it is instructive to place his understandings next to those of later important figures in the field of Old Testament theology. Unlike Otto Eissfeldt who viewed historical method and theological interpretation as working on independent planes (knowledge and faith),[97] Harper had devoted himself to a blending of faith and knowledge through his program of critical reverence. Harper was more responsive to the developmental nature of Israel's belief than was Walter Eichrodt, who tried to forge a unity of theology and history by tracking one fundamental idea, the covenant, through the biblical material.[98] But if Harper did not solve the problem of theology and history by placing the two types of knowledge on separate planes or by organizing the scriptural message around one fundamental theological idea, he nonetheless worked with a typological model similar to one that would be hailed by Hahn a half century later as a key

[94] Ibid., p. 153.
[95] Ibid., pp. 164–9.
[96] Ibid., p. 218.
[97] Ibid., p. 231.
[98] Ibid., pp. 232–33.

element in a "new theology" from Germany. Hahn described the Christocentric interpretation of Wilhelm Vischer:

> On the surface his method was historical: it began by setting the texts examined in their original contexts. But mainly his technique was typological, for the historical meaning of the texts was allegorized so as to serve as figures for their "eternal" meaning in relation to the "universal" revelation to which both Testaments testified.[99]

Others advanced Harper-like themes. H.H. Rowley, for example, called for critics to move beyond scholarship to cultivate a "spiritual receptivity to the basic message which the Bible conveys."[100] Notice of such resonances between Harper and elements of the "new theology" of neo-orthodoxy does not make Harper into a closet neo-orthodox interpreter. Instead he was an unusual mediator who could blend and reconcile a sense of God's immanent presence in the world, a progressive view of history, and an evangelical reverence for the biblical message.

Harper had anticipated what Hahn termed the "new historical definition of revelation" which neo-orthodoxy was to advance.[101] An understanding of Harper's typological model of interpretation and his new argument for the inspiration of Scriptures helps to qualify Hahn's evaluation of H. Wheeler Robinson's achievement in the 1940s:

> H. Wheeler Robinson's exposition of the process of revelation as the learning of God's will through a series of historical events, the meaning of which individuals of prophetic insight interpreted to the people, for the first time provided a successful synthesis of the historical point of view with theological exposition. Robinson succeeded in finding theological nexus between historical method and theological interpretation which Eissfeldt had been unable to perceive.[102]

Similarities between Harper and later scholars like Vischer and Robinson, who had moved beyond the liberal paradigm of biblical scholarship which prevailed in Harper's day in their efforts to forge a new understanding of the relationship of revelation to history, point to his selective appropriation of the new liberal approach. While he shared with biblical scholars of his generation a commitment to penetrate biblical texts in the search for the history behind them, he also held on to fundamental evangelical beliefs which would receive new articulation in the age of neo-orthodoxy.

This preliminary attempt to set Harper within the context of the field of Old Testament studies reveals significant and previously unnoticed convergence points between Harper and later scholars within his field. Hahn's

[99] Ibid., p. 236.
[100] Ibid., p. 239.
[101] Ibid., p. 241.
[102] Ibid., p. 244.

summary of developments within that field provides a horizon within which Harper can be placed. Within that context Harper seems to stand in a synthesizing rather than seminal posture towards the amazing explosion of biblical studies which began in his generation and continued long after. Because he died prematurely and because his Divinity School turned in different directions from those he had chosen, Harper's methodological cosmopolitanism has been forgotten. Yet when his work as a whole is assessed, it is clear that Harper incorporated into his distinctive vision many of the new directions in scholarship which shaped biblical studies for most of the twentieth century. That he held together what the age of specialization so quickly put asunder was a sign both of his genius and his datedness. At the same time that he welcomed the gifts of new knowledge Harper also refused to leave behind the enduring commitment of evangelical Americans to provide a coherent biblical framework for their nation's experience. The arena in which he worked most strenuously to provide coherence was higher education where a new organization of knowledge was emerging to affect the entire educational configuration of the nation.

# CHAPTER 4

# THE CRITICAL REFORMATION

Less than one year before the end of his life, Harper responded to a letter from a Nevada, Missouri, clergyman, the Reverend G.D. Edwards who inquired if Harper's "missionary zeal" had diminished under the impact of the "New Theology." Harper's answer indicated that the opposite of his interrogator's expectations had happened. "You will readily understand, of course, that all my work is in a very fundamental sense missionary work." His answer also revealed the common thread which wove together all his activities. He claimed that exposure to new types of biblical scholarship, which troubled many in his era, had, in fact, "greatly increased my sense of the value of Christianity for all men." Harper's mission, which he expressed in his various enterprises of scholarship, popular education, publication and university administration, was to spread his biblical message as widely as possible.[1]

With reinterpreted Bible in hand, Harper zealously set out on his career-long mission to reform the educational agencies of church and nation. Each of America's central educational institutions—Sunday school, public school, college, seminary, family and ministry—were recipients of scrutiny and calls for reform. As his "Bible study movement" developed, Harper boldly attempted to reshape the entire national configuration of education, and through it, the American people.

## THE BIBLE STUDY MOVEMENT

In the first issue of the first journal he published, Harper, then a newcomer to the seminary in Morgan Park, asked if someone would write an article entitled "A Revival of Hebrew Study." According to the fledgling editor, an article, much study and a revival were all needed. He wondered why "pastors so universally detest Hebrew" but found encouraging "indications of change" in the fact that "four hundred ministers from thirty-five states, and of thirteen denominations have within a year felt constrained to

---

[1] William Rainey Harper to Rev. G.D. Edwards, February 11, 1905, Personal Papers, Box 7, Folder 19.

take up a study so long neglected."[2] In fact the revival he called for had already begun, largely the result of his own early extracurricular efforts at making the study of Hebrew available beyond the walls of his seminary through correspondence study. The young editor was also a promoter who regularly called attention to aspects of the revival he wished to encourage, by providing readers with a vast array of statistical indicators which pointed to growth and progress.

Three years later, in September of 1885, Harper was certain that

> we have begun, but also only begun, a movement of immense proportions and one which is bound to be accompanied with significant and far reaching consequences.

By that time he had scoured the nation, locating 157 professors of Hebrew. Laboring systematically to build a network among his colleagues, Harper reported their publications, research efforts, and position changes on the pages of the *Student*.[3]

The study of the Hebrew Scriptures was the heart of the movement even if it would not always be its sole focus. Hebrew summer schools were an "instrument under God" for "bringing the Old Testament to the front in this country."[4] For those unable to commute to Harper's summer school, correspondence courses and "Semitics Clubs" provided access to Hebrew. Within Harper's program seminars no longer remained the private preserve of German-trained specialists at distant universities. Hebrew Clubs, which gathered to do linguistic study wherever a handful of interested students subscribed to Harper's publications, became American counterparts to the German model of higher learning.

In March of 1887 Harper, then a Yale professor, claimed that the nation was on the "eve" of a "revival of interest in the study of the Bible."[5] By this time his vision extended beyond the "Hebrew movement" to include a larger group of people who wished to study the Scriptures without the aid of Hebrew. Contacts with popular audiences at Chautauqua and Yale had expanded his public dramatically. But Harper did not abandon his earlier more specialized enterprises; instead he simply built on to his movement with additional programs.

Harper celebrated biblical interest wherever he discovered it. Although he and Dwight L. Moody did not share similar approaches to the Scriptures, Harper occasionally reported Moody's successes with approval.[6] Noting that lay people also predominated in his own Bible movement, Harper criticized

[2] William Rainey Harper, "Editorial," *The Hebrew Student* 1 (April 1882):11.
[3] William Rainey Harper, "Editorial," *The Old Testament Student* 5 (September 1885):37; "Editorial," ibid. 5 (December 1885):183.
[4] William Rainey Harper, "Editorial," ibid. 6 (September 1886):4.
[5] William Rainey Harper, "Editorial," ibid. 6 (March 1887):193.
[6] William Rainey Harper, "Work and Workers," *The Biblical World* 11 (March 1898):211.

pastors for their lack of ability and interest in biblical study.[7] As the number of parishoners interested in the Bible study movement increased while their clergy stubbornly failed to respond, Harper boasted of his success and attempted an end run around the ministers. Thus, the December 1893 *Biblical World* editorialized:

> With all due modesty, it may be claimed that *The Student* in former years, *The Biblical World* of today, has led thousands and thousands of men and women to a larger and better comprehension of sacred truth, has inspired many persons to work and strive for higher things, and has aided many a troubled soul which found itself in the midst of doubt and difficulty.[8]

Editorials alternated between celebration of movement gains and criticism of whatever obstacles impeded its advance. Harper was convinced that the Bible had never been more powerful in its influence than during those years when so many people were coming to terms with new ways of reading it. Biblical criticism was responsible for the new interest—all of it under God's "immediate supervision."[9]

The touch of history had "revivified" the Bible to such an extent that by 1901 the Bible study movement had become international in scope. Germany, France and England had come to share in the common spirit which fueled the "great popular movement in the churches" of America. The revival, supported by a belief in the "supremacy of the historical method," was participating in what Harper and his colleagues trusted was a "new revelation of God."[10]

In 1899 Harper could count 5,000 readers of *The Biblical World*—and those were more than mere subscribers. To Harper they were almost a family held together by a "bond" which was "deeper and higher than a common theological position." The desire to know the Scriptures made one movement out of many readers whose common goal was to "enthrone the Bible." That supreme purpose unified the journal's readers no matter how many theological differences existed among them.[11] Regular contributions by Jewish biblical scholars, for example, which began with the first issue of *The Hebrew Student*, indicated the inclusiveness of Harper's movement.[12]

To accomplish the enthronement of the Scriptures in America Harper made his popular journal meet diverse needs. In 1887 the Inductive Bible Studies Series appeared in *The Old Testament Student*, offering a monthly

[7] William Rainey Harper, "Editorial," ibid. 6 (September 1895):162.

[8] William Rainey Harper, "Editorial," ibid. 2 (December 1893):402.

[9] William Rainey Harper, "Editorial," *The Old and New Testament Student* 12 (April 1891):197.

[10] William Rainey Harper, "Editorial," *The Biblical World* 18 (September 1901):164–65.

[11] William Rainey Harper, "Editorial Letter," ibid. 14 (September 1899):147–48.

[12] See for example Rabbi I. Stern "Beams From the Talmud," *The Hebrew Student* 1 (April 1882):14.

program which sought to lead readers to the promised land of biblical knowledge by following a route of carefully crafted questions. Through the studies Harper ambitiously sought to develop both detailed knowledge of biblical history and comprehensive understanding of the Scriptures' fundamental ideas.[13] In addition to these study guides bibliographies were prepared to help more ambitious readers find needed books. For clergy there was a special series on expository preaching by W.H.P. Faunce, D.D.[14] Willis Beecher and Herbert Lockwood Willett each contributed series of Sunday school lesson materials to assist the teachers and pupils who were another important and distinct audience.[15]

As the Bible study movement's activities and participants increased, Harper created new institutions to respond to growing needs. The American Institute of Hebrew, for example, was formed in 1882 to serve as the umbrella organization for Harper's extra-seminary activities. In the principal's report for the year 1886 Harper gave a detailed breakdown of this initial effort to shape the study of Hebrew in America. With his penchant for statistics he pointed to 683 students in the Institute's Correspondence School. Thirty-two denominations were represented in a student population that included representatives from 48 states or provinces of North America and 11 foreign countries. Harper reported that the average age of enrolled males was 33 and called attention to the fact that eighteen females had joined the mostly male movement. Ninety-eight of that year's enrollees were not in the ministry.

In addition to its sizeable correspondence program, the Institute sponsored summer schools at Philadelphia, Morgan Park, Newton Centre, Chautauqua and the University of Virginia. During 1886, 37 different instructors from around the nation shared teaching duties at these schools where 205 students experienced more intense programs of instruction.

The volume of paperwork for the Institute's total program was staggering and Harper seemed to relish calling attention to it. In 1888, for example, 12,620 sheets of printed letter-head stationary, 366,023 pages of circulars, 8,356 dictated letters and 1,328 written letters were issued. With a good deal of understatement Harper admitted that it took a "large amount of *pushing*" to make the movement go. He logged his own labors: 425 hours of classroom work in the five summer schools; 6,700 miles of travel; 600 hours of office work, every one of the 8,350 dictated letters. The demands of the program required the help of 6 assistants to keep the paper flowing. Loans of $1,650

[13] William Rainey Harper, W.G. Ballantine, Willis J. Beecher and G.S. Burroughs, "Inductive Bible Studies," *The Old Testament Student* 7 (September 1887):21ff.
[14] W.H.P. Faunce, "Expository Preaching, I," *The Biblical World* 11 (February 1898):8lff.
[15] W. J. Beecher, "Sunday School Lessons for the Third Quarter, 1885," *The Old Testament Student* 4 (June 1885): 445ff; Herbert L. Willett, "The International Sunday School Lessons," *The Biblical World* 14 (July 1899):58ff.

to cover operating costs during that year signalled that the Institute's success created needs which threatened to exhaust the resources that Harper had managed to assemble.[16]

Nonetheless, the movement continued to expand. By 1888 Harper could boast of a Japanese chapter of the American Institute of Hebrew.[17] Still, he refused to let matters coast. An 1889 appraisal of the needs of his Bible students prompted an editorial question: "Why not have an American Institute of Sacred Literature?" Despite many impressive strides, he felt that biblical work was still "at loose ends." It needed "stirring up, systematizing, elevating."[18] By 1893 the revamped Institute, which had moved to a new home on the south side of Chicago, had grown even larger. The Correspondence School had expanded from its original one course of Hebrew instruction to a total curriculum of twelve courses, only four of which were Hebrew. At that time 448 students pursued Hebrew, while three delved into Arabic, 158 studied New Testament Greek, and 450 read the English Bible. More than 1,100 students were organized into 92 correspondence clubs. The total number of students participating in some form of correspondence work was 2,891. They mailed in their lessons from England, Ireland, Scotland, Wales, Norway, Italy, Turkey, Syria, India, Assam, Burma, China, Korea, Japan, Australia, West and South Africa, Brazil, Bermuda, West Indies, Mexico and Newfoundland.[19]

By 1899 the American Institute of Sacred Literature had 10,000 students involved in some phase of its program, including 4,500 in a new Outline Course designed to help those who could not devote large amounts of time to Bible study.[20] Harper's institutional creativity continued to express itself in constant innovation. The Institute's original structure of four departments (Correspondence School, Summer School, Special Courses and Examinations) was augmented by the addition of Local Boards to foster growth across the nation. Willett, one of Harper's proteges, became the field secretary responsible for developing local programs of Bible study.[21] Under Willett's leadership Bible Study Unions began to meet in large cities, chapters of the Institute took shape in congregations and a network of state secretaries brought order to the nationwide program. In addition, ministers belonged to their own Guild for Professional Reading, which boasted 248 members in

[16] William Rainey Harper, "Report of the Principal of Schools of the American Institute of Hebrew," *The Old Testament Student* 6 (February 1887):178–87.
[17] William Rainey Harper, "Report of the Principal of Schools of the American Institute of Hebrew (1888)," ibid. 8 (February 1889):225.
[18] William Rainey Harper, "Editorial," ibid. 8 (April 1889):282–83.
[19] C. Eugene Crandall, "The American Institute of Sacred Literature," *The Biblical World* 1 (January 1893): 36–37.
[20] William Rainey Harper, "The Council of Seventy," ibid. 13 (January 1899):47–48.
[21] William Rainey Harper, "The American Institute of Sacred Literature," ibid. 4 (October 1894):307.

1899.[22] A Bible Students Reading Guild was added to foster a thirty-minute-per-day program for novices who lacked time to do sustained work.[23]

When the October, 1902 issue of *The Biblical World* featured a prominent advertisement for "The Largest Bible School in The World," it was promoting a complex institution consisting of 10,000 students annually registered, an administrative council of seventy leading biblical scholars, a program of "Advanced Courses for Ministers, Teachers, Colleges and Schools," as well as "Elementary Courses for Laymen, working independently or in groups, in the Church, Sunday School, Young People's Society, etc."[24] The wide appeal of the Institute's programs can be seen in the rapid growth of the Outline Course program. Within its first six years more than 60,000 students had made use of the new Outline Courses.[25] Harper's program had come a long way from the solitary extra-curricular Hebrew course offered in Denison, Ohio.

Harper's frequently stated perception of an emerging revival of biblical study clearly had data to support it. The career of the Institute under his leadership was one of expansion and growth, even if financial troubles were always threatening. Never satisfied, Harper frequently tinkered with the movement's organization, always seeking to make it more efficient and more inclusive. When his efforts at fueling the Bible study movement are placed next to his responsibilities at Chautauqua the amazing scope of his moonlighting efforts becomes apparent. Through these two major efforts at popular education Harper had identified a significant public with a strong interest in his type of biblical study. Both his Institute and Chautauqua aimed at popular learning; both developed a variety of programs to reach into the homes and villages of Bible-reading America. Both responded to the energetic leadership of Principal Harper.

As Harper became the leader of a more visible and organized movement he called for more specific types of reform. In 1900, for example, an "Editorial Letter" urged "Bible Study Sundays" in congregations to awaken interest at the local level.[26] But more than that, Harper began to target individual educational institutions for precise changes.

## THE SEMINARY

Harper made his initial reforming foray into America's educational environment by calling for changes in the world of the seminary. Morgan

[22] Harper, "The Council of Seventy," ibid. 13 (March 1899):209.

[23] Harper, "Editorial," ibid. 3 (June 1894):403–4.

[24] "Advertisement," ibid. 20 (October 1902):ii.

[25] William Rainey Harper, "The American Institute of Sacred Literature: Announcements for the Year 1904–5," ibid. 24 (September 1904):228.

[26] William Rainey Harper, "Editorial Letter," ibid. 15 (May 1900):323.

Park Seminary was the place where he first sensed that perhaps he could reshape aspects of American education. On the basis of what he observed there and heard elsewhere about America's seminaries, he concluded that this peculiar institution was most responsible for American Protestantism's misinterpretation of the Scriptures. To counter this situation he offered a first reform proposal which when compared to his later ones seems tame enough. Old Testament departments needed two professors rather than the conventional solitary generalist. One professor should specialize in linguistic subjects, the other in exegetical or interpretive matters. Implicit in the proposal was Harper's inductive model. Only after careful analysis of linguistic facts could students begin the interpretive work of Old Testament theology. To facilitate full inductive study of the Scriptures Harper also urged the introduction of a whole new range of subjects into the field of Old Testament Studies. A student should begin with Hebrew, then move on to the cognate languages like Aramaic, Syriac, Assyrian and Arabic. Next, the history of the biblical material should be carefully investigated. Finally each particular section of Scripture had to be viewed as a piece of literature and compared with other similar types of literature. When the student was equipped with all those pre-requisite skills, then the task of interpretation could properly begin.[27]

From these initial concerns with the internal affairs of his academic specialty Harper then brashly struck at the heart of theological education by asserting that seminaries lacked "only one thing": the opportunity for potential preachers to study the Word. He sarcastically prophesied that the day was coming when seminary graduates "must know something of the Bible." From his vantage point real biblical knowledge had been crowded out of the seminary curriculum.[28]

According to Harper seminaries had a "duty" to perform. They were supposed to nurture "a renewed heart," or if one was not extant in the bosoms of young seminarians, the schools must help create it. But more than that each seminary was required to provide true, clear, full knowledge of biblical history, literature, and thought to its students. The institutions were "under obligation to require this knowledge . . . before graduation." Unfortunately the seminaries had fallen short of their duty. Instead of teaching students the fundamental knowledge required for ministry, Harper believed the institutions taught prospective pastors to "ignore the Bible." To address that fundamental failure the larger problem of the nature of theological education needed to be addressed. A true reformer, Harper exhorted

[27] William Rainey Harper, "Editorial Notes," *The Old Testament Student* 4 (November 1884):136–38.
[28] William Rainey Harper, "Editorial," *The Biblical World* 1 (February 1893):87; "Editorial," *The Old Testament Student* 6 (February 1887):162.

seminary educators to return their schools to study of "the fountain-head" and begin their educational efforts there.[29]

To understand the significance of Harper's challenge to the seminaries of his day it is necessary to place his attempt within the larger context of the history of these important institutions of theological education. Like so much of the history of religious education in America, the history of the seminary remains largely unwritten. In "Notes Toward a History: Theological Encyclopedia and the Evolution of American Seminary Curriculum, 1808–1968," however, Robert W. Lynn has made a pioneering contribution to this neglected field.[30] Lynn's research reveals that prior to the nineteenth century prospective ministers prepared for their callings by "reading divinity" under the tutelage of a respected clergyman. The Reverend Nathaniel Emmons, for example, minister of the Congregational Church in Franklin, Massachusetts, guided more than 80 students through a suggested list of books during a 50-year period. Sometime during his working day Reverend Emmons stopped to meet with students to "hear their compositions or to converse with them upon particular subjects." Lyman Beecher, author of *A Plea for the West* and later president of Lane Seminary recalled a similar manner of preparation for his calling. Once a week he and fellow aspirants to the holy calling met with President Dwight of Yale College. The group read papers, discussed questions and listened to lectures.[31]

According to Lynn, this divinity-reading model prevailed in America until the creation of Andover Seminary in 1808 under Congregational auspices. Previously ministers had given attention to a loosely structured reading program that concentrated on certain key emphases—exegesis, sacred rhetoric, and "the" theological system. Andover, "America's first graduate school," changed this pattern.[32] After several years of trial and error, the seminary's founders developed a specific curriculum for ministerial preparation. The first year was devoted to Sacred Literature, the second to Christian Theology, and the third to Sacred Rhetoric and Ecclesiastical History.

Andover began with an endowment of $75,000 from three donors, which grew during their lifetimes to $300,000—an amount twice that of Harvard's

[29] William Rainey Harper, "Editorial Notes: The Duty of the Theological Seminary in Reference to Bible-Study," ibid. 5 (January 1886):234–35; "Editorial," *The Biblical World* 6 (September 1895):166; "Editorial," *The Old and New Testament Student* 10 (January 1890):1–4.

[30] Robert W. Lynn, "Notes Toward a History: Theological Encyclopedia and the Evolution of American Seminary Curriculum, 1808–1968," unpublished essay, The Lilly Endowment, Indianapolis, Indiana, June 1979.

[31] Ibid., pp. 7–9.

[32] Norman J. Kansfield suggests that the Associate Reformed Church Seminary in Pennsylvania headed by John Mitchell Mason is older than Andover. See "Study the Most Approved Authors: The Role of the Seminary Library in Nineteenth-Century American Protestant Ministerial Education," (Ph.D. dissertation, University of Chicago, 1981), p. 48.

total endowment at that time. Such unprecedented resources allowed the school to experiment with specialization—Professors Leonard Woods, Moses Stuart, and Ebenezer Porter divided the "theological encyclopedia" among themselves, sharing what previously had been haphazardly covered by one busy cleric. By 1830 the "four-fold theological curriculum" (sacred literature, Christian theology, ecclesiastical history, and sacred rhetoric) had emerged; increasingly, it came to dominate American theological education until the 1880s.[33]

The half century from the 1830s to the 1880s Lynn characterizes as a period of "The Development of a Transatlantic Persuasion." During this period many Americans participated in a transatlantic migration to and from German universities. Students returned home with new visions for theological education, including the central notion of "theological encyclopedia," a scientific schema for the study of theology which divided theological inquiry into four separate departments: exegesis, *Dogmatik*, ecclesiastical history, and *Homiletik* or practical theology. Theological encyclopedia was the framework within which seminal figures like Friedrich August Gottreau Tholuck, Johann August Wilhelm Neander and Ernest Wilhelm Hengstenberg made distinct disciplines out of different areas of theological study. Under their leadership each discipline developed its own objectives, bibliographies, and methods of study. That which an exceptional seminary like Andover had groped toward, Americans encountered in breathtaking completeness in the seminars and libraries of German universities. Eventually, the theological encyclopedia of Germany, i.e., the modern structure of theological learning, was imported and tranplanted to institutions across the United States.[34]

It was at the end of this period of enthusiasm for German models of learning that Harper entered the plot of theological education in America. Unlike many who attempted to restructure the seminaries of America he did not study abroad and therefore did not harbor commitments to the German paradigm as deep as those of his predecessors. Further, the German organization of knowledge had moved beyond the earlier coherence supplied by classical paradigms and *Neuhumanismus* to an increasingly specialized style.[35] Barriers between disciplines had become increasingly insurmountable as overarching unity became less plausible. New disciplines like sociology and psychology challenged the coherence which once made the

[33] Lynn, "Notes Toward a History," pp. 5, 11–12, 18.
[34] Ibid., pp. 14–20. Edward Farley provides a thorough analysis of the development of "theological encyclopedia" from its eighteenth century pre-Schleiermacher origins, through its seminal formulation in Friedrich Schleiermacher's *Brief Outline of Theological Study*, to its dissolution in the "fragmentation" of twentieth century seminary curricular confusion in *Theologia: The Fragmentation and Unity of Theological Education* (Philadelphia: Fortress Press, 1983).
[35] See Chapter 2, p. 33.

fourfold curriculum a comprehensive system of knowledge. As scholars achieved competence in expanding numbers of fields, the neat fourfold curriculum began to fragment and new fields of study resisted assimilation under the old paradigm.

At first Harper seemed unconcerned about the larger context which posed new problems for America's theological educators. His interest was in the emerging Semitic discipline and its place within a curriculum that threatened to squeeze out what was most important, i.e. his own specialty. He conducted a symposium on Bible study in American seminaries through the pages of the *Old Testament Student* and concluded that "the Bible does not occupy the place in the theological curriculum which it deserves." To return the Scriptures to their rightful place he offered a series of far-reaching suggestions. More time had to be given to the study of the Bible—at least *one-half* of a student's program of study. Knowledge of Hebrew was mandatory—but it should be acquired in pre-seminary days so that seminary work could get on with biblical study. Harper's proposed seminary reform thus had implications for college curricula also. The "habit of Bible study" had to be formed in seminary students. Notions of academic vacation time had to be reconceived, as cherished ideas of summer time off had to yield to the constant work of scholarship. Biblical history needed to become a required subject; how else would the critical perspective so essential to Harper's reforms be grasped? Finally, the Bible must be studied in English so that students would be at home in the book and truly understand it. To that end Harper called for a new department to be added to the unravelling fourfold curriculum—the department of English Bible study.[36]

Problems with the seminary curriculum were so pervasive that Harper eventually moved beyond editorializing for his own cause to a more thorough reappraisal of theological education in general. In 1899, from the vantage point of a university president who led an institution through the transition from seminary to Divinity School, Harper authored a penetrating and critical analysis of theological education entitled "Shall the Theological Curriculum Be Modified, And How?" His answer to his own question revealed that the experience of constructing a complete edifice of learning had widened his horizons to include concerns barely discernible in previous calls for reform.[37]

Harper began his final proposal for reconstructing theological education by noting the perceptions of modern churchgoers. He believed that

> Many intelligent laymen in the churches have the feeling that the training provided for the students in the theological seminary does not meet the requirements of modern times.

[36] William Rainey Harper, "Editorial," *The Old Testament Student* 5 (April 1886):321ff.
[37] William Rainey Harper, "Shall the Theological Curriculum Be Modified, And How?" *The Trend in Higher Education in America* (Chicago: University of Chicago Press, 1905), pp. 234–67.

In addition, he claimed that ministers who had completed their training looked back upon the seminary experience with similar disapproval. So widespread was disenchantment with the seminary that Harper heard students preparing for ministry asking, "Is there not some way of making preparation other than through the seminary?" Some went so far as to pursue alternative routes in graduate schools or "short-course" plans. The basic problem was that the seminary curriculum and organizational structures were "survivals from the oldest times." They were simply "out of harmony with the whole situation as it exists today."[38]

Two basic principles lay beneath the specific suggestions Harper wished to make. First, any modifications in the theological curriculum "should accord with the assured results of modern psychology and pedagogy" as well as the demands made by "common experience." Second, seminary work had to be adjusted "to render it attractive to the best men." In another essay Harper asked, "Why Are There Fewer Students For the Ministry?" Citing a 15 percent decline in enrollments at northern Protestant seminaries—from 2,522 in 1894 to 2,133 a decade later—he answered this question by pointing to the rise in prominence of other professions and the decline in "general influence of the minister." No longer did ministers tower in stature above the rest of the community. Other factors such as a "gradual decay of religious expression" in modern times and the "theological uncertainty" of the era complicated the ministerial situation. It was quite clearly a "time of transition" for Christianity. Small salaries furthered the ministry's slide down the status ladder. Harper dared to prescribe an immediate solution for the money problem: "If the present salaries could be doubled within ten years, the influence of the average minister would be doubled."[39]

But if America's widening embrace of modernity had done great damage to the status of the ministerial profession, the seminaries had made matters worse. Harper was appalled by the "promiscuous admission of ignorant candidates" to the schools and subsequently to the profession. While other professions were raising their standards, this one, he felt, was lowering its requirements.[40]

With the grim seminary reality before him and his two key principles in hand, Harper posed specific alternatives to the conventional model of theological education. Rather than push all students into a prescribed mold, the curriculum had to be "adapted to the individual taste and capacity of the student." Only one essential core was required of all students: "a general and comprehensive knowledge of the Scriptures." Beyond that limit choice should prevail. A new conception of the seminary's function was offered; it

[38] Ibid., pp. 234–35.
[39] Ibid., p 236; "Why are There Fewer Students For the Ministry?" ibid., pp. 195–202.
[40] Ibid., p 203.

was "not a place in which men are to learn certain views, or to receive and adopt certain opinions." Instead it had to become "a place in which men shall be taught to think."[41]

A key verb in Harper's reforming lexicon was "adapt": seminaries needed to help individuals adapt to their environments. To accomplish that goal, the institutions needed to become aware of the "present state of society." Still much more like a medieval monastery than a modern professional school, the seminary had to come to terms with the "modern democratic situation." Convinced on the basis of his critical and progressive reading of the Scriptures that "Christianity is democratic through and through," Harper felt that problems had occurred when religious leaders moved from the pure world of Christian ideals to the real one of institutions and history. In the real world of history the church had to a large extent "antagonized the democratic spirit." In addition to the pressing demand to adapt to modern democratic society Harper also asked the seminaries to come to terms with the "greatest factor in modern civilization," science. Furthermore, the new economic realities in which these schools functioned meant that seminaries also had to learn how to deal with another modern phenomenon, "men of wealth."[42]

After sketching the major contours of the changed environment for theological education, Harper proceeded to offer close-up analysis of academic programs. Certainly one of the most distinctive and cherished tasks of the ministry in his era was preaching; but Harper was not afraid to aim sharp criticisms at the way seminaries were preoccupied by this one element out of the many needed to adequately equip would-be ministers. Popular expectations and financial motives compelled students to "preach constantly" during their early years—assuring both an undue emphasis on this one function and the development of poor habits of preparation. If seminarians were diligently preparing lessons during the week, they could not be in "fit condition to preach regularly on the Sabbath." Negative learning resulted from such a system, since students acquired the "habit of slovenliness" in sermon preparation and classroom work. Harper was unsparing in his condemnation of this tradition, calling preaching in early years of seminary training an "evil." Instead of encouraging or requiring student preaching, he felt that seminaries "should forbid it."[43]

The practice of providing free tuition and board for seminarians, a "survival of mediaevalism," was also singled out for criticism. Harper argued that such coddling degraded students and fostered attitudes of dependence that could color an entire ministry. For pastors to function effectively in

[41] Harper, "Shall the Theological Curriculum be Modified, And How?" pp. 237–38.
[42] Ibid., pp. 238–41.
[43] Ibid., pp. 243–44.

democratic America, they had to cultivate a habit of independence from their earliest seminary days.[44]

The scientist in Harper deplored the "lack of sufficient amount of laboratory work in science" in the ordinary course of pre-ministerial study. Scientific knowledge was as necessary for the modern cleric as a knowledge of Greek. To contend with "the greatest enemy Christianity is called to contend with," materialism, Harper believed that students needed to know how scientists thought and worked. His proposed solution was advocacy of established chairs of science like the one occupied by Henry Drummond who probed the relationships between theology and geology at Free Church College of Glasgow, Scotland.[45]

Harper balanced his call for including science in the theological curriculum by placing strong emphasis on the need for the study of English literature. In his estimation mastery of this field of knowledge was "second in importance only to the mastery of the sacred Scriptures." In the classics readers could encounter "common feelings of the soul of humanity," primary material for ministerial reflections. Harper doubted if he would be "going too far to assert that every minister should be a specialist in English literature."[46]

Ignorance of English literature seemed to accompany a general weakness in the ability of seminary students to express themselves properly in "strong and forcible English." Harper called for regular "theme work," if necessary at the expense of technical theological work, in order that students might learn to communicate clearly. The fourfold curriculum received one more jolt as Harper advocated yet another "special chair" for "every well-organized theological seminary"—one in English language.[47]

The wide-ranging curricular suggestions that Harper proposed at the turn of the century reflected a much broader concern than the main interest which dominated his earlier days: encouraging Hebrew and biblical study by seminary students. But he had certainly not abandoned his original purpose; for along with all his other suggested innovations came the familiar request for a department of English Bible. To explain why this reform was needed "most of all," Harper reiterated the main concern of his Hebrew and Bible study movements:

> The theological seminaries are sending men into the ministry who have no proper knowledge of the growth and development of Biblical thought, and who even lack familiarity with the most common material of the Biblical books . . . . Of the great movements of national life, of the contemporaneous history of the social development, of the gradual growth of religious thought, he [the seminary graduate] remains largely ignorant.

[44] Ibid., pp. 244–45.
[45] Ibid., pp. 245–46.
[46] Ibid., p. 250.
[47] Ibid., pp. 250–51.

So acute was the need for students to know the plot and thought of the Sacred Scriptures that Harper found it necessary to modify his stance on the subject closest to his heart, Hebrew. His earlier calls for mandatory Hebrew had been so successful that the study had become compulsory in many schools by 1899. According to Harper's calculations one-fifth of the average seminarian's time was spent in pursuit of Harper's specialty. Lest his Hebrew movement end in a pyrrhic victory Harper felt constrained to urge making "Hebrew an elective." Ironically, the zealous Semitics teacher who in the 1880s watched students come alive as they studied Hebrew admitted at the turn of the century that "the requirement of Hebrew has worked incalculable injury to the morale of many students." Harper surveyed the results of his movement and judged them: "No greater farce may be found in any field of educational work than that which is involved in the teaching and study of the Hebrew language in many theological seminaries." The subject must be made "voluntary."[48] Experiences at Yale, Chautauqua and the University of Chicago had taught him lessons which made him view his initial reform as inadequate for the more pervasive set of problems and the larger public which could not be addressed through the advancement of one specialized solution.

After sealing the fate of the fourfold curriculum and reforming his own reformation, Harper moved to another group of proposals which he gathered under the heading of "specialism." The present curriculum required the same work of every student and turned out a uniform product. Some day, Harper felt, "the churches will . . . learn that one man, whatever may be his ability, cannot meet all the demands of modern times." It was "practical suicide" to pursue singlemindedly the old model of the pulpit-centered ministry. The new environment of modernity called for people specially prepared for particular aspects of ministry. Training for a career as a medical missionary would take on a different form than preparation of someone entering the new field of church administration, or that of the person developing gifts in church music. Harper looked ahead and predicted: "Twenty years from now young men will announce from the beginning their purpose to prepare themselves for college and university presidencies and for the secretaryships of our great missionary societies, and will undertake long years of training especially adapted for such work."[49]

Specialism within the field of ministry paralleled specialism within the academic world of theological education. Linguistics, history, sociology, philosophy, pedagogy, rhetoric and literature were parts of a theological world too broad for any one individual to master. The existing theological curriculum encouraged dilettantish dabbling in several fields and mastery of none. Such "superficiality" had to give way to "the student habit" by which

---

[48] Ibid., pp 247–49.
[49] Ibid., pp. 251–55.

individuals pursued a "single problem" from one field of inquiry to the next. Problem-centered education that dealt with "fundamental subjects" through personal investigation was the new goal.[50]

Old ways of teaching, primarily the lecture, were inadequate for the new types of learning. The seminar, comparative study and "theological clinics" that specialized in various aspects of practical church life were needed. Harper anticipated the program of modern seminary education normally called "field work" when he suggested that at least three months of a student's time be spent working in a church under the direction of a pastor. In order for a student to accomplish all this, Harper uncharacteristically recommended that the curriculum be expanded from three to four years. First-year work was to be "prescribed": work in Old and New Testament history, literature and theology, a survey of ecclesiastical history and an outline of what would be covered in the field of systematic theology. In addition a series of weekly lectures in sociology should be offered. At the end of the first year, a student would select a specialty from the various fields of study. Individuals sharing a common field of inquiry would form a group around their interest and be under the guidance of an advisor. Out of the minimum six departments in Harper's theological *Gestalt*—Old Testament, New Testament, church history, systematic theology, sociology and homiletics—each student would pick another department in which to do secondary work.[51]

Having completed his theoretical revamping of the internal components of seminary education, Harper turned his attention to its external circumstances. Seminaries should no longer hide in "out-of-the-way" forests or hamlets. They should move to the city, preferably next to a university where students, like Israel of old, could "intermigrate" between points of view and fields of knowledge. Harper's ideal, which he began to develop at the University of Chicago, was the cluster of seminaries around a university. Students were encouraged to journey through them, adapting, absorbing, purifying. A part of his grand vision was that eventually seminaries would themselves specialize, agreeing to concentrate on certain fields rather than foolishly attempting to cover all areas of knowledge.[52]

Theological education was destined for one last reform and Harper saved it for the last line of his essay on seminary curricula. The scope of the seminary enterprise was too narrow. If necessary the schools could be

[50] Ibid., pp. 256–59.
[51] Ibid., pp. 258–64. It should not be assumed that Harper was the only successful seminary reformer. Chester David Hartranft instituted a number of important changes at Hartford Seminary in Connecticut during the same years that Harper advocated his reforms. There are similarities between Harper's and Hartranft's reforms, most notably in concern for scientific study and practical education. See Kansfield, "Study the Most Approved Authors," pp. 82–96, for a description of Hartranft's efforts.
[52] Harper, "Shall the Theological Curriculum be Modified, And How?" p. 266.

renamed in order to communicate that "instruction for Christian workers of all classes" would be given. With that suggestion Harper revealed that at root he was reforming the seminary to serve a redefined conception of ministry. Earlier in his essay he had reduced his argument to a single proposition, which showed the relationship between specialization and comprehensiveness. "The day has come for a broadening of the meaning of the word minister, and for the cultivation of specialism in the ministry, as well as in medicine, in law and in teaching." What he intended to create was a diversified ministry, grounded in a common core, the properly interpreted Scriptures. He united the many emerging specialties around one center, the "God-given word."[53]

In his "Notes" Robert Lynn sees in Harper's reform a "prefiguring" of many twentieth-century developments in theological education. After Harper, theological education moved away from the encumbered traditional fourfold curriculum and toward a new, twofold one that divided theological work into a two-part encyclopedia of theory and practice.[54] As the twentieth century progressed students increasingly became seminar specialists and clinical experimenters. That Harper fore-shadowed this change is clear. Yet his main goal was not merely to balance theoretical work by introducing practical dimensions. As always his fundamental concern was to introduce a properly understood Bible into the daily lives of modern Americans. To do that Harper wanted to reshape theoretical education in the seminary, and he called for new forms of practical education to further that larger aim. Both theoretical and practical work had to be shaped by the single most needed reform: restoring the Scriptures to their central place in American life. That overarching goal impelled him beyond the confines of the seminary with results that affected most of the major forms of education of his era.

### THE SUNDAY SCHOOL

One of the primary areas of Harper's concern was the Sunday school. Deeply troubled by the quality of Sunday school education, Harper staged a "revolt" against the predominant methods of Sunday school instruction and cheered as he watched it become a "revolution."[55] To people at the opposite end of the twentieth century Harper's revolt against the Sunday school can sound quite tame. With the exception of certain fundamentalist groups and Southern evangelicals, most denominations have watched the Sunday school slide into desuetude. For most contemporary observers the Sunday school evokes images of harmlessness and irrelevance.

[53] Ibid., pp. 267, 256.
[54] Lynn, "Notes Toward a History," p. 28.
[55] William Rainey Harper, "Popular Bible Study: Its Significance and Its Lessons," ibid. 18 (September 1901):163.

Yet during Harper's years the opposite was the case. The Sunday school was at the zenith of its influence, reaping results of more than a century of growth in America. Robert W. Lynn and Elliot Wright have told the story of this often overlooked institution in their narrative history, *The Big Little School*. According to these scholars the Sunday school began in England in the 1780s when a Gloucester newspaper publisher, Robert Raikes, became concerned about the "pit of misery" surrounding the pin-making industry of his town. On Sundays unsupervised children wandered around in bands, doing damage to property and causing nervousness among genteel Anglicans. Raikes hired a teacher in 1780 to provide education for the children and to keep them under control. By 1785 Raikes' beginnings had developed into a movement. Another layman, London draper William Fox, led others in forming "A Society for the establishment and support of Sunday-Schools throughout the kingdom of Great Britain." Two years later English Sunday school enrollments exceeded 250,000.[56]

American beginnings took place contemporaneously. In 1780 Philadelphians created a First Day Society which numbered Roman Catholic Mathew Carey among its sponsors. Although the Sunday school thrived chiefly within the orbit of evangelical Protestantism, this Philadelphia venture into early ecumenism revealed a basic nondenominational character which prevailed in the Sunday school movement for much of its history. Mrs. Joanne Bethune of New York gave the fledgling movement one of its first institutional shoves in 1816 with her Female Union for the Promotion of Sabbath Schools in New York City. Her husband responded to a similar impulse by supporting the New York Sunday School Union Society.[57]

The initial impulse for Sunday schools was charity mixed with some concern for social order as Raikes and his followers sought to aid children in harsh urban circumstances. The American context, however, provided circumstances for the transformation of its purpose. An "exercise in charity was converted into a prep school for the whole of evangelical America." The American Sunday School Union, formed in Philadelphia in 1824, passed a resolution six years later pledging that within the next two years it would create "a Sunday school in every destitute place where it is practicable, throughout the Valley of the Mississippi." Its ensuing Valley Campaign stretched from Pennsylvania to the Rocky Mountains, seeking to bring the Sunday school gospel to every hamlet along the booming frontier. People from a variety of denominational backgrounds crossed barriers in the common enterprise of spreading these new institutions across the landscape. Most famous of the frontier agents was Stephen Paxson, who began his

---

[56] Robert W. Lynn and Eliott Wright, *The Big Little School: Sunday Child of American Protestantism* (New York: Harper & Row, 1971), pp. 3–7.
[57] Ibid., pp 10–12.

career in Illinois during the 1840s. Riding his horse, "Raikes," Paxson established some 1200 schools during a twenty-year period.[58]

The frontier provided special opportunities for the Sunday school. Lack of trained clergy and booming populations that constantly shifted as the frontier moved westward required new portable forms of Christianity. Circuit riders, colportuers and Sunday school agents became the carriers of a simplified, quickly grasped message. Books were scarce, so Sunday school leaders moved to fill the gap. An 1859 *Manual of Public Libraries* in the United States reported that of the more than 50,000 libraries in the land, 30,000 were operated by Sunday schools.[59]

The American Sunday School Union kept an eye on the eastern cities also. In 1856 it published an alarmist report about the "refuse population of Europe, rolling in vast waves upon our shores." As the tide of immigrants moved westward it deposited its "dregs upon our seaboard." Sunday school leaders worried about children of these newcomers, "a wretched progeny," and called for response from the Union members.[60]

Lynn and Wright describe the failings of this "big little school." Evidences of nativism appeared frequently in the rhetoric of leaders and in their convention resolutions. The leaders of the schools seemed unwilling or unable to speak out on major social issues like slavery, and appeared for the most part to be wedded to conservative social stances. Yet the fact remains that the Sunday school became a primary carrier of the Christian faith and literacy on the frontier and in the cities during the nineteenth century.

Harper's challenge to this important institution came shortly after the movement went through its "second birth" in 1872. Following the Civil War, an "Illinois Band" led by Benjamin F. Jacobs, John H. Vincent, and Edward Eggleston had moved into leadership roles in the Sunday school movement. By 1875 they had developed a voluntary network in most of the states and provinces of the United States and Canada. With the assistance of the new International Sunday School Conventions, which met every three years, the Illinois leaders sought to systematize the Sunday school movement. Troubled by inefficiency and lack of order in most of the schools, Vincent and Jacobs responded with several innovative ventures. Vincent began "Sunday School Teacher's Institutes" like the one which led to the creation of Chautauqua. With his new publication the *Sunday School Teacher*, he advocated a "uniform lesson plan" model of Sunday school instruction. Jacobs enthusiastically backed the idea of a seven-year cycle of plans in which "each lesson would be studied by *every person*, from infants to the infirm, in *every Sunday school*."

Dwight L. Moody described the decision made in 1872 to adopt the

[58] Ibid., pp 14, 17–20, 28–29.
[59] Ibid., p. 31.
[60] Ibid., p. 33.

international lesson system as a "holy event." On a more mundane level the uniform plan made it possible for any Sunday school pupil to attend a class anywhere in the English-speaking world and study the same lesson on a given Sunday. Successful businessmen like Lewis Miller, John D. Rockefeller, H.J. Heinz and John Wanamaker became leaders of local schools and promoters of the International Sunday School system. At the same time that Harper came into prominence the organizing efforts of the advocates of international systems for the schools achieved their greatest success. In 1889 the First World Sunday School Convention was held. Thirteen years later an enthusiastic delegate to the 1902 Convention of the ISS proclaimed a sense of destiny that seemed to permeate the movement and the age:

> God seems to be offering to America the leadership of the world . . . . In a peculiar and special sense this International Convention seems to have been put in trust of the Gospel and of the world's destiny.[61]

Thus in 1895 when his *Biblical World* proclaimed that nine-tenths of Sunday school teaching was a "farce," Harper was positioning himself against the flow of a widespread popular movement. What was necessary, his journal claimed, was a "conversion of the Sunday School" into a genuine educational institution. Problems of modern religious doubt could be "traced to the instruction in the Bible received in the Sunday School."[62] A great deal of the blame finally had to fall on Vincent and Jacobs' great invention, the uniform lesson system.

Editorials in the *Biblical World* relentlessly scored the state of affairs in the conventional Sunday school. The "low intellectual ability" of the teachers did not escape criticism. There was an ever present "danger" that younger students would confuse activities like marching and "a general good time" with authentic religion. Adolescents, on the other hand, lost respect for materials that treated the biblical message in the same manner they were used to in grammar school. The chief difference between materials prepared for children and those for adults seemed to be the pictures. There was a "fundamental evil" in Sunday school instruction: uniformity in subject and method. The first element in Harper's proposed reform of the Sunday school, therefore, was the "principle of grading." Children should learn stories, young people should spend their time on biblical facts and history. Adults needed to grapple with abstract doctrinal issues and relate them practically to everyday life.[63]

Harper and his colleagues intended to turn every Sunday school teacher

---

[61] Ibid., pp. 56–71.
[62] William Rainey Harper, "Editorial," *The Biblical World* 3 (September 1895):164; "The Teaching Ministry," ibid. 15 (March 1900):167.
[63] William Rainey Harper, "Teacher Training," ibid. 24 (October 1904):245; "Editorial," ibid. 12 (August 1898): 66ff.

into an "interpreter." They prepared a complete curriculum of specialized materials which would teach genuine biblical knowledge. Two distinct series of courses appeared, a "Comprehensive" or "Outline" series and a variety of special courses which focused on particular topics or books of the Bible. Children and adolescents were divided by age groups, 5–9, 10–14, and 15–19. Materials stressed repetition, review, independent thought, and definite demonstrable results. If a young pupil completed the entire program which Harper and his colleagues had devised that individual would be forty years old by the time every course had been taken.[64]

Some of Harper's innovations seem implausible seventy-five years later. He proposed a regular program of examinations for Sunday school classes, and he had the American Institute of Sacred Literature create a special department to assist in preparing the tests. In effect the Sunday school became a little "seminary" with seminar methods as the norm. Students were to prepare before coming to class. A problem-centered approach was to be used, with pupils presenting reports on independent work. Prizes were to be awarded, not for attendance or memory work but for real scholarly achievement.[65]

For Harper the "singular oversight" in the Sunday school of his day was the teacher. Authoritarian and poorly disciplined teaching forced pupils to a mystical type of faith rather than to a thinking one. Aids for teachers to use in preparation shortcircuited their learning and therefore robbed the students. The chief problem was that these aids "do all the work" for the teacher rather than requiring inquiry and serious preparation. These teachers needed to learn a new sentence which would indicate a change in their status: "I don't know" could make them co-inquirers rather than junior authority figures.[66]

Responsibility for the teachers' poor preparation was laid at the door of clergy—whose job it was to train them. Harper's solution for this problem was to evangelize for a new calling, the Bible teacher. One thoroughly trained teacher in each Sunday school could instill a critically reformed perspective in the remainder of the teachers. To accomplish this the AISL announced a series of "Teacher-Training Courses" in June of 1904.[67]

[64] William Rainey Harper, "The Necessity of Biblical Training For Lay Workers," ibid. 16 (December 1900):405; "A Plan of Bible Study For Sunday Schools," *The Old and New Testament Student* 11 (October 1890):198–206.

[65] William Rainey Harper, "American Institute of Sacred Literature: An Examination on the Gospel of Luke," ibid. 10 (January 1890):57; "Editorial," *The Biblical World* 13 (March 1899):14–49.

[66] Harper, "The Teaching Ministry," p. 164; "Editorial," ibid. 12 (October 1898):228; "The American Institute of Sacred Literature," *The Old and New Testament Student* 12 (June 1891): 381.

[67] William Rainey Harper, "Editorial," *The Biblical World* 6 (September 1895):165; "The Teaching Ministry," p. 166; "American Institute of Sacred Literature: Training Courses for Sunday-School Teachers under the Direction of the Institute," ibid. 23 (June 1904):467.

Instead of merely exhorting other Sunday school leaders from the safety of their new gothic towers at the University of Chicago, Harper and his colleagues entered the fray themselves. One journal editorial proclaimed: "nearly every member of the editorial staff of the *Biblical World* is directly connected with practical Sunday-School work; that is, doing work in a Sunday school." In addition, the journal came to regard Sunday school teachers as its main area of concern, and announced that decision in its August 1899 issue.[68]

In addition to building his university on Chicago's south side Harper presided over the Hyde Park Baptist Church Sunday School where ideas expressed in the *Biblical World* took concrete shape. Harper tested ideas in this "laboratory" and published them for use elsewhere. In May 1899, the "Work and Workers" section of the *Biblical World* gave a glimpse into this model school. It was staffed by a superintendent [Harper], assistant superintendent, secretary, treasurer, and directors of spiritual work, instruction, public exercises, benevolence, and the library. 554 students were grouped in three divisions: elementary, intermediate, and adult, each headed by a principal. Students were placed into grades not on the basis of public school status, but biblical knowledge. Grades 1–3 concentrated on biblical stories, 4–6 on biblical biographies, 7–8 on separate books of the Bible, 9–12 on biblical history. Adults selected electives from an extensive menu of subjects. Sessions lasted an hour and a quarter. The first half of a period was for instruction, the second half for worship.[69]

Underneath Harper's innovative materials and administrative suggestions was an understanding of the Sunday school quite different from that of the evangelical mainstream that had fostered it. Was biblical revelation static or progressive? Was the purpose of the Sunday school preaching or instruction? Were people to be molded into one uniform system, or clustered in grades according to ability and knowledge? In each case Harper opted for the latter alternative and led the protest against the predominance of the former.[70]

## THE PUBLIC GRADE SCHOOL

One of the reasons for Harper's concern for a reformed Sunday school was an awareness that family life in America had significantly changed. Families no longer seemed able to provide the religious instruction that Harper believed had once been their primary responsibility.[71] Concern about this situation impelled him, if only in preliminary ways, to venture occasionally into another arena, the public grade school. He searched the

---

[68] William Rainey Harper, "Editorial Letter," ibid. 14 (August 1899):85.
[69] William Rainey Harper, "Work and Workers," ibid. 13 (May 1899):353–54.
[70] William Rainey Harper, "Editorial," ibid. 11 (March 1898):145ff.
[71] William Rainey Harper, "Religious Education in the Home," ibid. 21 (January 1903):3.

grade schools of his day for some evidence of biblical instruction. Without this chief "instrument of character building" the schools were operating with a serious handicap. Therefore the *Biblical World* pleaded for a restoration of the Bible to the common schools, viewing these institutions as places where the study of fundamental religion should occur. The solution the journal advocated for this lack at home and school was nonsectarian Bible study—but in a new location, the public classroom. While the idea failed to mature from proposal into program, it was of sufficient interest to receive backing from eminent educators like Nicholas Murray Butler at the 1902 convention of the National Education Association, an indication that the American educational world was still sufficiently Protestant-tinctured not to be immediately alarmed at the idea of religious instruction in public schools.[72] What Harper and people sympahetic to this suggestion did not bother to ask was whether this variety of biblical study might also have its own sectarian character.

## THE COLLEGE CURRICULUM

The properly interpreted Bible had to be inserted into the curricula of all of America's educational institutions, not merely those affecting children. Therefore, Harper asked, "Shall the study of the Bible have a place in the college curriculum?" In 1886 he challenged his readers with the observation that the study of the Bible in America's colleges was an "outside work." There was no place for the Bible in these schools' curricula—and this charge was not confined merely to the newer secular institutions in the land. Even the denominational colleges, founded under impulses of biblical faith, had made no curricular room for biblical instruction.[73]

Harper's experience at Yale provided a paradigm for launching a college Bible study movement. At Yale he began his teaching within the confines of the Semitics Department and the Divinity School. Only as he built a popular following did study of the Bible in English begin to take its place within the college curriculum. By 1890 Yale had an official chair of English Bible; the first incumbent—Harper. As he previously had done with the study of Hebrew, Harper converted personal triumph into a national campaign. Before long he was coaching a movement that sought to teach the English Bible, train competent Bible teachers, and place academic value on biblical study. The "most serious blunder in the American education of the last half-century," he claimed, was ignoring the Bible in higher education.[74]

---

[72] William Rainey Harper, "The Bible and the Common Schools," ibid. 20 (October 1902):244–47; "Notes and Opinions: Should the Bible Be Taught As Literature in our Public Schools?" ibid., pp. 302–5.

[73] William Rainey Harper, "Editorial," *The Old Testament Student* 7 (September 1887):1; "The Study of the Bible by College-Students," ibid. 6 (March 1887):196ff; "Editorial," ibid. 8 (November 1888): 83.

[74] William Rainey Harper, "Editorial," ibid. 7 (October 1887):38; "Bible Study Versus

To accomplish his objectives Harper reiterated his call for a new approach to the Scriptures, one informed by his critical perspective. In addition, however, the Bible needed to be studied because of its "classic" value. Believer and unbeliever alike needed to know the contents of the book because of its unparalleled role in human history. To succeed in this setting, he argued, the book should be approached in a collegiate manner, not in the old style associated with traditional methods employed in Sunday schools. Students needed to develop a method of inquiry that was reverent, historical, logical, comprehensive, rigid and productive of definite results. To achieve these kinds of results Harper again resorted to specialization. Just as he sought to create a new calling—that of the Bible teacher—in the Sunday school, so within the college environment he called for another "new calling," the college teacher of English Bible.[75]

To orchestrate this movement Harper sent H.L. Willett, formerly his student at Yale and Chicago, and subsequently field secretary of the AISL, to the University of Michigan in 1893, where the latter initiated "the first attempt ever made to provide formal religious instruction in connection with an American state university." Soon there was a Chair in English study of the Bible at Ann Arbor, and the Scriptures began to assume an academically respectable position in other secular institutions. Willett aided the spread of the movement from Michigan to the universities of Virginia, Georgia, Texas, Missouri, and Illinois. Beginning on the perimeter of these institutions the new courses of instruction worked their way into the official curricula: "Gradually these institutions granted academic credit for the courses taken, and in some instances the instructors were made regular members of the university faculty and their courses included in the university curriculum." In some cases, Willett claimed, whole departments of biblical literature sprouted from the efforts of those who responded to Harper's call.[76]

Harper's critical reformation had reached into many forms of popular and theological education. One educational institution remained to be revamped: the new modern American university. The University of Chicago became Harper's chosen vehicle for continuing his effort to develop a new biblical world for moderns. In his new institution in Hyde Park Harper strove to unite all of his programs into a larger whole, one that could lift a nation to the higher life.

---

Theology," *The Old and New Testament Student* 10 (February 1890):120; "Editorial," ibid. 10 (April 1890):l98.

[75] William Rainey Harper, "Editorial," *The Old Testament Student* 7 (October 1887):38; "The Study of the Bible by College-Students," ibid. 6 (March 1887):199–202; "Editorial," *The Biblical World* 1 (February 1893):86.

[76] Herbert Lockwood Willett, "The Corridor of Years," unpublished autobiography, The Archives of *The Christian Century*, Chicago, Illinois, pp. 92–94.

# CHAPTER 5

# THE UNIVERSITY AND THE RELIGION OF DEMOCRACY

The unanimous invitation made on September 18, 1890, by a two-month-old Board of Trustees of a not-yet existent university in Chicago to assume that institution's presidency presented Harper with the kind of decision which William James called a "forced, living and momentous" option.[1] It also gave him an unprecedented opportunity to carry insights gleaned from his scholarship into a much larger and more public realm than the one customarily inhabited by his colleagues in biblical studies. No other biblical scholar of his era attempted to translate a vision shaped by modern biblical scholarship into a master plan for American educational life on a scale comparable to that of Harper's effort at Chicago. No other university of that period was based on a plan that so strenuously sought to keep the critically interpreted Scriptures integrally related to modern scholarship.

All of Harper's associates shared the sense that he stood at a critical juncture. Some of them felt that he was on the verge of a colossal mistake. Yale colleague George T. Ladd, for example, bemoaned the possibility of Harper's abdication of the most "perfectly unique" position in the land from which to influence biblical and Semitic studies. Yale's president, Timothy Dwight, felt betrayed, having just accomplished his goal of raising $50,000 to establish Harper in a third endowed chair. To these and other associates Harper seemed a fool, chasing a vision that could never match what already existed in New Haven.

Harper's former colleagues in Morgan Park, on the other hand, were elated. For years many of them had believed that the entire enterprise of building a new institution of learning in Chicago under Baptist auspices depended upon him. Thomas Goodspeed, a primary agent in wooing John D. Rockefeller with the dream of a Baptist university to replace the defunct older University of Chicago, had admitted to Harper on New Year's Eve in 1888 that "I have from the first had but one desire, that you should take the headship of the University." Baptist fundraiser and subsequent organizer of

---

[1] William James, "The Will To Believe," *Pragmatism and Other Essays*, intro. by Joseph L. Blau (New York: Washington Square Press, 1963), p. 194.

the Rockefeller family philanthropy, Frederick T. Gates, also had felt that Rockefeller's ultimate decision "hinges at last on your acceptance of the presidency." Harper alone seemed to possess the vision, drive, stamina and talent to raise the phoenix of a new school out of the ashes of the defunct old University of Chicago.[2]

While colleagues and friends around the nation waited, Harper dragged his feet and pondered the offer to head the institution he had been so successful in selling to John D. Rockefeller in earlier private conversations. Six months passed before he indicated on February 16, 1891, that he would make the change. Part of Harper's reluctance was due to the longstanding lack of Baptist support for their old University of Chicago which had existed from 1857 to 1886. When offered the presidency of that struggling institution in April, 1886, Harper had declined in view of the larger possibilities of a position at Yale. That he had also made a realistic assessment about the future of the old university became clear when the institution ceased instruction two months after Harper decided to cultivate New Haven's greener pastures. Faced in 1890 with this new offer, he met once again the old problem of a lack of tangible local support for a strong university in Chicago. In addition he encountered disagreements about the basic character of the proposed institution. Throughout the years of preliminary discussions, Harper had lobbied for a full-fledged university. Rockefeller, although intrigued by Harper's expensive ideas, was reluctant to commit the funds necessary to make possible the birth of a modern university in Chicago. The earlier failure of Chicago Baptists to support their first university raised concerns in the oil tycoon's mind that he might end up as the sole means of support for this new venture. Other key figures like Goodspeed and Gates wavered, torn between the grand vision of a full-fledged university and the much less costly desire to have something—even if only a college—for Chicago. They were willing to start small and eventually, if possible, expand the institution from a good college into a great university. Harper's position, on the other hand, had remained consistent through the years of negotiations. What Chicago, the West and the Baptists needed was a university. In 1889, when it seemed certain that Chicago would be the home of a mere college, Harper signalled his disapproval of the less ambitious plan by signing a six-year commitment to Yale. Two years later, he turned back to Chicago, accepting the presidency only after the Cleveland oil baron

---

[2] George T. Ladd to William Rainey Harper, July 27, 1890, Personal Papers, Box 12, Folder 16; Timothy Dwight to William Rainey Harper, August 11, 1889, Personal Papers, Box 12, Folder 16, and July 18, 1890, Personal Papers, Box 1, Folder 13; Samuel H. Lee to William Rainey Harper, July 15, 1890, Personal Papers, Box 1, Folder 13; Frank K. Sanders to William Rainey Harper, July 20, 1890, Personal Papers, Box 1, Folder 13; Thomas W. Goodspeed to William Rainey Harper, December 31, 1888, Personal Papers, Box 9, Folder 5; Frederick T. Gates to William Rainey Harper, January 5, 1889, Personal Papers, Box 8, Folder 17.

committed an additional $1,000,000 to his original pledge of $600,000, impressive proof that Rockefeller was willing to pursue Harper's larger vision.[3]

Another factor had clouded Harper's decision about the Chicago presidency. The Morgan Park Baptists, with their appealing candidate named Harper, were in competition with others who wanted to build *the* Baptist university for America. Dr. James C. Welling had argued for Washington D.C. as the site for the new institution. A much more serious rival was Augustus H. Strong, president of Rochester Seminary and advocate of a scheme calling for a Baptist university in New York City. Strong was close to the Rockefeller family, an occasional guest, like Harper, at the Rockefeller home, and father of a son destined to marry into the Rockefeller family. Strong's scheme was more extravagant than was Harper's. He called for $20,000,000 from the Rockefeller coffers and intended to erect a modern version of the medieval university, in which theology would sit as queen over an ordered graduate curriculum. Harper's talent had not escaped Strong's eye. As the Baptist visionaries hawked their academic wares, Strong sought to include Harper within his scheme by offering a leadership position in his proposed New York enterprise. When that tactic failed to diminish enthusiasm for the Chicago idea, Strong suddenly became concerned about Harper's orthodoxy and attacked him by raising doubts in Mr. Rockefeller's mind about Harper's approach to the Scriptures.[4]

Deeply wounded by Strong's accusations, Harper received contradicatory letters from Gates, Goodspeed and George W. Northrup suggesting both public defense against Strong's charges and withdrawal from candidacy for the Chicago presidency. Gates counseled reticence. Goodspeed assured Harper of his confidence in him and in his orthodoxy. Seminary president Northrup wondered if his former colleague should state his beliefs clearly to find if they were radically divergent from those of other Baptist leaders. If so, Harper "should not identify with great public interests which would thereby share in [his] troubles." Because of the innuendos being voiced, the call to the presidency became a moment of truth for Harper. More was involved

[3] Thomas W. Goodspeed, "The Beginnings of Things in The University of Chicago," unpublished manuscript (n.d.), Personal Papers, Box 12, Folder 11; William Rainey Harper to the Board of Trustees of the [old] University of Chicago, May 8, 1886, Personal Papers, Box 12, Folder 14; Thomas W. Goodspeed to William Rainey Harper, December 31, 1888, Personal Papers, Box 9, Folder 5; Frederick T. Gates to William Rainey Harper, November 23, 1888, Personal Papers, Box 8, Folder 17 and April 27, 1891, Personal Papers, Box 8, Folder 19; Thomas W. Goodspeed to William Rainey Harper, February 18, 1889, Personal Papers, Box 9, Folder 6; Frederick T. Gates, *Chapters of My Life* (New York: The Free Press, 1977), pp. 118–19.
[4] Frederick T. Gates to William Rainey Harper, April 18, 1889, Personal Papers, Box 8, Folder 17, and *Chapters of My Life*, p. 95; Goodspeed, *A History of The University of Chicago*, p. 39; Storr, *Harper's University*, p. 27; William Rainey Harper to Augustus H. Strong, January 4, 1889, Personal Papers, Box 1, Folder 8.

than accepting the challenge of building a new institution. Harper's views were on trial before Rockefeller and acceptance of the offered presidency seemed possible only if his carefully achieved biblical perspective was approved by the tycoon and his associates.

Rockefeller chose not to get involved in technical doctrinal matters. Strong's questionable timing of his accusation, plus a misguided letter which stressed the oil millionaire's unpopularity while praising the New York plan as a chance for Rockefeller to secure the "favorable judgments" of posterity, did much to mute the magnate's concern about Harper. Unhesitating endorsement by Thomas W. Goodspeed and several other Baptist patriarchs was sufficient testimony to convince Rockefeller to commit his dollars and his reputation into the hands of the biblical scholar. Strong's expression of concern about Harper's orthodoxy, while possessing a potential for a prolonged debate, amounted to little more than an exchange of several letters; it was followed by an eventual hatchetburying after Rockefeller made his decision for Harper and Chicago.[5]

Installation as president of the new Baptist university in Chicago in the face of the preceding allegations of doctrinal impurity gave Harper added incentive for revealing his biblical stance. As late as 1889 Harper had expressed nervousness about claiming responsibility for the critical views expressed in his technical journal, *Hebraica*. After opening his university, however, Harper publicly declared himself on many sensitive issues of biblical interpretation. As the only professional educator on the original board of trustees of the university, Harper held a unique position as the only expert on biblical study and university design among all who would shape the policy of the new institution. Clearly, there was ample room for his vision for both enterprises to take shape.[6]

It is not the purpose of this chapter either to recount the details of Harper's years of forming and leading his university or to pick apart the structure he raised. These tasks have been done in Goodspeed's dated *A History of The University of Chicago*, Storr's *Harper's University* and Gale W. Engle's "William Rainey Harper's Conceptions of the Structuring of the

[5] Frederick T. Gates to William Rainey Harper, January 11, 1891, Personal Papers, Box 8, Folder 18; Thomas W. Goodspeed to William Rainey Harper, April 12, 1888, Personal Papers, Box 9, Folder 5; George W. Northrup to William Rainey Harper, January 4, 1891, Personal Papers, Box 1, Folder 16. H.L. Morehouse's letter of encouragement to Harper, which also informed him that Rockefeller "has neither the time nor the inclination to decide mooted theological questions," was written on February 2, 1891 and is quoted in Goodspeed, *A History of The University of Chicago*, pp. 126–27. Augustus H. Strong to John D. Rockefeller, November 26, 1887, is quoted in Gould, *The Chautauqua Movement*, p. 43.

[6] See above, p. 50. Frederick T. Gates to William Rainey Harper, May 31, 1890, Personal Papers, Box 8, Folder 18; Storr, *Harper's University*, p. 43.

Functions Performed by Educational Institutions."[7] Instead, the focus here is on the religious vision that Harper carried into his university presidency and the significant implications that accompanied it. His professional advancement from biblical scholarship to university administration offered Harper the unparalleled opportunity to channel his reforming impulse into new efforts to reshape or at least reconceive the total configuration of higher education in America. Harper, like Tammany Hall's "boss" George Washington Plunkitt, saw his opportunities and "took 'em."[8] Functioning as the conceptual architect of his new institution he fashioned a university which sought to reshape the nation. Seizing many significant educational innovations from the last half of the nineteenth century, Harper formed a distinctive educational edifice with an overarching religious purpose.

In each previous transition in his life, Harper had left little behind. When he moved to Yale from Morgan Park, for example, all the apparatus of the fledgling Hebrew movement went along. Returning to Chicago, Harper brought with him the American Institute of Sacred Literature, the Chautauqua movement and all the concerns of his critical reformation. Counseled by Mrs. Rockefeller and Gates to give up his Chautauqua work, Harper did the opposite. Instead of shedding the time-consuming responsibilities of overseeing Chautauqua's complex program, he reorganized his schedule to permit frequent commuting back and forth between western New York and northeastern Illinois. In the process he attempted one more effort at reorganization of the Chautauqua system. When his attempt to separate the Chautauqua Literary and Scientific Circle from the New York-based Chautauqua institution and bring it to Chicago failed to gain support from the Chautauqua leaders, Harper reluctantly scaled down his efforts for them, and eventually resigned, but not without incorporating many aspects of Chautauqua's system into his university program.[9]

His university sought to incorporate the Bible movement with its concerns for religious education, seminary reform, and popular education into its new organization of learning. Somehow in this institution religious and biblical concerns would co-exist peacefully with emerging specialized education. The challenge of building such a university provided Harper with the opportunity to widen his vision once again. From 1891 on, Harper's gaze extended to the edges of the American educational enterprise, and occasionally peered across the ocean to appraise the status of European

[7] Engel, "William Rainey Harper's Conceptions of the Structuring of the Functions Performed by Educational Institutions."

[8] William L. Riordan, ed., *Plunkitt of Tammany Hall* (New York: E.P. Dutton & Co., Inc., 1963), p. 3.

[9] Frederick T. Gates to William Rainey Harper, July 20, 1891, Personal Papers, Box 8, Folder 19; William Rainey Harper to George E. Vincent, August 5, 1898, Personal Papers, Box 4, Folder 11; William Rainey Harper to John H. Vincent, May 31, 1899, Personal Papers, Box 4, Folder 29.

learning. As he proceeded, Harper began to grapple with the fundamental problem of integrating pluralistic American life. In his occasional writings on university education and life, Harper began to articulate an understanding of a new form of public religion which he believed could respond to modernity and its pluralism. This understanding, expressed in the piecemeal manner of an individual who always had a list of 50 items needing immediate attention, was rooted in his biblical perspective, nurtured in a new educational system and participated in by all who breathed the spirit of democracy.

SOURCES FOR THE VISION

As long as his colleagues in Chicago had toyed with the idea of a college rather than a university, Harper's interest in the enterprise had remained moderately warm. Gates's stationery during those days carried a letterhead which indicated the pervasive uncertainty about the identity of the proposed school: "The New Institution of Learning in Chicago Under the Auspices of The American Baptist Education Society." For a short time during the period prior to his formal invitation to be president of an authentic university, Harper considered being part of a triumvirate which would shape such a school during its first five years. He would remain at Yale but share responsibility with others for building the institution. Requested to come forth with his own model for the less ambitious enterprise, Harper stalled, unwilling or unable to offer a scheme for a smaller western version of Yale College.[10]

On September 10, 1890, John D. Rockefeller, E. Nelson Blake, Marshall Field, Frederick T. Gates, Francis E. Hinckley, and Thomas W. Goodspeed took the step that fired Harper's passion and propelled him into action. They became incorporators of a university and filed a charter which declared that Chicago would soon be the home of an institution that would contain "all departments of higher education," "one or more academies," "manual training schools," "one or more colleges," and

> maintain a University, in which may be taught all branches of higher learning, and which may comprise and embrace separated departments for literature, law, medicine, music, technology, the various branches of science both abstract and applied, the cultivation of the fine arts, and all other branches of professional or technical education which may properly be included within the purposes and objects of a university. . . .

Eight days later the Board of Trustees elected Harper President.[11]

---

[10] Frederick T. Gates to William Rainey Harper, June 20, 1889, Personal Papers, Box 8, Folder 17; Goodspeed, *A History of The University of Chicago*, pp. 56–57, 132.
[11] "The Charter of the University," *The University of Chicago Official Bulletins*, (1891–92), The Department of Special Collections, The Joseph L. Regenstein Library, The University of Chicago, p. 4.

Harper's train ride home from the Chicago Board meeting was momentous. Although he asked for six months to consider the Board's offer, he did
not hesitate to let the idea of the new university come to life on paper. Upon
reaching New Haven, he wrote to Rockefeller:

> On my way from Chicago the whole thing outlined itself in my
> mind and I have a plan which is at the same time unique and
> comprehensive, which I am persuaded will revolutionize study in
> this country. . . . It is very simple, but thoroughgoing.

In December of 1890 Harper presented his plan to the Board of Trustees.
Although its author was still one month away from accepting the appointment to serve as president, his plan was published in January 1891 as the
first official publication of the University of Chicago. Five other "official
bulletins" followed during the next seventeen months, filling in details of
the vision hastily scribbled into one of Harper's everpresent notebooks on
the train ride to New Haven.[12]

Harper's six Bulletins provide a *locus classicus* for his vision of his new
task: the construction of a university with room for a critically studied Bible
at its heart. The *Bulletins* are Harper's first public statements on the subject
of university education in America. There is no evidence to suggest that he
sat down and read carefully on the subject of university education; on the
contrary, his writings on the subject are remarkably free of references to
authorities on the subject. Engel argues that because of Harper's lack of
reference to them it is not possible to determine how much influence the
failed attempts to import the tripartite Prussian model of elementary,
gymnasium and university education made by Presidents Henry P. Tappan
at the University of Michigan and William W. Folwell at the University of
Minnesota had on Harper. It is true that the new president went to Europe
to study German educational models, but he did so only after preparing his
own initial plan.[13]

Instead of turning to Germany for his paradigm, Harper drew upon
American sources. Johns Hopkins University under the leadership of Daniel
Coit Gilman held out new possibilities for graduate education. In an essay
on the twenty-fifth anniversary of Johns Hopkins, Harper did acknowledge
the significance of the school's founding for American higher education.[14]

But Joseph E. Gould has called attention to another source for Harper's
ideas, one given little or no attention by Goodspeed, Storr, or Engel.
Reproducing the organizational proposal John H. Vincent had presented to
the Chautauqua trustees in 1885 alongside the one offered by Harper in his
*Bulletins* six years later, Gould found significant parallels.

[12] Goodspeed, *William Rainey Harper*, pp. 110–11.
[13] Engel, "William Rainey Harper's Conceptions of the Structuring of the Functions
Performed by Educational Institutions," p. 175.
[14] Harper, "The Contribution of Johns Hopkins," *The Trend in Higher Education in
America*, pp. 151ff.

> Harper's University Proper corresponds to the formally orga-
> nized and accredited College of Liberal Arts, or "Chautauqua Uni-
> versity," the difference being that the Chicago institution was to meet
> four times a year (in four assemblies, so to speak) and Chautauqua
> only once. The C.L.S.C. (Literary and Scientific Circles) had its
> counterpart at the new institution, as did the newly devised system of
> extension lectures under university auspices and for university credit.
> The plan for affiliation of colleges with Chicago may have had its
> inspiration from the many "little Chautauquas" that had sprung up all
> over the country....
> Instead of regarding the summer quarter as an appendage to the
> regular college year, it is possible to regard the autumn, winter, and
> spring quarters as extensions of the Chautauqua idea; to offer four
> sessions rather than one. "Majors" and "minors" have their counter-
> part in the course work offered in the Chautauqua College of Liberal
> Arts, with its emphasis on intensive work during a relatively short
> period of time. The concept of the extension of university resources to
> everyone, regardless of age or academic preparation, was a
> Chautauqua idea, as was the proposal to allow work toward a degree
> to be distributed over a long period of time, or concentrated or
> divided between work in residence and work by correspondence.[15]

It is not necessary to accept every one of Gould's judgments in order to
appreciate the significance of the Chautauqua experience in the formation of
Harper's vision. At the same time, one can see the rudiments of Harper's
vision in his autochthonous Hebrew movement. Disturbed by waste of time
in traditional academic calendars, Harper had filled his summer and holiday
vacations with Hebrew study prior to his affiliation with Chautauqua. His
publishing ventures antedate the Chautauqua years as well, and may be the
authentic harbingers of Harper's concerns for a university press. Correspondence study was at the heart of his Bible study movement; it was part of
Harper's program before he became associated with Chautauqua.[16]

The Gould hypothesis, plus the recollection of Harper's own educational innovations in the early 1880s, are resources for understanding the
vision that emerged in the *Bulletins*. Harper did not need to turn to Europe
for his model, nor did he need to read the catalogues and speeches of
university leaders who preceded him. His model had been under construction from the beginnings of his interest in Hebrew in New Concord, Ohio.
Yale and Chautauqua were other primary sources for forging the personal
vision which altered the educational terrain of modern America.

## A NEW INSTITUTION

What was the vision? The university's Charter stipulated that the
institution would be governed by Baptists, requiring that two-thirds of the
trustees and the president had to be "members of regular Baptist churches."

[15] Gould, *The Chautauqua Movement*, pp. 60–61.
[16] See Chapter 4, pp. 82, 84f.

This initial and "forever unalterable" requirement could "not be amended or changed at any time." But if Baptist colleagues breathed a sigh of relief after reading about the institutional leadership, a subsequent sentence should have given pause. "No other religious test or particular religious profession" could be made requisite for any other position in the university. A careful balance between Baptist auspices and nonsectarianism set the religious tone of the new institution.[17]

Within that religious context Harper announced an ambitious and unprecedented plan. This university would have "three general divisions," the University Proper, the University Extension Work, and the University Publication Work. With his first official sentence about his new institution, Harper had widened the scope of university education to include aspects of education which previously had been regarded as non-university matters. In the same breath he called for the creation of the first university-owned press in America.[18]

Harper envisioned an edifice of complementary institutions within what he called the University Proper. There would be Academies for pre-college level students. Colleges of Liberal Arts, Science, Literature and Practical Arts took places on the next rung of the educational ladder. Colleges from other parts of the nation would "affiliate" with the university, thus allowing Harper to extend his university's influence beyond its walls. A Graduate School and the Divinity School were to be organized at once, with Schools in Law, Medicine, Engineering, Pedagogy, Fine Arts, and Music added "as soon as funds permit."[19]

Harper's University Extension program would offer regular courses of lectures, evening courses, correspondence programs and library extension services to carry learning to a wider circle than those who could travel to the university and enroll in its programs. Only one academic subject merited individual attention in his first bulletin: "special courses in a scientific study of the Bible in its original languages and in its translations" would be a primary component of the extension program. The Hebrew movement thus would make its way into the modern American university. For those who could not participate in his extension program Harper created the third division, the University Publication Work.[20]

After sketching the outlines of his blueprint, Harper turned his attention to a series of specific suggestions for the new institution. Faculty meetings would be held once a month. All university officers, "including the President," were required to teach. The academic year would have four twelve-week quarters which would begin on the first day of October, January, April

[17] "Official Bulletin," No. 1 (January 1891), p. 5.
[18] Ibid., p. 7.
[19] Ibid., pp. 7–8.
[20] Ibid.

and July respectively. The quarters were to be divided into two six-week terms. Students would concentrate efforts in major and minor courses. Entrance to the university was by examination, and certificates from other institutions were not acceptable.[21]

For the quarterly fee of $25.00 students put themselves into rigorous circumstances. It was not enough to pass a final examination at the end of a course; Harper called for a second examination on course material to be taken twelve weeks after the first one—a proposal that can still send chills down the spines of test-takers and graders alike. Completion of six majors and six minors enabled a student to advance to "the next higher class." No longer were students to be grouped as freshmen, sophomores, etc. Instead they moved along at their own speed. Harper veered away from the fixed curriculum still prevalent in the majority of America's colleges, but he did not go quite as far as Harvard's President Charles W. Eliot who made students arbiters of their own fates with his elective program. Instead Harper sought a balance—"the proportion of required and elective courses necessary for a degree shall be equal." To make certain that the university's academic character would be clear from the beginning, Harper declared a prohibition of honorary doctorates, a policy he would amend several years later.[22]

One other detail completed Harper's first venture into university design. Attendance at 12:30 weekday chapel and 9:30 Sunday services was "required" of undergraduates and "requested" of graduates. Individual departments and schools within the university were free to hold "special chapel service for the members of that School" as long as the concerned faculty and the university Board had given prior approval.

Harper's academic blueprint for the new university filled exactly nine pages; it was a comprehensive plan, embracing all levels of education. But it also sought to foster specialization, allowing students, teachers, and particular institutions to concentrate their efforts on fewer tasks. There was room for choice in his vision, but there was structure also. This university would be an institution with a religious character; devoted to arduous education; reaching out to all areas of American life.[23]

In the next year and a half Harper filled in the blank spaces in his vision. "Official Bulletin" #2 dealt with "The Colleges of the University," and here Harper proposed a novel distinction between Academic and University Colleges. By dividing college work into two types Harper hoped to preserve some of the "advantages of the small college." He also sought to overcome an inherent problem in the American educational system—one that he had encountered at Muskingum College as an undergraduate. The nation's

[21] Ibid., pp. 9–12.
[22] Ibid., pp. 12–13.
[23] Ibid., pp. 14–16.

colleges had a tendency to lump together students with elementary educational skills and those who were prepared for more advanced work. The academic college would complete the preparatory work of the high schools and academies of the land; only during the latter part of a college career would a student be allowed to pursue university-level work. The sharpness of the distinction between colleges was to have geographical reinforcement since much of the academic level work would occur away from his new university campus:

> The Academic College work of the University will, it is hoped, be accomplished in large measure through its affiliated colleges. This will permit the University in Chicago to develop its energies mainly to the University Colleges, and to strictly University work.[24]

The academic college would divide its work into ten departments, one of which was the Department of Biblical Literature in English, while the envisioned university college expressed its similarity to the proposed graduate program of the university by offering work in twenty-two distinct schools. The School of Biblical Literature in English and the School of Semitic Languages and Literature shared curricular status in Harper's plan with other more conventional areas of instruction, testifying once again that the properly studied Bible was to have its place.[25]

Harper's third Bulletin, "The Academies of the University," testified to the new president's intention to extend his reforming reach into preparatory education. Existing high schools and academies would be strengthened by their affiliation with the University of Chicago; new ones would be planned in light of the reorganized college program which Harper's grand design called for. To guarantee that the work of academies would not be confused with that of college level, Harper stipulated that these schools could not exist on the campus of his new university. The plan was as ambitious as it was self-confident.

> The University will be enabled to adjust the curriculum of the academies more closely to that of the earlier college work and thus not only to avoid what in many cases is a worse than fruitless repetition of work, but also to prevent abrupt transition from one to the other.

This innovation would simultaneously "reduce the age at which students may be admitted to college" and "increase considerably the requirements for admission." Harper unabashedly acknowledged that he was proposing a system of "feeders" from which students of "the best class" would be channeled toward the university. At the same time such a network of academies made possible an academic "farm system" where university

---

[24] "Official Bulletin," No. 2 (April 1891), pp. 2–3.
[25] Ibid., pp. 13–16.

graduates could develop skills that in future years would be attractive when the university recruited "its own teaching force."[26]

The university began its efforts at affiliating prepatory schools by building its own academy in Morgan Park, the former home of the old Baptist Theological Seminary. Ever the systematizer, Harper intended to divide this and other preparatory schools into Lower and Higher Academies. Lower work would be non-elective; choice could enter the curriculum in the higher years. Students and faculty of the academies would live by the calendar of the parent university, sharing the same option to select vacation time during whichever quarter best fit personal needs. Nine academy departments, including "Biblical Literature in English," were placed "under the general supervision" of the appropriate university departments. To insure that the academies would share the same religious character as the university, Harper's plan specified that chapel attendance would be mandatory just as at the university.[27]

The proposals Harper advanced in his first three bulletins established the basic blueprint for an attempt to restructure the entire configuration of American education. By joining upper-level college work with that of the university, and by similarly combining upper-level academy work with the lower work of the college, Harper was inching toward the German model advocated by Tappan almost forty years earlier. These proposals also carried clear imprints of both his Bible study movement and the Chautauqua program, with Harper consistently finding room in whatever curriculum he was proposing for the Bible to be read and studied with academic seriousness.

When Harper turned to plans for the Graduate Schools of the University in "Bulletin" #4, he proposed twenty-one distinct schools. His personal commitment to scholarly publication was apparent in the proposal that each graduate school publish its own journal.[28] Most startling of all the suggestions he offered about graduate education was provision for the addition at an unspecified date of a post-Ph.D. degree program that would result in the LL.D. degree. According to this never realized scheme the exalted final degree of the German universities, the Ph.D., would become a pre-requisite to be followed by three years of resident work, a thesis and a final exam.

While Harper had the rare mandate to create a full-blown modern university on a grander scale than had been seen elsewhere, he did not begin with a completely free hand. The Baptist Union Theological Seminary of Morgan Park was part of the initial package that included Rockefeller dollars and the Harper vision. The seminary traced its roots to early informal educational efforts of Dr. Nathaniel Colver and Reverend J.C. Clarke who began teaching would-be ministers in Chicago in 1865. One year later Dr. George W. Northrup left a post in Church History at New York's Rochester Seminary to teach systematic theology and organize the fledgling seminary. For a decade it existed on the southern edge of the city, but financial difficulties forced relocation to Morgan Park in 1877. During its first decade Danish-Norwegian and Swedish departments were added to the institution as immigrant populations placed new needs before earnest Baptist leaders.[29]

Harper set out to transform the seminary into a Divinity School, and in the process created the university's first professional school. Since several leaders of the Baptist university movement were associated with the seminary, it was assured prominence within the new institution. Some things had to change, however. As president of the university Harper became president of the Divinity School, signalling a change in status for Dr. Northrup. Further, Old Testament Studies would be removed from the Divinity School. Item #11 on Harper's list detailing the relations of the Divinity School to the university specified: "The Union shall cease to conduct the department of Old Testament and Semitic studies. . . ." Instead, item #16 decreed:

> The instruction in the Old Testament and Semitic department shall be provided by the University: that is, the instructors of the department shall be members of the faculty of the graduate school and shall receive their salaries from said University.

After leading a national campaign to open college curricula to serious Bible study, Harper was not about to allow his enterprise to slip out of sight behind the professional walls of a Divinity School. The decision to locate his field of study in the wider context of graduate studies was consistent with his career-long attempts to give the Bible a more prominent place in American education. But Harper's decision to move his field of studies out of the Divinity School may also have unwittingly doomed his passion, Old Testament studies, to a precarious institutional existence. In this plan critical study of the biblical texts was separated from the official ministerial curriculum, providing room for a wedge to be driven between criticism and reverence, the two essential components of his approach to the Scriptures. Ironically, while protecting his specialty's place within the larger university, Harper may have sacrificed its impact in the Divinity School and upon its faculty and students.[30]

Those familiar with the Divinity School's distinguished history of preparing scholars of religion would search in vain for a commitment to religious research in the fifth "Official Bulletin." Instead, Harper continued the pastoral course of the School.

---

[29] "Official Bulletin," No. 5 (March 1892), p. 2.
[30] Ibid., pp. 4–5. See Chapter 3, pp. 72–76 for discussion of the obscure relationship of Harper to the subsequent intellectual history of the Divinity School.

> *Its Purpose*: The purpose of the Seminary is primarily and chiefly to fit men to become preachers of the Gospel. To this end students are instructed in the great doctrines of the Bible, in the chief facts and teachings of Church History, in the critical translation and interpretation of the Old and New Testaments, in the constitution and management of churches, in the composition and delivery of sermons, and in the practical duties of the pastorate.

Four groups comprised the targeted constituency of the school: those preparing for or practicing ministry, those preparing for or practicing missionary work, Christian teachers, and other Christian workers. Toward the end of his life Harper anticipated the need for a center devoted to graduate academic study of religion. In his report on the occasion of the university's tenth anniversary, for example, he suggested that the line between "scientific Divinity" and "practical Divinity must be more sharply drawn and such reorganization of the work should be brought about as will adapt it more closely to the needs of different classes of students."[31]

Despite its explicitly ministerial character, this Divinity School, however, would be different. For example, it was open to "students of all denominations of Christians." Furthermore, to secure the degree of Bachelor of Divinity a student had to enter this school with a bona fide B.A. degree. There was room for women—but with a catch.

> Women will be admitted to the Divinity School upon equal terms with men. They will receive no encouragement to enter upon the work of public preaching, but, on the contrary, are distinctly taught that the New Testament nowhere recognizes the ordination of women to the Christian pastorate.

In keeping with his frequently expressed dissatisfactions with the conventional theological encyclopedia, Harper proposed an eightfold departmental structure which included: 1) Old Testament Literature and Exegesis (apparently something distinct from what Harper intended to do in the University graduate school), 2) New Testament Literature and Exegesis, 3) Biblical Theology, 4) Apologetics, 5) Systematic Theology, 6) Church History, 7) an omnibus Homiletics, Ecclesiastical Polity, and Pastoral Duties Department, and 8) Missions and Mission Work. In addition Harper made provision for "instruction in Elocution, Music, and Physical Culture."[32]

Not satisfied with reforming the theological content of the seminary's curriculum, Harper turned to "various kinds of religious work open to students." The concern for practical work and theological clinics described in the previous chapter can be seen in a less explicit form in Harper's initial model for the new Divinity School.[33] Preaching would be allowed, but only

[31] William Rainey Harper, *The President's Report, July 1892–July 1902* (Chicago: University of Chicago Press, 1903), p. lxxv.

[32] "Official Bulletin," No. 5, pp. 6–8.

[33] "Official Bulletin," No. 5, p. 11; see above pp. 95f.

"to a limited extent." Students were expected either to assist parish pastors, or engage in city mission work and the programs of various Sunday schools. Further, this religious work was a mandatory part of the curriculum.

> The practical religious work . . . is to be regarded as a regular part of the Divinity course, and is not undertaken merely by those who need financial help. This work is under the charge of an officer specially appointed to superintend it. Every student who is a candidate for a degree, or for a certificate, will be required to do a certain amount of practical work in addition to such preaching as he may do from time to time.

The last of Harper's blueprints for the new university dealt with "The University Extension Division." In a spirit reminiscent of Chautauqua, he maintained that

> to provide instruction for those who, for social or economic reasons, cannot attend in its class-rooms is a legitimate and necessary part of the work of every university.

Here and in the bulletin dealing with the academies, Harper departed most sharply from existing notions of the university. Clark and Johns Hopkins had narrowed their academic focus to graduate study—at least as much as nervous trustees and founders would permit. Harper, on the other hand, was attempting to create a complete edifice of learning that could reach all people in need of higher learning. The University of Chicago became the pivotal institution for Harper's larger enterprise of constructing this new configuration.[34]

Clearly there were "dangers" in the proposed extension program. Work that was substandard in quality could be passed off as acceptable, and the good name of the university would experience "reproach."

> But if the work is an organic part of the university, directed and controlled by the university, and if the distinction between university work and university extension work is clearly indicated, the danger is reduced to the minimum.

Harper wanted a separate faculty for the extension—one which would, however, be accorded the "same rank" as members of other faculties.[35]

The Chautauqua paradigm is evident in the structure of the various departments of the Extension Division, which would include Lecture Study, Class Work, Correspondence-teaching, Examinations, Library and Publication, and District Organization and Training. At each place where university work might be offered around the city and nation, Harper hoped for the creation of "a Local Centre, governed by a Local Committee." These centers had to take on "bricks and mortar" as soon as possible.

[34] "Official Bulletin," No. 6 (May 1892), p. 2.
[35] Ibid., pp. 2–3.

The ease with which Harper blended his goals for a new modern university and his evangelical commitments became obvious in his descriptions of the extension program. Most of the institutions which Harper suggested as possible cooperating agencies in this effort possessed explicit Christian identities or affiliations. Moreover, Harper went so far as to claim that since "the University Extension is a great missionary movement, the missionary spirit must never be stifled." Ever the publicist, he proposed a new publication for this division, *The University Extension Gazette of Chicago.*[36]

If there were no other sources for mining Harper's vision for the University of Chicago than the *Official Bulletins*, it would nonetheless still be possible to isolate several dominant elements in Harper's vision. These initial writings reveal that for Harper the university became the pivotal institution for reshaping the existing structure of American education. Further, they show that his efforts at reconfiguration, in turn, were governed by the biblical perspective and passion which had motivated him in his pre-presidential years. Every aspect of the educational configuration he proposed provided ample opportunity for study of the sacred Scriptures. In addition, the *Bulletins* reveal Harper's commitment to specialized education: educational tasks were distributed among institutions and people moved from one institution to another. He wanted system, and strove to provide it by careful delineation of various schools, departments, and divisions. With satellite academies and local extension centers he sought to make his university a national institution. Finally, the university was not an end in itself; it had a mission to fulfill.

As he periodically released installments of his vision for university education, Harper labored in his customarily driven manner to establish the plan at once. The University of Chicago opened in 1892 with an Academy, ✗ Divinity School and Graduate School. Quarterly convocation reports soon informed the world of promised new buildings, new gifts, new areas of study.

The dimensions of Harper's public success in Chicago, however, have kept observers from noticing the larger vision of which the university was only a part. Harper's private correspondence reveals an astonishing range and variety of efforts to reshape American education. Letters discussing girls' schools in Paris, France and Oak Park, Illinois, show the scope of his concern to affiliate academies and preparatory schools with the university. Harper sought to link technical schools such as Bradley Polytechnic Institute of Peoria, Illinois, with the university. Colleges in Stetson, Florida, and Kalamazoo, Michigan, were also officially affiliated.

Harper seemed to grasp any occasion that might extend the impact of his new creation. For example, he tried to convince the new president of Brown

---

[36] Ibid., pp. 3–21.

✗ LABORATORY SCHOOL

University, W.H.P. Faunce, to take steps toward some kind of cooperative relationship with the university. His vision of the new possibilities for American education led him to join an elite group of national educators in a call for a new university at Washington, D.C., which would sit as the capstone of an emerging but still-to-be-organized national educational system. Harper cooperated with a generation of university presidents like Eliot of Harvard and Benjamin Wheeler of California to form the Association of American Universities in order to raise the standards of these new institutions and assist them in developing cooperative approaches to their peculiar problems. On one occasion Harper admitted privately to Rockefeller that his goal was to build an "educational trust," a coherent system of American education.[37]

The only limits on his achievements seemed to be dollars. Luring acknowledged academic giants from comfortable positions at established institutions to the new one emerging from the swampy midway on Chicago's south side required large salaries and costly promises of facilities, journals and ample funds for supporting research. As Harper worked to bring his vision into limestone, steel and flesh, he had to count dollars. Rockefeller consistently sought to keep from being the fail-safe mechanism for Harper's dreams and, indeed, Harper's vision eventually stretched beyond the oil magnate's patience. Although he seemed never to lose his respect for Harper, Rockefeller finally stopped the flow of dollars, and sent in an independent accountant to attempt to force Harper to live within the budget.[38]

Although his visions were costly, Harper was not profligate. He abhorred inefficiency and lack of system. In 1899 Harper expressed his intolerance for America's obsolete and costly educational configuration in an address to the Regents of the University of New York on "Waste In Higher Education." Adopting the "method of a businessman," Harper developed his own economics of education, in which dollars were not the primary datum. His economics dealt with the personal, social, and academic costs of

[37] William Rainey Harper to Miss Julia H.C. Haly, December 4, 1897, Personal Papers, Box 3, Folder 20; William Rainey Harper to Miss [?] Jones, June 24, 1898, Personal Papers, Box 4, Folder 9; William Rainey Harper to Nathaniel Butler, February 5, 1897, Personal Papers, Box 3, Folder 8; William Rainey Harper to Mr. [?] Stetson, May 21, 1898, Personal Papers, Box 4, Folder 7; William Rainey Harper to A. Gaylord Slocum, December 14, 1895, Personal Papers, Box 2, Folder 20; William Rainey Harper to Rev. W.H.P. Faunce, April 4, 1899, Personal Papers, Box 4, Folder 25; William Rainey Harper to J.P. Carney, May 1, 1895, Personal Papers, Box 2, Folder 12; William Rainey Harper to Martin Ryerson, March 3, 1900, Personal Papers, Box 5, Folder 15; William Rainey Harper to John D. Rockefeller, November 15, 1888, is quoted in Storr, *Harper's University*, p. 24.

[38] Thomas W. Goodspeed to William Rainey Harper, March 29, 1905, reported that a Rockefeller auditor, Starr J. Murphy, had concluded after an investigation that "we are here, not conducting a great educational institution, but rather an organized conspiracy to rob Mr. Rockefeller of his wealth" (Personal Papers, Box 9, Folder 9).

educational practices which schooled students in "dissipation." Providing a smattering of knowledge in an increasing number of subjects only set students on a course destined to be strewn with waste. Furthermore, he argued that failure to teach students "the habit of accuracy" did incalculable damage to society. In Harper's opinion, one of the most glaring examples of waste in the current American model was the division placed between the fourth year of high school and the freshman year of college, which he termed a violation of "the laws of nature." It seemed obvious to him that students were not ready for university methods until the sophomore year at the earliest. Premature use of advanced methods resulted in the "waste of interest" of the student. Furthermore, Harper claimed that high school and elementary preparation had been drawn out much too long. The net result of America's present practices was tragic waste; by the time a student became a junior in college he or she had wasted two or three years of life.[39]

To Harper the wasteful American structure was a "sin," the problem was "utter lack of system" caused by the "injurious independence of our separate institutions." He gratefully noted signs of "this archaic system's" break-down. But there was still a long list of problems needing resolution. Traditional notions of the four-year college, for example, were nothing but a "fetish," which had to be eliminated along with other debilitating customs. Sixty to 70 percent of college instructors' time was wasted during summer vacations. And lack of concentration by students and teachers on a few subjects had to be changed. Harper countered existing scattershot practices with the claim that "no student can profitably conduct more than three lines of study at the same time." Challenging the entrenched model of the professor as generalist he also argued that no instructor should pursue more than two or at most three courses of teaching at any given time.[40]

After looking at systemic matters in preparatory and college teaching, Harper turned to three basic perceptual changes that needed to occur if American education was to be free from waste. First, "the principle of individualism" had to be applied to college education. In the old "class" idea, there was no room for individuals. Harper's alternative was a suggestion that schools do "a diagnosis of each student," treating each one "as if he were the only student" in the institution. Efforts to offer more than one required curriculum were praiseworthy because they fostered individual development. Harper speculated that as many as five or six distinct groups of interests should be offered to students. His foil was an unnamed "prominent president" of an eastern university who felt that

> the purpose of the university in its dealing with its students is to impose upon each of them a like impression; to remove the individ-

---

[39] Harper, "Waste in Higher Education," *The Trend in Higher Education in America*, pp. 78–86.
[40] Ibid., pp. 87–92.

ualities of the students, and to send them out as if all had been formed in a given mold.[41]

The second problem of perspective was the tendency of teachers to regard every student in each course "as if he were going to make a specialty of that department." Doctors of Philosophy who taught at lower college levels tended to "germanize everything," i.e., to treat each subject in a specialized manner, appropriate for graduate students but inappropriate for those who did not seek to master a narrow specialty. Elsewhere Harper remarked that he often thought that it took students who had completed European doctorates two or three years back in America before they overcame the deficiencies of German specialization. What was needed was a type of teaching which discovered the "interrelationship" between fields of study. Harper bemoaned the fact that "more than half of the students who leave college are as ignorant as babes of the organic and logical relation which exists between the various courses in the ordinary curriculum." Departmental divisions were "artificial and misleading."[42]

Finally Harper tried to overcome his generation's wasteful practices by advancing an image of cooperation between institutions. Students should "intermigrate" between schools, participating in a process that presupposed that colleges and universities would abandon illusory goals of trying to cover all fields of knowledge equally well. Instead of competing with one another, the institutions in Harper's new configuration would specialize in one or two areas of work. When institutions sought to cover the total academic encyclo- pedia, he believed they were inevitably forced to settle for mediocrity.

Under the prevailing circumstances of the period, Harper believed that standards for teaching competence and student admissions would continue to decline. More than 200 colleges and universities were guilty of a "sin against reason and against God" which brought "shame and reproach upon a cause so holy as that of higher education." These institutions literally "stole" money from students in their early college years to fund the work of higher education at more advanced levels. Denominational schools were among the worst offenders of this common "practice of fraudulent waste." Harper concluded his indictment of the existing configuration with the claim that the American system had "actually murdered hundreds of men" by making them teach too many subjects while paying miserly wages.[43]

As a partial solution to the waste problem Harper advocated acceptance of certain German notions—especially those which nudged America's edu- cational system toward a six-year institution which combined the high school

[41] Ibid., pp. 93–96.
[42] Ibid., pp. 97–99; William Rainey Harper to Miss Ella Young, January 28, 1899, Personal Papers, Box 4, Folder 22.
[43] Harper, "Waste in Higher Education," pp. 102–13.

and lower college. The high schools in fact became the colleges of the new configuration.[44]

Harper, the efficient systematizer, has received considerable attention from scholars who have acknowledged his role in the creation of significant academic reforms like the quarter system or the junior college. But all too often they have failed to see a larger pattern which becomes apparent when this educational work is put beside his work in popular and religious education; in essence Harper was attempting to redesign American education from top to bottom. The missionary character of Harper's educational efforts has been equally neglected. Whether attempting to reform the Chicago public high school system, raiding the faculty of a sister institution, or landing another bequest for a building, Harper was striving for nothing less than the redemption of America.

## The Messianic Role of the University

On February 22, 1905, immediately prior to undergoing a serious operation for the carcinoma which took his life less than a year later, Harper prepared the preface to a collection of his own occasional writings on topics related to the university. Entitled *The Trend in Higher Education*, this book would serve as his final public statement on key educational themes. Harper did not live long enough to develop his educational philosophy beyond what appears in this hastily assembled collection of essays. But in those unsystematically arranged fragments, the reader encounters Harper's final vision of the relationship between the university and religion.[45]

With the same assuredness that accompanied his conviction that science could demonstrate the facts of the Scriptures, Harper turned to American higher education and interpreted the facts. He had no doubt that there was a trend, a plot, to the American story. Harper traced the movement of education from east to west and viewed the west as the locus of the new and significant developments of higher education. Indeed he interpreted his own moment as the beginning of a second era in the history of the American university, surpassing the one inaugurated with the founding of Johns Hopkins in 1876. Now the institutions of the east had to look to the west for their models and guides. The essays collected in *The Trend* were simply entries in "a notebook in the great educational laboratory" of America.[46]

[44] Ibid., pp. 114–17. Harper's efforts to reshape the American high schools took the form of affiliating various academies, institutes, and high schools with the University of Chicago. In addition, he served on the Board of Education of the Chicago Public Schools and proposed a plan which would affiliate the city's high schools with the university, Personal Papers, Box 2, Folder 24.

[45] Harper, "Preface," *The Trend in Higher Education*, pp. vii, viii.

[46] Ibid. "Dependence of the West upon the East," ibid., pp. 135–39; "Higher Education in the West," ibid., pp. 140–50; "The Contribution of Johns Hopkins," ibid., pp. 151–52.

No more compelling picture of Harper's ultimate vision of the modern university can be found than the one offered in his essay, "The University and Democracy," first given in 1899 as a Charter Day address at the University of California. There Harper revealed the place of the university in his total schema. There Harper the biblical scholar joined Harper the university president in fashioning a philosophy of education which was overtly religious and overtly American.

In this essay Harper traced the "slow and tortuous progress" of humanity "toward a higher civilization." Democracy, "the highest ideal of human achievement," was rising, like the "glorious and golden sun lighting up the dark places of all the world." The university had a peculiar relationship to this rising sun in the human cosmos, a relationship with origins in the guilds of the medieval period. Side by side, Harper believed, the university and democracy had developed, flowing from a common "beginning of that spirit" which emerged in the "spontaneous confederations" of these associations. "The university had its birth in the democratic idea; and from the day of its birth this democratic character, except when state or church has interfered, has continued."[47]

The university became a place where people from diverse nationalities could intermingle. In these places "secular" disciplines like medicine and law found a home. New methods of instruction and freedom of expression were additional "birthmarks" of the university, which was fundamentally an "institution of the people." Harper embraced the tradition. A university was

> a self-governing association of men for the purpose of study; an institution privileged by the state for the guidance of the people; an agency recognized by the people for resolving the problems of civilization which present themselves in the development of civilization.

The university was the place where humanity's "great problems" could be addressed. Such a responsibility required people of "the greatest genius, equipment of the highest order, and absolute freedom from interference of any kind, civic or ecclesiastical."[48]

The special vocation of the university was the preparation of leaders and teachers for "every field of activity." By preparing this intellectual elite, the highest group in the multilevelled but interconnected educational world, Harper believed that the university could relate itself to everything:

> The university touches life, every phase of life, at every point. It enters into every field of thought to which the human mind addresses itself. It has no fixed abode far away from man; for it goes to those who cannot come to it. It is shut in behind no lofty battlement; for it has no enemy which it would ward off. Strangely enough, it vanquishes its

[47] Harper, "The University and Democracy," ibid., pp. 1–2.
[48] Ibid., pp. 3–5.

> enemies by inviting them into close association with itself. The
> university is of the people, and for the people whether considered
> individually or collectively.

As he began to unfold the social mission of the university Harper revealed an assumption about education. The people of America "must be an educated people." In fact, the first and foremost policy of democracy "must be" education. Education "is the foundation which underlies all else." Parting company with Rousseau and others who trusted "an innate and instinctive wisdom" in people, Harper sought to erect modern life on university foundations.[49]

The preceding remarks would be noteworthy simply as representative of the broad, progressive educational stance of an age if Harper had not linked them to religion. Others had seen the relationship between democracy and new forms of education. Theoretical giants like John Dewey went beyond Harper in efforts to make explicit the connection between democracy and education. But none of them turned to the Old Testament for the key categories to describe the relationship between democracy and the new American university. Both Harper's personal distinctiveness and the character of an age in which many could find plausible such public linkages of university, democracy and biblical particularity come into view when Harper's argument is carefully considered.

Beginning cautiously, Harper stated cherished American assumptions:

> Democracy has nothing to do with religion and yet it has
> everything; nothing with the specific form in which the religious
> feeling or religious teaching shall express itself, but everything in
> making provision for the undisturbed exercise of religious liberty.

But then he turned to a different source. Asking his listeners' pardon for a digression, President Harper became the Old Testament expert who probed sacred texts for new revelation. Repeating a point frequently made in lectures and articles on biblical themes, Harper pointed out that the Hebrew people were unique:

> In the course of their long-continued history they passed through
> nearly every form of life, from that of savages to that of highest
> civilization, and they lived under nearly every form of government,
> from the patriarchal, through the tribal, the monarchical, and the
> hierarchical. The history of no other nation furnishes parallels of so
> varied or so suggestive a character.

This history could speak to "all men who have religious sympathies"— Protestant, Catholic or Jew. Harper had found his key integrator in the history contained within Old Testament. No subject of study was more open

[49] Ibid., pp. 6–9.

to all the specialized university disciplines than biblical scholarship. No history was as universal as that of the Hebrews.[50]

Then came a startling statement from a precise Old Testament scholar. He invested the terms "university" and "democracy" with key meanings taken from the Old Testament:

> Democracy has been given a mission to the world, and it is of no uncertain character. I wish to show that the university is the prophet of this democracy, and as well, its priest and its philosopher; that, in other words, the university is the Messiah of the democracy, its to-be expected deliverer.[51]

The temptation for the late twentieth-century reader is to regard these words as mere hyperbole, the excited utterance of an individual swept away in the first flush of his success as university builder. Such an approach does not do justice, however, to Harper's preceding history. A more meaningful approach is to view these words in the light of Harper's career as biblical interpreter. Prophet, priest, sage (philosopher) and Messiah were technical concepts employed within a highly developed craft. Harper knew what the words meant and intentionally reapplied them in his new setting. He was attempting to fit modern American educational reality into biblical categories, to fashion a new biblical world.

No category was as central to Harper's thought as "prophet." A major part of his scholarly career had been devoted to reviving the study of prophecy; it was the distinctive element in Israel's history. Prophets interpreted history, they discerned divine activity in the events of past, present and future. Now Harper prophetically interpreted a piece of history, the present modern setting. A divine plot was discernible in the midst of the ebbs and flows of modernity.

How did the university serve as prophet? First like Elijah or Isaiah the university served as spokesperson for the democracy. The university's vocation was to read the history of the past fifty centuries and to discern the "laws of life" operating therein. As Elijah attempted with the religions of Canaan so the prophetic university was to be the purifier of democracy. Traces of past ages, of medievalism, needed to be purged in order that democracy could emerge in pure form.

Just as prophecy developed over centuries of Israel's history so democracy developed slowly over the centuries; it made its way by degrees. Now, Harper believed, democracy existed in American government, but social life, the arts, literature and science had not yet been fully touched by its spirit. He granted that Christianity had its democratic elements, "but the church is too frequently hostile to the application of democratic principles."

[50] Ibid., pp. 10–11.
[51] Ibid., p. 12.

Modern prophets were needed to carry the singular message of democracy to those areas of life still lacking the liberating word.[52]

The prophetic university, like Second Isaiah, bore "the words of the comforter." In modern society the university was called to soothe the minds and hearts "of the great multitude of men and women in our great cities, for whom as individuals there is no hope in life. . . ." It was to bring hope to "a democracy despondent."[53]

Democracy, like the chosen people of the Old Testament, had a mission, and it was one the prophet could formulate. Again Harper dipped into his Old Testament lexicon. The mission of democracy was, in a word, righteousness. "The world is waiting for the working out of the doctrine of national righteousness through democracy. . . ." The university was to use the "object-lessons" of the world's history in order to guide the present development of the democratic impulse.[54]

The prophet also had a responsibility to look ahead:

> Mounting the watch-tower of observation, the true leader of democracy will make a forecast of the tendencies, in order to encourage his followers by holding up the glory that awaits them, or, by depicting the disaster that is coming, to turn them aside from a policy so soon to prove destructive.

Harper, the university president, was a modern version of the minor prophet Habbakuk, who more than 25 centuries previously had strained from his watchtower to see what was coming for the people of Israel. The university had the same task.[55]

The Old Testament prophet based his message on the fact of Israel's divine chosenness, and Harper was willing to posit just such a ground for the university's vocation. "The university, I contend, is the prophet of democracy—the agency established by heaven itself to proclaim the principles of democracy." Individual universities thus became the prophetic schools of the modern age. They took up their dwellings "in the very midst of squalor and distress" to provide help and to pronounce judgment on corruption and scandal. Prophets were some of the "greatest souls the world ever knew." With hearts touched "by the spirit of the living God," eyes opened "to visions of divine glory," and arms steeled by "courage born of close communion with higher powers," they sallied forth on their holy mission. "It is just so with universities."[56]

The second element in Harper's tripartite conception of the university was that of "priest." A priest must have a religion.

[52] Ibid., pp. 12–15.
[53] Ibid., pp. 15–16.
[54] Ibid., pp. 16–18.
[55] Ibid., pp. 18–19.
[56] Ibid., pp. 19–20.

> Is democracy a religion? No. Has democracy a religion? Yes; a
> religion with its god, its altar, and its temple, with its code of ethics
> and its creed. Its god is mankind, humanity; its altar, home; its temple,
> country. The one doctrine of democracy's creed is the brotherhood,
> and consequently the equality of man; its system of ethics is con-
> tained in a single word: righteousness.

Here Harper revealed the religious core of his vision. The university was to
nurture a religion for modernity, a religion that could unite all the dimensions of life which modernity separated. Harper found much of Judaism and
Christianity in this religion of democracy. After all, Jeremiah had discovered
one of its cardinal tenets, the "idea of individualism." That idea was given
fundamental place in the teaching of Jesus, "the world's greatest advocate of
democracy." But democracy's religion was truly eclectic, gathering ideas
from more than these two great traditions. Just as Israel had done during its
centuries of intermigrating, democracy had "absorbed many of the best
features of various religions and systems of philosophy." Centuries had
passed before Israel's people accepted the full form of its own religion. So
the modern world still had to be changed before this "world-wide religion"
could be generally accepted.[57]

As mediator between humans, the university was to bring the people of
the world "into close communion with their own souls" and then with each
other. By studying the self, the university could lead into communion with
God. The consecrated task of the university was "lifting up the folk of her
environment." No responsibility was more holy.[58]

As "keeper" of the holy mysteries, those sacred and significant traditions
of the "church of democracy," the university was to protect them from
"profane hands." At the same time its priestly vocation was to include in the
list of the initiated, "who handled the mysteries," the whole world. The
priestly service of the university was to take place in the homes of the land.
The home was "the altar of democracy, the most sacred altar known to
mankind." Cloaking his educational configuration in priestly vestments,
Harper sought by teaching the nation's teachers to bring "every family in this
entire broad land of ours" into "touch" with the university. As this task was
accomplished the nation would become the "great temple of democracy."
Mediating between rival parties within the land, the university served as
crucible for widely divergent ideas, a place for their mingling. This institution could hold up consecration to truth as the standard of conduct, reveal the
strange secrets of history and provide ways for discordant notes of pluralism
to come together in the "harmonious sound" which lifted "the soul to higher
and purer thoughts of patriotic feeling."[59]

Harper had discovered the priestly tendency in Old Testament religion

[57] Ibid., pp. 20–22.
[58] Ibid., pp. 22–24.
[59] Ibid., pp. 24–26.

to identify the ways of God with the destiny of the chosen few, the Israelites. Because of lessons learned in study of the prophets, Harper broadened the priestly vocation of the university to include concern for all humanity. "The most profound act of worship" occurred when an individual's thoughts were lifted "beyond home and country to humanity at large, mankind." The priestly university had the duty to enlarge the vision of its followers. As priest it took

> infinite trouble to teach men that the ties of humanity are not limited to those of home and country, but extend to all the world; for all men are brothers.

The university stood "as mediator between one country and another." All of humanity had a "common soul"; the university's ministry was to bring humans and nations into close communication with it. To be sure, Harper had a religious vision that stressed America's uniqueness in the divine plan. But his biblical understandings carried him beyond a "religion of the republic" or "civil religion" toward an inclusive world religion. The same scholar who had found similarities in the various stories of the world's great religions viewed the university as the agency that could bring people together in the world-embracing religion of democracy.[60]

A third element in the historic three-fold office of Old Testament leadership remained—that of sage, or "philosopher." In Harper's own biblical scholarship the office of sage had received proportionately less attention than that of prophet or priest. Sages, who appeared in the moment of Israel's great trial of captivity and defeat, were unique individuals who could look beyond the boundaries of Israel and see the universal dimensions implicit in this particular people's monotheism. They were people who struggled with the "great problems" of history and life.

In the age of the emergence of democracy and the university with its "serious demands for severe thinking," the philosopher/sage moved to center stage in Harper's vision. Specifically, the university as philosopher needed to address itself to three key problems: "the origin of democracy," "the philosophy of history," and "the formulation of the laws or principles of democracy." Harper surveyed the new realities of industrial urban life and identified problems which threatened the existence of democracy. Social-ism, population increases in the large cities, concentrations of great wealth in the hands of a few, the emergence of great business corporations, floun-dering "lawmaking bodies" that seemed unable to cope with party ma-chines, demagogues and bosses, a church that seemed unable to respond to

---

[60] Ibid., pp. 26–27. Sidney E. Mead described America's "religion of the republic" in *The Nation with the Soul of a Church* (New York: Harper & Row, Publishers, 1975), pp. 65ff. America's "civil religion" was named and outlined in Robert N. Bellah's, "Civil Religion in America," *Beyond Belief: Essays on Religion in a Post-Traditional World* (New York: Harper & Row, Publishers, 1970), pp. 168–89.

the needs of "workingmen"—all were new problems which the university as philosopher must solve for the sake of democracy.[61]

The "problem of problems" was the future of democracy, whose ability to last was being tested. Traditionally, pragmatic Americans sneered at theorizing, but only as the university concentrated on the great theoretical needs of democracy would the idea come to full flower.[62]

Harper remembered that another of the key offices of leadership in Old Testament thought was the kingly one. Ideas of kingship, however, had no place in the democratic scheme. For proof of the historically limited character of the kingly office he turned to Jesus. When the Messiah came "he was no king in any sense that had been expected." The Old Testament theocracy had dreamed of this Messiah. Prophets, priests and sages labored to hasten "the realization of this magnificent ideal."[63]

In essence Harper had carried his typological interpretation of Scripture into the next spiral.

> Now, let the dream of democracy be likewise of that expected one; this time an expected agency which, in union with all others; will usher in the dawn of the day when the universal brotherhood of man will be understood and accepted by all men. Meanwhile the universities here and there, in the New World and in the Old; the university men who occupy high places throughout the earth; the university spirit which, with every decade, dominates the world more fully, will be doing the work of the prophet, the priest, and the philosopher of democracy, and will continue to do that work until it shall be finished, until a purified and exalted democracy shall have become universal.[64]

Harper had chosen the secular University of California's 1899 Charter Day celebration as the moment to reveal his understanding of the religious mission of the university. His startling combination of secular setting and religious content on that occasion point to an identification of divine activity with a peculiar agency which challenged both traditional religious under-standings and emergent patterns of higher education. As biblical scholar, Harper had penetrated the texts of the Scriptures to find the divine element in history. As university president, he asserted that the same divine element was at work in contemporary educational history. That he identified the workings of God with an agency which seemed to many anti-, or at best, non-religious reveals how far Harper's religious understandings had moved from those of New Concord, Ohio.

George Hunston Williams's essay, "The Theological Idea of the Uni-versity," helps locate Harper's model of the university within the context of

---

[61] Harper, "The University and Democracy," pp. 28–32.
[62] Ibid., p. 32.
[63] Ibid., pp. 33–34.
[64] Ibid.

centuries of theological thinking about the place of the university within society. Williams did not mention Harper, but did find a distinctive "triadic arrangement" or pattern involved in Christian thinking about the relation of university to church and state. This triadic arrangement of society in turn corresponded to the three-fold office of Christ: prophet, priest and king.

Beginning with the asceticism of early Christianity, Williams traced the development of a special Eden-like place for Christians to be prepared for "learned warfare" against corruptions in both church and state. St. Jerome's idea of the role of the monastery thus was a precursor of the medieval notion of university. By the thirteenth century, the university had emerged as a distinct institution which merited recognition by Pope Gregory IX as a third sector in the social structure of his age. A German cleric, Alexander of Roes argued at the end of Gregory's century that the peace and order of Christendom depended upon the harmonious working of three powers: papacy, empire and university.[65]

Williams claimed that the tripartite medieval social configuration of church, state and university was placed on a more overtly christological basis by John Calvin and other reformers at Geneva. There Calvin followed the lead of Martin Bucer and explicitly developed the christological model of prophet, priest, king as a paradigm for his new social structure. The new Geneva configuration was church, academy and magistracy. Calvin increasingly came to accentuate the role of Christ as prophet/doctor, emphasizing the importance of the teaching office in society.[66]

Williams's theological history traced the emergence of a distinct "third force" function for the university in medieval and post-reformation life. In his reading, the advent of the German university muted the corporate function of the institution, making it a place where individual scholars prepared for solitary battle for truth against error. Arguing that "an expressly or distinctively Protestant theory of the university was never fully and clearly enunciated in Germany or elsewhere," Williams felt that as the gap between church and university widened, the university came to be viewed as a secular entity, and a new institution appeared to fill the gap, the Protestant seminary. The difference between the social places of the post-reformation seminary and the medieval university was the seminary's marginal relationship to the social structure, a signal of the fracture of the tripartite model.[67]

This brief detour through the main avenues of Williams's argument allows the distinctiveness of Harper's vision for the modern university to become more apparent. His application of a three-fold biblical model to the

[65] Williams, "The Theological Idea of the University: The Paradise Theme and Related Motifs in the History of Higher Education," *Wilderness and Paradise*, pp. 157–58, 66–67, 70.

[66] Ibid., pp. 187–92.

[67] Ibid., pp. 196, 220.

problem of relating the university to its context can be seen as continuous with a long Christian tradition. What should be noticed is that in addition to its more traditional prophetic role, his ideal university had taken on the priestly role which once belonged to the church. Further, the kingly function had dropped from view in this reconstruction. Harper's democratic reading of the Scriptures had made the king obsolete. The wisdom of the sage who grappled with the great problems of modern life for the sake of society had replaced the authoritarianism of the king.

Williams's reconstruction of university history around the christological pattern of prophet, priest and king also brings into clearer perception Harper's attempt to resist the trend toward the marginalization of religious learning in modernity. Harper did not seek to build secure seminaries on the margins of America's new social structure. His university can be seen as an attempt to continue an older tradition of viewing the university as a third force to counteract the evils that infect both church and state. At the heart of his attempts to reform American education was an attempt to conserve a public religious role for the modern univerisity.

RELIGION IN THE UNIVERSITY

Harper's model of world salvation, although expressed in terms of one institution as the key transformer of the world, was an individualist model. One by one, students would be lifted to the higher life as they experienced university life. Harper, the prophet of the new type of biblical religion, was also its priest. As university president he served as mediator, comforter and servant of students and faculty. His personal papers are filled with letters which show him functioning as an unordained minister: comforting the troubled, counseling the searching, rebuking the errant.[68]

[68] For example, see William Rainey Harper to Mr. Williamson, October 18, 1900, where he writes: "I have just learned of the illness of your daughter, Miss Kate Williamson and of the fact that it has been found necessary to take her home. I wish to express my very great sympathy with you and her in this illness and also to express the hope that she will soon recover" (Personal Papers, Box 5, Folder 13). On November 12, 1900, Harper requested Mr. Gale of Snell Hall and other households to send him notice of serious student illness or deaths in student families (Personal Papers, Box 5, Folder 24).

People from around the nation requested Harper's help in personal religious matters. Lloyd W. Bowers, General Counsel of the Chicago & North-Western Railway Company, for instance, wrote Harper on February 22, 1898, that "after a life of inattention," he desired "to study now the religion that his wife cherished and that it will now rest with him in some way to teach to two little children for whose Christian care she was anxious." Requesting a course of reading, Bowers admitted that "I would give all I have for Christian confidence. . . ." Harper responded with an invitation to discuss Bowers's religious questions over lunch (Personal Papers, Box 4, Folder 2).

Harper felt free to give advice which he himself did not always follow. Thus he urged Mr. Thurber on June 14, 1898, to "take a bit of fatherly advice and do not work so hard. Why do you not enjoy life and have a good time as I do? I should like to make one other

As religious leader of his institution, Harper had opportunity to mold the religion implicit in his university vision. Convinced that the colleges and universities of the land "are not performing their full function in the matter of religious education," Harper published a series of "talks to students" in a volume entitled *Religion and the Higher Life*. In his talks Harper moved his new form of biblical religion beyond the conventional notions of his contemporaries. He admitted that the responsibility for the religious needs of his students "weighed upon me more heavily than any other connected with the office which I have been called to administer."[69]

These inspirational addresses revealed that Harper had rejected anthropological models that forced human development into rigid categories. Instead, he advocated the vague sounding "higher life," a notion which steadfastly avoided any universal standard for all to meet. According to Harper the concept had to be adjusted to each individual.

> It is only the man who lives *the highest life possible for him to live*, that may be said to live the higher life; the failure at any time, to put forth his utmost endeavor—a failure of which in every case he is unquestionably conscious—degrades him, from a higher to a lower position.

On the basis of this individualist understanding, Harper endeavored to aid all forms of development. Religion had a central role to play in this enterprise. It was "essential for the fullest development" of all other important phases of the higher life. As the "oldest sister of the family" of art, science, philosophy and ethics, religion did not dominate these important areas of life; instead it integrated them and helped each to flourish.[70]

Harper carefully distanced "religion" from any identification with church. The church was "of a transitory and variable character," sometimes taking on a particular form, sometimes passing out of sight. Unconcerned with the passing phenomena of religious expressions, Harper sought the essential within them. In this understanding of religion Christianity, "in its broadest form," became "the highest and most perfect form of religion thus far developed."[71]

Religion had an intrinsicality; it was "something in itself and for itself, fulfilling a separate role." Unique in offering "peace of soul," religion held the various "faculties" of the human spirit in "even balance." It addressed a person's "whole being." When normal religious development took place, "every function of life" was strengthened.[72]

---

suggestion. Give up drinking coffee or tea with milk in it and I will guarantee that you will be free from all future bilious attacks." (Personal Papers, Box 4, Folder 8).
[69] Harper, *Religion and the Higher Life*, pp. vii–viii.
[70] Ibid., pp. 3–5.
[71] Ibid., pp. 6–7
[72] Ibid., pp. 9, 12–13.

For Harper, the essence of religion was "belief in God." Beyond that essential element one encountered countless varieties of belief and practice—the results of a multitude of tastes and sympathies. Such differences were not merely "of creed, nor of forms of worship, but of standards of morality, of external accompaniments, and of subjective ideals." Still, Harper claimed, "there must be some things in common." Running through the varieties of religious expression were six characteristics that seemed essential for all in search of the higher life. Modern religion, therefore, had to be: simple, reasonable, tolerant, idealistic, ethical and consoling. As the example of such a religion Harper cited "the religion of Jesus Christ." It was "capable of adjustment to any and every individual, however peculiar his temperament, however exacting his demands." Indeed, it met each of the six criteria:

> Its simplicity, as the Master himself presented it, is marvelous. In its proper form, it has always stood the most rigid tests; and it appeals as strongly to the reason as to the heart. It will permit you to respect your friend's religion; if he is a Jew, because it came out of Judaism; if a sincere follower of Islam, because much of Islam came from it, if a disciple of some eastern faith because its founder, Jesus, was broad-minded and tender, and saw truth wherever truth existed, without reference to the name it bore. It is a religion of ideals, not wierd and fanciful; but chastened, strong and inspiring to true service. It is ethical in a sense peculiar to itself, for it is the religion of the beatitudes and the Golden Rule. It is a religion that says: "Come unto me all ye that labor and are heavy laden, and I will give you rest."[73]

Harper deliberately refrained from urging any special form of this religion upon his audience. Instead he advocated "its very essence" which was common to all its forms. In the teachings of Jesus and the Old Testament sages, Harper found his core—"the fear of the Lord." Religion in this reading equalled "belief in and acceptance of One who has power to help, even to the uttermost." Moving beyond issues of creeds and denominations, he claimed that "The dividing line runs, not between this and that form of religious faith, but through all forms. The name is insignificant; the serious thing is the character of your religion." Each individual had to find her own.[74]

As he reasserted what he believed to be the essence of biblical religion, Harper clearly had transformed traditional understandings of it. A career of biblical scholarship had enabled him to penetrate layers of interpretation and come nearer to what he considered essential religion. As a modern biblical historian Harper had joined contemporaries like Julius Wellhausen in tracing the development of biblical religion through three distinct phases which seemed to set the terms for the emergence of the new understanding he was advocating. In Israel's earliest phase worship had been the main

[73] Ibid., pp. 15–20.
[74] Ibid.

religious activity of priests who focused their followers' attention on proper ritualistic actions. Belief, the main emphasis of the second phase, became the dominant concern of the Hebrew prophets, whose passion for proper religous ideas ruled religion for the next cluster of centuries. Part of the heritage of this prophetic emphasis on belief was fragmentation of Judaism and Christianity into a multitude of sects and denominations. Although they played marginal roles in their own times, Old Testament sages proleptically introduced the element of ethics which finally came to prominence in modern religious expression. In this third phase belief lost its central religious role. "A man's life, at least in civilized countries, is not dependent upon his theological belief, as it once was." Instead, in Harper's era, greater emphasis was being placed on conduct. Once again, Harper used the particular history of Israel to encompass the universal human story. Israel had experienced the progression of religious concern from worship to belief to behavior. The religious evolution of the Hebrew people from priestly to prophetic to sagely styles was similar, he believed, to the general historical development of religion. Israel's experience with these religious stages of development was "essentially their history everywhere."[75]

For any human life to be complete, for any human to develop to her highest potential, all three of these stages had to be experienced. Harper encouraged listeners to "study *yourself*." Symmetrical development was the goal. "The day of special priesthood is past—everybody must be his own priest; the day of special prophetism is past—everyone must be a prophet; the day of specialism in morality has never existed and will never come." If a student's religious growth was lopsided the weak area should be cultivated and developed. The exemplar for any student to follow was Jesus—"the best representative of this religious spirit." Careful study of Jesus' life and teachings would provide the pattern by which to assess religious development. But while he clearly gave Jesus a pivotal role in his new understanding of religion, Harper also was careful to note the distance between Christianity and its founder. Christianity had "almost forgotten that there was a Christ, or, perhaps more accurately, had so changed him that he could no longer be recognized as Christ." The "glory" of late nineteenth-century thought was its restoration of the Christ "who had been forgotten or ignored."[76]

Arguing that the Bible was necessary for genuine religious development because of its teachings about worship, belief and ethics, Harper based his claim upon the uniqueness of Jesus.

> In order that the world might have such perfect illustration of it
> (the religious life), and illustration which all men might see and study,
> and by which humanity might be lifted to a still higher plane than that

[75] Harper, "The Religious Spirit," ibid., pp. 22–29.
[76] Ibid., pp. 31–35.

which it had reached through the divine help already furnished in other ways, Jesus Christ was born, and therefore he lived and taught and died. His attitude of reverence and homage toward God, in its simplicity and sublimity, in its irrepressible aspiration was the perfect presentation of the true worship, in itself, and in its relation to the other factors which constitute the religious experience. His teaching concerning God as Father of the world, of humanity as a single, closely related family, every member of which had responsibility for every other member, his teaching of the kingdom of heaven, and the ideal social life in which justice and peace shall reign, constitute a creed from which nothing may be subtracted; while the making of additions to it, as history has shown, leads surely to confusion and controversy. His life, in the perfection of its purity, in the pathos of its self-sacrifice, in the loftiness of its unselfish achievement, has furnished the world principles which underlie and control all right living.

The pattern set by Jesus thus became the norm by which all religious experience could be tested. But in the process of making him the normative exemplar for all religions, Harper refrained from including many traditional teachings about him, an omission which would make it impossible for all to follow his type of Jesus.[77]

Throughout his career Harper labored on two of the three fronts he identified as crucial for religious development, beliefs and ethics. Certain that worship had received ample attention, Harper initially concentrated his reformation on biblical interpretation, intent upon clearing away the debris of inadequate beliefs that blocked access to the message of the Scriptures. He followed the spirit of modern scholarship and asserted that one had "to go to the original sources" for correct information. "The one source, the only source, as well as the original source, for help . . . is the Bible."[78]

Harper also sought to develop an academic ethic that retrieved the concerns of the sages and reiterated the fundamental idea of the Scriptures: suffering for others. When true to their vocations both college and university had an overarching religious purpose: to teach one to suffer. The messianic responsibility of the university was to suffer for society. In so doing it also equipped individual members of society for personal encounters with suffering.

In a talk on "Fellowship and Its Obligation—Service," Harper sounded simultaneously modern and biblical. He began by noting that the "worlds we live in grow in number and in size as life proceeds." Consistent with his own experience he pointed out that one never left behind the old worlds of his or her past but that new ones were continually "super-added."[79]

Speaking in a manner which seemed to echo his Chautauqua mentor

[77] Harper, "Bible Study and Religious Life," ibid., pp. 161–62.
[78] Ibid., p. 163.
[79] Harper, "Fellowship and Its Obligation—Service," ibid., p. 36.

John Vincent, Harper asserted that the "college world" merited special attention because it served as "a kind of epitome" of the "great world." Within that special world the student met, in compressed form, all of life's temptations, struggles, successes, failures, ambitions, and despairs. In addition, collegians encountered in that distinctive context a "world-fellowship" which embraced all humans. Harper likened this encounter to a second birth, in which individuals were transformed and prepared to sustain "a peculiar relation to the world" and to occupy "a peculiar place in its fellowship." Individuals initiated into the higher or larger life of the college world had a special burden or responsibility of acting as parent or instructor to those still living the first type of life in smaller worlds of family and friendship.[80]

The higher life was arduous:

> With every increase of knowledge there is an increase of the capacity for sorrow. To the unthinking mind the man of wealth, living in his mansion, is an object of envy. If the real facts were known the life of such a one would be found in many cases, to be a life of care and responsibility, for which the satisfaction of physical life is no fair remuneration.

Harper was advocating an academic version of *noblesse oblige*. The person of privilege had to use opportunities "for the advantage of others." An obligation went with college life—"one of service." The service was "hard and rigorous," "continuous and never ending." In "one form or other" Harper's educational elite were invited to become modern ascetics who "give to others everything that has been given to you." Harper labored to equip the strong for service in order that they might equip the weak.[81]

For Harper "service" was more than altruism. He translated what he believed was the most fundamental idea in the Old Testament into a code of ethics for college educated individuals. Even his cherished academic principle of individualism had to give way to the servant ethos he advocated. "The world today needs more of the spirit of voluntary sacrifice and less of that spirit, called independence, which is in essence real selfishness." To move his student listeners beyond such self-centeredness, Harper once again turned to biblical themes, claiming that the kind of service he described was "the real essence, not only of true manhood, but of divinity itself." Harper challenged underlying theological beliefs which would hinder the development of the servant style. The image of God as royal taskmaster seated upon a high throne had to be seen as "a thing of the past."

> We now think of him as actually existing in every human being, and as working out through man in all the multiformity of man's

[80] Ibid., pp. 39–43.
[81] Ibid., pp. 46–50.

activity. God himself is the great servant of humanity; and in the ideal man, Jesus, this spirit of service found its highest example.

Harper challenged his listeners to let the great servant work within them. He called for commitment: "Will you consecrate your body, your mind, and your heart to the cause of humanity? Or will you be a miser . . . ?" In this spirit of sacrifice, Harper recognized the same spirit that had been at work in university life for ten centuries. This spirit was also, he believed, the spirit of "the true church."[82]

Harper further developed the theme of suffering in his talk "Trials of Life." No life escaped suffering, which was both a universal fact of life and the place for encountering God. The proper posture for the human who encountered suffering was reverence and resignation. Human struggle,

> if it is a struggle, is with God himself. Face to face as with an enemy; face to face with the closest friend, and face to face as standing in the very presence of God, one must meet the sorrows and disappointments, the pains and the suffering of life.[83]

Harper encouraged students to "begin at once to suffer." If they had not experienced life's darker side they should "try to find a disappointment." By participation in someone else's vexing situation, the college student prepared for the inevitable future encounter. To complete this unusual form of college preparation, students needed to "hold relationship with that unique character in the world's history who suffered as no man ever suffered before or since." Jesus' "sympathy with a suffering humanity was so great that only God himself could have experienced and expressed it." From his suffering came "light and life to all who will accept them." For Harper suffering, from the earliest days of Israel through the life of Jesus and into the lives of modern college people, was the locus for humans to encounter the vision of God.

> How easy it is for us, in these days, to have this sight, this vision of God! It was for this purpose that Jesus came to men, from God the Father, to represent him as only he could be present to humanity. This above all things else, was his mission to make God known to man; Jesus, the brother, through whom the Father might be revealed to those who also were brothers. To see Jesus is to have had a sight of God.[84]

The ethic of suffering was also Harper's personal code. Just as Jesus was brother to humanity so Harper saw himself as older brother to his college students. The powerful position of university president became in his perception primarily an office of suffering. The extent of Harper's suffering can be seen in private admissions that he had made a tragic mistake in

[82] Ibid., pp. 53–56.
[83] Harper, "The Trials of Life," ibid., pp. 58–65.
[84] Ibid., pp. 66–68.

assuming the presidency of the university and forsaking his scholarly career. On less dark days he viewed his office as "an office of service."

In 1904 Harper collected his thoughts on "The College President." Smarting under accusations that one had to be "mad" to assume such an office, he recited the usual epithets hurled at presidents. The list included "boss," prevaricator, naysayer, despot, czar. Such labels obscured the true picture of presidential life.[85] To counter the bad press given to his colleagues in college administration, Harper reapplied the themes of vicarious suffering to his own vocation. "In no other profession, not even in that of the minister of the Gospel, is vicarious suffering more common." Harper felt that in reality presidents were "slaves" of their environments, whose work was surrounded by the feeling of "great loneliness." As years of tenure passed, incumbents came to regard their feelings of separation and isolation as a permanent part of the calling.[86]

Presidents were also frequently victims of persecution through misrepresentation, some of it "malicious." Occasionally they experienced "times of great depression" when faced by the enormity of the task. These misunderstood leaders became "sick at heart," and knew the feeling of "utter dissatisfaction" with their own work. Because of the complex character of these institutions, each college president had to stand back and watch others do the things "which in his heart he would desire to handle." Never permitted "to finish a piece of work," presidents became masters of the "art of letting others do things." The one thing that compensated for these and other presidential burdens was the "close association with life confessedly higher and more ideal than ordinary life."[87]

Between Harper's lines the frustration of the biblical scholar who suffered for the sake of others is visible. Harper seized his ideal of vicarious suffering from the biblical material. In his vision for the modern university, that ideal shaped the sacred calling of the institution as it suffered for society and world. It also determined the university ethos Harper wished to pass on to students as they were shaped religiously in their academic experience. It was also the personal code of the first President of the University of Chicago.

[85] Harper revealed his second thoughts about his decision to accept the presidency of the University of Chicago in a letter to Mr. Lincoln Hulley, on September 5, 1895. He counselled Hulley not to accept the presidency of Colby University, arguing that "I think you are too young in your scholarly career to assume such a handicap as the presidency of an institution. I am confident that every man who enters upon administrative work at an early age, diminishes immensely his probable usefulness in life. I know that I have made a mistake and hardly a day passes that I do not feel it" (Personal Papers, Box 2, Folder 17). The speech "The College President," is in *The William Rainey Harper Memorial Conference*, Robert N. Montgomery, ed. (Chicago: University of Chicago Press, 1938), pp. 24–29.
[86] Ibid., pp. 29–30.
[87] Ibid., pp. 30–32.

## THE AMERICAN AGE

To complete the picture of Harper's religious vision for the university, it is necessary to ask what he believed about the American setting for his educational labors. In "America as a Missionary Field," Harper revealed a religious understanding of his nation that simultaneously participated in and transcended the "manifest destiny" ideology of his age. Harper believed that he could trace the world's history through three periods of twenty centuries each. The Old Testament patriarch Abraham served as benchmark ending the Babylonian epoch, Jesus marked the end of the Syrian, and the coming of age of America would end the English period. After following the progress of civilization westward from Babylon to America, Harper looked forward in a postmillennial manner to a fourth era of twenty centuries dominated by the Americans.[88]

Harper believed that the nineteen centuries following the birth of Christ had been shaped by "piecemeal" demonstrations of Christianity's "better, truer knowledge" of God and humanity. Although articulated relatively clearly in the New Testament this new knowledge had "not yet received . . . perfect demonstration in human history." Nineteenth century America was "the arena" in which Christianity's superior ideas would receive their "great trial."

> Here in this great country, provided by God himself with all the facilities needed, preserved in large measure by God himself from the burdens and trammels of dead institutions and deadly traditions, the consummation of Christian life and thought will be realized. This is the message written on every page of our nineteen centuries of history.[89]

All of Harper's efforts came together in his vision of America's religious role. Sounding like a prophet on the watchtower, Harper rejoiced in "the days that are coming" which would surpass any "except that one day which saw God take the form of man, the day which saw him live as man, and die as man, and rise again as God." America was destined to be the scene of divine action. The main lesson learned from the Old Testament received a twentieth-century application: "God is in the world as of old."[90]

America was the chosen nation in which all of Harper's other visions would come to fruition. The new Christianity he anticipated "will have no room for ignorance. Education will be its watchword." In spite of previous cautions about adding on to the messages of Jesus, Harper built on to the traditional Christian dispensation. What the world needed and what he had labored to provide were "the gospel and education." In Harper's eyes "the

[88] William Rainey Harper, "America as a Missionary Field," *Religion and the Higher Life*, pp. 173–75.
[89] Ibid., pp. 177–79.
[90] Ibid.

gospel, as it is commonly understood . . . is not sufficient." To be sure it contained within itself "the elements" which could "incite" to education. But more attention had to be given to developing those elements. In light of this grand view Harper's efforts at biblical and educational reform can be seen as distinct but essentially related elements in an overarching evangelical endeavor. The distinctive feature in Harper's version of the nineteenth-century evangelical imperative was that "education will constitute a larger part of the work of evangelization than in the past, both at home and abroad." Clearly, for Harper, education was missionary work.[91]

The call to educate previously overlooked native Americans and black people, or to grapple with the problems of the city was a "call from heaven." America was to be another Palestine, a laboratory for God's ongoing experiment. It could become a place where people of different nationalities could mix and commingle. If the world was to be evangelized, Harper believed "America must do it." Evangelization took place when America responded to the "call to equip all our academies and colleges and theological seminaries, and to see to it that the instruction given in these institutions bears upon its face the mark of truth; has its roots in the established principles of the faith." In one sentence he had summarized his life's work. It was time for humanity to move out of Kindergarten and to learn mature lessons of divine love. The "great Teacher" may have been patient but Harper could not hold his own impatience in check as he looked forward to the time when "Jesus the Christ will come to reign in the hearts of men." The educational work which would make this vision a reality depended on America, "the training-school for teachers."[92]

### THE BIBLICAL INTEGRATOR

Harper's biblically-based university-nurtured understanding of religion was one of a variety of religious options which were presented to modern Americans. Many, indeed most, Americans continued to cling to traditional models of religious belief and behavior. Others, like Harper, sought to mediate between traditional religious understandings and the new environment. A few turned to new sources for their religious authority. And some, like William Graham Sumner, put religious concerns away in one of the infrequently searched drawers of the mind, where they would remain ignored and harmless.

To better locate Harper's understanding of the nature of religion, it is helpful to compare his vision with alternatives posed by three of America's most important religious thinkers who sought to respond to the modern context in quite different ways. William James (1842–1910), John Dewey (1859–1952) and Alfred North Whitehead (1861–1947) were contemporaries

[91] Ibid., pp. 180–81.
[92] Ibid., pp. 181–84.

of Harper. Although two of them lived and published long after Harper's death in 1906, all three of them were part of a cohort who passed through the tumultuous religious changes of the late nineteenth century. Like Harper, they sought to respond to religious and social pluralism, and the impact of scientific and historical knowledge, with new inclusive understandings of religion. Unlike him, they turned away from scriptural data to new sources of religious knowledge. Further, all three rejected specialized religious institutions as the primary mediators of religious nurture and development.

Perhaps the clearest contrast can be seen in the radical empiricism of William James. In 1902 James published his classic series of Gifford Lectures, *The Varieties of Religious Experience*. The book's title indicated his decisive move. James turned to religious experience as his primary source. Adopting a psychological approach, he decided to place himself on the personal side of the "great partition" between institutional and personal religion. Believing that personal religion was "more fundamental" than the institutional varieties which merely recycled experiences of founders into less interesting secondhand commodities, James proposed "to ignore the institutional branch entirely." Personal feelings and conduct, on the other hand, comprised the "short circuit," the irreducible minimum of religion, out of which

> she carries on her principal business, while the ideas and symbols and other institutions form loop-lines which may be perfections and improvements, and may even some day all be united into one harmonious system, but which are not to be regarded as organs with an indispensable function, necessary at all times for religious life to go on.[93]

James's "experiential point of view" led to a redefinition of religion as consisting of "feelings, acts and experiences of individual men in their solitude, so far as they apprehend themselves to stand in relation to whatever they may consider the divine." The result was a pluralistic understanding of religion. The "breadth of the apperceiving mass" of human religious phenomena meant that "religion cannot stand for any single principle or essence, but is rather a collective name."[94]

Things became "more or less divine" and boundaries became "misty" as James developed what he called a "piecemeal supernaturalism." As the psychologist/philosopher probed human consciousness, he found at its core "a sense of reality"—that there was "something there." This undifferentiated "More" became the center of his religious understanding. The fact that in the human subconsciousness one could find the evidence for more in life than the individual could be aware of became the ground for "building out"

[93] William James, *The Varieties of Religious Experience: A Study in Human Nature* (New York: The New American Library of World Literature, Inc. 1958), pp. 22, 40–42, 381.

[94] Ibid., pp. 44, 42, 38–39.

a religious understanding. The core "psychological fact" of the subconscious became the mediating discovery which connected humans to an inclusive more. James had turned to the "hither" rather than the "farther" side of the more. He built his religious understanding on the basis of an analogical understanding of human consciousness.[95]

Alfred North Whitehead delivered his pivotal set of lectures—which were subsequently published as *Religion in the Making*—shortly after his arrival in America in 1924 to become professor of philosophy at Harvard. The 63-year-old philosopher made a turn similar to that of James when he argued that religion "is what the individual does with his own solitariness." But when he penetrated to the basic structure of the universe, Whitehead discovered an evolutionary process which linked various religious manifestations together.

> The religious idea emerged gradually into human life, at first barely disengaged from other human interests. The order of the emergence of these factors was in the inverse order of the depth of their religious importance: first ritual, then emotion, then belief, then rationalization.[96]

"Rational religion" was the Whiteheadian candidate for the modern age. The components of earlier forms of religion were "reorganized with the aim of making it the central element in a coherent ordering of life." If the result of rationalization was a "very low temperature" form of religion in comparison with earlier instances, Whitehead nonetheless advanced this form as adequate to account for several important religious facts. There was, he claimed, "no consensus" about God. People did not have verifiable direct visions of a personal God; rather, they had intuitions, which were, in fact, "private psychological habits." The belief in God was an inference drawn from the data of religious experience. A different ground, however, could be found for building an understanding of religion. There was, Whitehead claimed, a "large consensus" in favor of "the concept of a rightness in things." This "general character inherent in the nature of things" became the "ultimate religious evidence." There was no question that individuals had religious experiences, and these were expressions of a human "longing for justification" which was addressed in the "direct apprehension" of a basic rightness in the character of what is.[97]

James had found his evidence for the "More" in the human subconscious. Whitehead found evidence for "God" in the "epochal occasions" where one encounters a "concretion" of both the "boundless wealth of possibility" and a "non-temporal actuality." In the multiformity of nature

---

[95] Ibid., pp. 47, 392, 61, 384, 388, 386.
[96] Alfred North Whitehead, *Religion in the Making* (New York: New American Library, 1974), pp. 16, 18.
[97] Ibid., pp. 30, 52, 64–65, 61, 63, 83–84.

and history, Whitehead discovered a "binding element": God. The core religious insight that he discovered as he viewed the world as a whole was the perception of infinite possibility bound together by an ideal harmony. God was the "one systematic, complete fact" present in the "primary actual units" of human experience, the epochal occasions. Each such occasion was a microcosm "representing in itself the entire all inclusive universe." Whitehead's process-shaped Platonism rested on a "final principle of religion." There was "a wisdom in the nature of things."[98]

Educator-philosopher John Dewey advocated a "natural piety" that had some similarities to Whitehead's rational religion. In the Terry Lectures, which were published as *A Common Faith* in 1934, he sought to "wipe the (religious) slate clean." Like Harper he wanted to allow the "basically religious" to express itself without the encumbrances of traditional religions. What was necessary was a "dislocation of the religious" from religions. The religious became "a comprehensive attitude" or perspective. It was "morality touched by emotion" and "supported by ends so inclusive that they unify the self."[99]

For Dewey there was "one sure road" to religious truth—inquiry. The cherished idea that there were special "religious" truths which were not susceptible to investigation and ordinary ways of knowing had to be surrendered. He posed a "method of intelligence" which was open and public in place of the "doctrinal method" which was limited and private. Sounding very much like Whitehead, Dewey described God as the "*active* relation between the ideal and the actual*." When one had a sense of the connection between the human and the world, one was participating in a natural piety.[100]

The current situation in which religion was confined to specialized institutions within "secular" society, according to Dewey, was an innovation. There had been a "change in the social center of gravity in religion." The modern alteration in the social place and the function of religion had been the "greatest change that has occurred in religion in all history."[101]

In place of the sacred/secular division of reality posited by supernaturalists, Dewey offered a relational unity. Wherever one perceived the "mysterious totality of being," there one was religious. The old "doubleness of mind" of the supernaturalists was unnecessary once the relations between things were discerned through the exercise of "passionate intelligence." The sectarian religions of his age allowed the religious to be crowded into a corner. With his natural variety of piety, Dewey hoped to make such

---

[98] Ibid., pp. 88–91, 152, 148, 137–38.
[99] John Dewey, *A Common Faith* (New Haven: Yale University Press, 1934), pp. 25, 6, 15, 22–23.
[100] Ibid., pp. 32–33, 39, 51–53.
[101] Ibid., pp. 60–61.

sectarian religion "catholic" again.[102]

This brief overview of the religious understandings of three of the most important philosophers in the American tradition cannot pretend to do justice to the fullness and richness of their thought. But it does provide a historical context for Harper's understanding of religion. Together with these philosophers of religion, Harper shared a passion for facts, concreteness, naturalness. His biblical exegesis had been an effort to uncover the historical facts underneath the accretions of traditions. Just as Whitehead had sought to penetrate to the essential nature of things beneath numerous epochal occasions, so Harper sought to penetrate to the essential reality of the religion of Israel beneath the variety of interpretations and historical understandings which surrounded it. Harper and Whitehead shared evolutionary perspectives which allowed them to celebrate religious development and to argue for movement from lower to higher forms. With William James, Harper was responsive to the reality of religious experience and wanted to know more about it. Like Dewey, Harper was interested in an approach to religion which was public and all-embracing.

Harper's distinctiveness is clear in his tenacious advocacy of biblical study as the best avenue to religious truth. While James, Whitehead and Dewey all knew the biblical traditions, they decisively turned away from that sacred book to follow other avenues of religious truth. There can be no doubt that Harper sought to be open to the new sources of knowledge which these contemporaries celebrated—self, nature, history. But he still found the Scriptures to be uniquely paradigmatic, inspirational and integrative.

A second distinctive feature in Harper's religious construction was his attempt to find a new mediating institution for religious knowledge. By bringing together people and the new knowledge, his messianic university would fill the gap created by sectarian denominations and compartmentalized local churches. With his three contemporaries, Harper shared a dissatisfaction with current institutional expressions of religion. Unlike them, he strove to create a new institution which could carry on the special task of fostering religious growth.

[102] Ibid., pp. 66, 85, 69–70, 79, 82–83.

# CHAPTER 6
## ASSESSING A VISION

In 1970, Morris Philipson, Director of the University of Chicago Press, published a Foreword for a pamphlet containing a reprint of Harper's essay, "The University and Democracy." Seventy-one years after Harper had first revealed his vision for the American university, Philipson searched for what could be salvaged from the "shambles" of Harper's idealistic oratory. He wanted to assist a new generation of readers to discern the difference between a ruin and a relic.

> The rhetoric has decayed and tumbled down; the style of expression is a ruin. Not all ruins are worthy of respect. But a relic is a ruin that is honored, not because it can still "work," but because it is the remains of something that was intrinsically good or beautiful or true. As a relic it can still evoke some degree of the intended original response, although our intelligence and imagination are required to flesh in what is missing. President Harper's speech is a relic of tightly reasoned American inspirationalism at the end of the nineteenth century.[1]

The tone of Philipson's Foreword is that of the wistful custodian of a sacred shrine. Perhaps, if one could draw people toward the holy relic, some spark of the old life might be rekindled in a new generation.

There was warrant for Philipson's harsh-sounding "shambles." Within a few years of Harper's death, his vision had broken apart. The University Congregation, Harper's attempt to make a community out of the varied academic disciplines, faded into obsolescence by 1909. The hoped-for national university, a would-be capstone for the complete system Harper proposed for American education, did not develop beyond the private musings of a handful of educational magnates. Ambitious plans for a complete system of affiliated institutions were abandoned.

Some of the key components of Harper's plan survived much longer, but not without significant shifts in direction and purpose. Although it still

---

[1] Morris Philipson, "On the Difference Between a Ruin and a Relic," in William Rainey Harper *The University and Democracy* (Chicago: University of Chicago, 1970), pp. vii–x. I am grateful to Professor J. Ronald Engel of Meadville/Lombard Seminary, Chicago, Illinois, for calling this Foreword to my attention.

survives, the Religious Education Association, for example, Harper's last and most far-reaching attempt to consolidate all religious education in America under the umbrella of one coordinating institution, proved unable to resist the pressures of specialization and professionalism. As Stephen Schmidt's recent study of the Association suggests, during the post-Harper years the Association experienced a narrowing of its horizon from its initial general public concerns to those of the emerging profession of religious educators.[2] Harper's beloved American Institute of Sacred Literature lasted until the mid-1940s when its Director, Sidney E. Mead, mercifully allowed the comatose organization to die. The Sunday school, a key institution in Harper's efforts to reach the American Christian community, could not live up to his ambitious proposals and slipped into a second-class role which challenged few to think critically about the Scriptures. Biblical criticism, instead of serving as the new integrating force in American religion, became an enduring source of conflict for Christians who wanted to trust the Sacred Scriptures. The Bible movement in higher education succeeded in gaining limited curricular space for scriptural study but lost its missionary and integrative character. Instead of becoming America's public book, the Scriptures became increasingly marginal to the nation's public life. Congregations, seminaries, divinity schools and religion departments continued to search them, but usually at a distance from the more public realms of commercial and civic life. As Americans became more aware of their pluralism they became more wary of public instruction about the Scriptures and more willing to keep silent about them.

Does something remain of the vision which originated in small-town circumstances and developed to its most mature statement in the occasional writings of a president on the run? While an occasional Harper story told in the halls of his own university may carry a vague intimation of a once compelling vision, the overriding impression is that his fundamental ideas and purposes have been relegated—either intentionally or simply by erosion of memory—to the ruins of American religious and intellectual history.

Before attempting to pose an alternative to the ruin or relic question, it is necessary to confront contemporaries of Harper who found little in his career except ruin. Three of his most outspoken critics, Robert Welch Herrick, Upton Sinclair and Thorstein Veblen, each described Harper as woefully deficient in one fundamental area; in their judgment he lacked a vision that could constructively shape American intellectual and cultural life. Through caricature, satire, muckraking and impassioned argument, they exposed what they believed to be the essential flaws in the person and work of William Rainey Harper. Their criticisms are clearly colored by their own alienation from American religious, intellectual and cultural life. Each of

---

[2] Stephen A. Schmidt, *A History of the Religious Education Association,* (Birmingham: Religious Publication Press, 1982).

these critics had alternative futures in mind for American education from the one offered in "The Official Bulletins" or *The Biblical World*. Notwithstanding the prejudices of their aversion toward religion and animosity toward late nineteenth-century American cultural elites, their responses provide a more complete picture of what was at stake in the era the three shared with Harper.

### THE BIG BARNUM OF EUREKA UNIVERSITY

One of the most fascinating portraits of the University of Chicago's first president was offered by an English professor hired by Harper in the institution's early days. Robert Welch Herrick came to the university in 1893 to organize and administer the composition and rhetoric program. Herrick's impressions of Harper's role in the founding of the university simmered in the professor's consciousness for more than thirty years before he published an account of them. In 1926 the novel *Chimes* appeared, a *roman á clef* about a young dramatist (Herrick) who joined the new Eureka University in the west. There the protagonist suffered disillusionment as he experienced the failure of the institution and its inhabitants to meet his high ideals for university education. The thinly disguised characters reveal Harper, Herrick and many of the earliest members of the university faculty.[3]

*Chimes'* opening sentences revealed the chasm between Herrick's ideals and the reality of Harper's new creation. "The new university! . . . A river of yellow prairie mud lay between the young man and the flat campus dotted with a half dozen stone buildings, some still unfinished." Dr. Alonzo Harris (Harper), Eureka's president, struck Beaman Clavercin (Herrick) as a "new meteor in the University world." Recalling his initial interview with the president who had lured him from Harvard to the mud of Chicago, the young professor noted several telling shabby details:

> President Harris's shoes had not been shined for days and showed traces of campus mud. They were of soft leather with elastic sides, a kind of shoes one should not wear outside his bedroom. Also, his trousers were too short, with curling frayed bottoms, and they bagged at the chubby knees. His new black frock coat was plentifully sprinkled with dust and dandruff, and down the black ministerial waistcoat there was a visible stain, possibly from coffee drip. . . .

Later, Clavercin attended a trustee dinner which afforded another memorable portrait of the president.

> Short, thick, with the round face of a gnome beneath the gold tasseled flat cap, his mussed silk gown swelling comically about his bulky body, the President of Eureka University was in total contrast with the stately figure that in Clavercin's experience embodied academic dignity.

[3] Robert Herrick, *Chimes* (New York: The Macmillan Company, 1926).

Herrick placed his initial impressions of Harper in the mind of Clavercin, his fictional counterpart. Harris lacked social graces; the polish of the academic statesman which Herrick had become accustomed to in New England was sadly absent at Eureka. The first presidential speech Clavercin heard was so impassioned in its delivery and so unusual in its content that it made him uncomfortable. He had, he felt, encountered a "new religion."[4]

Clavercin seemed unable to recover from the encounter with the crudities of Eureka and its first president. The institution was ugly, and the demeanor of President Harris verged on the ludicrous. Especially unseemly were Harris' notorious early morning bicycle rides. Zealously bent over the handlebars, he cut a "grotesque" figure peddling alongside faculty members before breakfast to "get in touch" with them. After sharing such a presidential spin around the campus Clavercin pronounced Harris a "big Barnum" caught up in the "comic process of growth."[5]

More than presidential rough edges troubled Herrick's protagonist, however. The university was mimicking the "factory process" of the business world. "Standardization" and the forces of "system" were at odds with his ideal for university education. Clavercin mourned over what he encountered among his colleagues at the faculty club.

> With the increasing degree of specialization they were cut off from each other in little provinces of thought and interest; knowledge had become an archipelago of small islands instead of a single continent.

University life became oppressive for this exile from the Ivy League. On the one hand examinations and other teaching duties seemed purposeless. On the other, students wasted themselves in activities like athletics and fraternities. Innovations such as the business school, or school of journalism seemed to be "meretricious devices" for raising funds for an empty dream. Herrick surveyed his colleagues and concluded that

> each felt that in some way he had been trapped by an illusion, when he had entered what Clavercin called "the pleasant walls of Academe," a dream of something that did not exist in America or if it had once existed faintly in the older colleges of the East had been choked by the rapid growth of national wealth.
>     "Look at our master!" (a colleague) cried, pointing to the flaming smokestacks of the steel city.[6]

Clavercin's disillusionment did not prevent him from an occasional expression of sympathy for President Harris. Noting that a phalanx of intermediaries came to separate the president from the university's founder,

[4] Ibid., pp. 1–4, 16–17.
[5] Ibid., pp. 40, 44.
[6] Ibid., pp. 64–72, 104–5.

the disillusioned professor observed that "somehow Aladdin had lost his magic touch." It was clear that the president's burden grew as his patience thinned.

> He could not wait on time. What it had taken centuries and many generations of men heretofore to accomplish, slow accretion of a shell, must grow beneath his touch in a few short years. His dream was pressing him, and something already whispered to his spirit that he might not live to see the Plan wholly inked in, with buildings roofed and pinnacles boldly soaring into the sky. . . .

The dramatist believed that Harris was aware of the discontent, grumbling and doubt among his faculty colleagues. Pressure mounted for the beleaguered administrator to produce some fresh miracle.[7]

There was more than the president's tragic illness to darken Herrick's narrative. A "spiritual canker" gnawed at the root of the entire enterprise. Ironically, as Harris labored to salvage his dream in the face of personal illness and the recalcitrance of the university founder, he grew in both author's and protagonist's estimation.

> The last spurt of life in him must be spent in redeeming his pledges, fulfilling all the promises he had so prodigally made in his buoyant days, assuring so far as he could the lives of those whom he had persuaded or permitted to attach themselves to his dream.

Occasionally Clavercin caught a glimpse of a valiant president. In those moments Harris seemed "another kind of being," transformed by his suffering for others. There was a "dignity, a grandeur about him that Clavercin had never suspected all these years." The final image Herrick offered of Harper was emblematic. The president died in his swivel chair behind his desk, at work.[8]

In his novel Herrick developed the character of Clavercin many years beyond those of Harris's presidency. Following the outbreak of World War I, Clavercin returned from Europe with a new understanding of the university and his place within it. For the first time he grasped "the meaning of the university."

> It was, it should be, the home of the human spirit, removed from the merely passing, the fluid, the accidental, the one withdrawn place of modern life where all the manifestations of humanity could be gathered in essence—and handed on! The enduring, the significant thing was—the Idea, the university itself! Men made universities as once they made great temples, blindly, not conceiving the ultimate ends to which they would be devoted, out of some inner necessity of their spirits, as Harris, that great-hearted combination of prairie boy

---

[7] Ibid., pp. 129–31.
[8] Ibid., pp. 137, 152–56.

and prophet, had built Eureka. Temples! Caravansaries of the human spirit—that was what universities were.[9]

Room must be made for the license of a novelist to develop his characters. Yet the similarities between the worlds of Herrick's novel and Harper's reality are striking. After learning of his terminal condition, Harper did engage in a frantic effort, largely successful, to place the university and his many other enterprises on solid financial footing. The morning bicycle rides, the lines in the office to see him, the red morocco leather notebooks, are authentic details which the novelist felt no need to mask or omit. But these interesting details cannot hide the character development of the protagonist, Clavercin, who was, after all, Herrick. The young, disillusioned Harvard graduate, so disenchanted with the vulgarities and the new religion he encountered in Chicago, became an advocate of part of the vision which Harper proclaimed in his speech on the university and democracy. In retrospect, Herrick affirmed that the university was a temple, and Harper was, above all, its prophet.

### "EDUCATION F.O.B. CHICAGO"

The transition from Herrick the storyteller, to Upton Sinclair, the alienated systems analyst, is almost a quantum leap. Herrick knew the Chicago story from the inside; Sinclair never served on the faculty of the university. Herrick occasionally commented upon the American educational situation in general, but for the most part confined his attention to the particular plot of his novel. Sinclair, on the other hand, indicted the whole American educational configuration. His book *The Goose-Step* is a savage *tour de force* which found nothing to praise in higher education in America. He aired all of higher education's dirty linen in the hope that reform would follow.[10]

According to Sinclair, the fundamental problem with American university education was an "interlocking directorate" chaired by J. P. Morgan, Sr. Sinclair believed that together with the Rockefellers, the Pillsburys, the Stanfords, and the Mellons, plutocrats like Morgan either directly or indirectly controlled all of the educational institutions of the land. In this vituperative polemic the National Education Association, which at that time was dominated by Nicholas Murray Butler, the university president who fared worst at Sinclair's hands, became the "Tammany Hall of Education." By means of his shrill expose, Sinclair intended to oppose what he perceived to be a well-oiled machine which held the educational life of the nation in a

---

[9] Ibid., p. 168.

[10] Upton Sinclair, *The Goose-Step: A Study of American Education*, rev. ed. (Pasadena: Upton Sinclair, 1923).

strangle-hold. The sad result of such a system was that it produced over-whelming dullness.[11]

As Sinclair took his readers on a verbal tour of the nation's campuses he told the "truth" about Wilson of Princeton, morality at Yale, and the study of the "classics" in California ("the annual Stanford-California foot-ball game, and the intercollegiate track meet, and the Pacific Coast Tennis doubles"). Never relenting, he exposed an "academic pogrom" being waged against Jews. Next, he turned to alumni, traditionally one of the most privileged university constituencies, who became "a semi-simian mob" in his version of the story. But, his basic concern remained with an entire educational structure dominated by a "psychology of submission" orchestrated by the tycoons of Wall Street.[12]

In the fiftieth chapter of his book, Sinclair focused attention on the University of Chicago. The muckraker began with a description of Harper:

> an educator—one of these typical American combinations of financial shrewdness and moral fervor, a veritable wizard of a money-getter, a "vamp" in trousers, a grand, impressive, inspirational Chautauqua potentate.

John D. Rockefeller did not fare any better at Sinclair's hands. The oil magnate had a "pathetic trust in education, as something you could buy ready-made for cash." It never occurred to Rockefeller, Sinclair claimed, that he "might not be able to order the whole of the human spirit, F.O.B. Chicago, thirty days net."[13]

Sinclair was especially outraged at the emergence of University-Gothic in American architecture. He envisioned a conversation between the "he-vamp," Harper, and his architect. The architect opened by suggesting an economical floor plan. Harper demurred because the donor wanted "culture." To that the architect countered with a suggestion of pyramids. Harper declined.

> He would think that was heathen. He's a religious old bird—a Baptist, like me; that's how I got him, in fact—met him at an ice cream festival.
> "Oh, well, then, it's plain," says the architectural wizard. "What we want is real old Gothic—stained-glass windows, mullioned, and crenellated battlements, and moated draw bridges—"
> "That sounds great!" says the educational wizard. "What does it look like?"

To Sinclair there was no better way to expose "the elaborate system of buncombe which is called 'higher education'" than to look at prevailing notions of university architecture. He was aghast that

[11] Ibid., pp 19, 29–37, 59–61.
[12] Ibid., pp. 111, 122, 141, 361–63, 457.
[13] Ibid., pp 240–41.

here in twentieth century America, where we know of bows and
arrows only in poetry, and have the materials and the skill to build
structures of steel and glass, big and airy and bright as day—we
deliberately go and reproduce the architectural monstrosities, the
intellectual and spiritual deformities of a thousand years ago, and
compel modern chemists and biologists and engineers to do their
research work by artificial light, for fear of arrows which ceased to fly
when the last Indian was penned up in a reservation.[14]

Sinclair's tour of the nation's universities produced no exception to the
general pattern he perceived of their subservience to the plutocracy. The
University of Chicago, in fact, fared better than most he surveyed. He
admitted that

during the early days of the university President Harper stood for
liberalism in religion, and thereby lost much Baptist money; . . .

The system would not be free, however, until professors united as laborers
against the financial tyrants. Sinclair's socialism, never far from the surface in
this work, came into full view as he prescribed his solution for America's
academic woes:

freedom for the college professor awaits the overthrow of the pluto-
cratic empire. And since the only force in our society which can
achieve that overthrow is labor, it follows that the college professor's
hopes are bound up with the movement of the workers for freedom.[15]

The penultimate goal of Sinclair's book was "to bring about a strike of
college professors." For him Harper was a lackey of the party of the past.
Only when Harper and his kind were out of power would education be free.

### The Captain of Erudition

In a biographical sketch of Thorstein Veblen, Joseph Dorfman called his
subject a "man from Mars." In some ways Veblen never seemed to fit into
the world he inhabited. Consistently out of step with the styles and
expectations of his age, Veblen never found a secure niche in academia. But,
of the three critics examined here, Veblen is the most important. More
systematic than Herrick and less impassioned than Sinclair, Veblen penned
a reasoned, if personal, memorandum titled *The Higher Learning in America: A Memorandum on the Conduct of Universities by Business Men.*[16]

For Veblen the problem with university education in America was not
that it failed to live up to the image of Harvard or that it failed to join the
battle against the plutocracy. Instead the problem was the unique American

[14] Ibid., pp. 241–42.

[15] Ibid., pp. 246, 457ff., 472f.

[16] Thorstein Veblen, *The Higher Learning in America: A Memorandum on the Conduct
of Universities by Business Men*, intro. by Louis M. Hacker (New York: Sagamore Press,
1957), p. v.

invention called the university president. Not content to tell a story of dashed and rekindled illusions or to reveal all the sordid parts of early university history in America, Veblen attempted to probe for root causes of American higher educational trouble. At bottom, the problem was a group of university leaders typified by William Rainey Harper.

Veblen knew Harper from firsthand experience. A Yale Ph.D., Veblen had been unable to secure an academic position in the last years of the 1880s until Harper hired him as a junior member of his initial teaching faculty. Veblen's ineffectiveness in the classroom and less-than-orthodox life-style resulted in a request for his resignation within a very short space of time. His resentment found its outlet in a criticism of university presidents that almost always held up Harper as a target. Veblen admitted that his argument drew "largely on first-hand observation of the conduct of affairs at Chicago, under the administration of its first president." Although he originally intended to release his bombshell at the time that the "Great Pioneer" (Harper) died, Veblen kept his manuscript from publication for several years for reasons of decorum. That interval of more than a decade between first draft and publication convinced Veblen that faults which he had first believed idiosyncratic to Harper were actually generic to the office of university president. Belatedly, in 1918 his book appeared.[17]

Veblen began his analysis of American higher learning by positing "two certain impulsive traits of human nature: an Idle Curiosity, and the Instinct of Workmanship." The problem in his era was the intrusion of a habit of workaday thought which had "imposed" itself upon the quest for knowledge. As he surveyed the problems of higher education, Veblen continually returned to this epistemological problem. "Matter-of-fact" knowledge, extremely useful to the newly emergent business culture of America, was imposing ends and means upon learning which were throttling its soul. What was emerging in America was a "barbarian University tradition." There seemed to be no place left for idle curiosity—for the pursuit of knowledge for its own sake. Instead a "habitual" practical bias was ruining education in America. Worse, the "cult of Knowledge" which had been created around this kind of matter-of-fact learning had usurped the privileged position which religion had occupied in earlier ages. No great fan of any religion, Veblen was an enemy of the new "cult" which was tyrannizing the mind of America.[18]

The source of the problem in American higher education was, he thought, the "current system of private ownership." An economic system which permitted unprecedented concentrations of capital in relatively few hands fostered a set of values that was at odds with learning.

[17] Ibid., pp. vi, x–xi.
[18] Ibid., pp. 3, 5, 26, 30, 43.

> Business principles are the sacred articles of the secular creed,
> and business methods make up the ritual of the secular cult.

These culture-wide values permeated academia, turning the university into a "business house" run according to accounting techniques. The department store—the exemplar of the new business culture's ethos of marketing, packaging, and competition—became the basis for a sarcastic analogy. In the modern university, a glossy commodity, erudition, was "standardized" to fit a market. The university had become a corporation rather than a seminary of learning.[19]

In essence, Veblen believed that the university had escaped from one tyranny, "clerical control," only to fall under the domination of another, "business administration." The results of this second captivity, he felt, became all too apparent in the accomplishments of people like Harper. Under their leadership universities became preoccupied with appearances as they engaged in "tawdry" exhibitions of "quasi-scholarly feats." Veblen, like Sinclair, lampooned the business-minded educators' costly "architecture of notoriety" as one more marketing device that kept donors and students coming. He questioned the "fitness of housing the quest of truth in an edifice of false pretenses." The academic ceremony which played an important part in the university life of Harper's era resulted in what Veblen derided as an "efflorescence of ritual and pageantry" strikingly similar to the grand openings of department stores. "Public song and dance," routines of "polite dissipation, ceremonial display, exhibitions of quasi-scholarly proficiency and propagandist intrigue" received more attention from the university executives than did serious matters of learning.[20]

Veblen believed, however, that these publicity devices, the products of the dominant competitive ethos of his day, were only surface symptoms of deeper troubles in higher learning. As he singled out additional items for criticism, Veblen managed to challenge most of Harper's innovations. Thus, he viewed the connection of undergraduate and professional education to the university (one of Harper's important legacies) as a lethal threat. Creation of the "senior college" allowed the collegiate type of learning to spill over into and further pollute the purity of university education.

Other distinctive features of Harper's vision for the modern university received similar assessments. Academic departments became in Veblen's eyes "bureaux of erudition" which competed for funds, equipment, and clienteles. "Scholastic accessories" like athletics and fraternities taught values of "genteel dissipation" and "conspicuous consumption." Systems of grading and credits resulted in "sterilization of the academic intellect." The practice of affiliating a variety of institutions only furthered the misguided process of grafting extraneous enterprises onto the basic university purpose

[19] Ibid., pp. 57, 60, 62–65.
[20] Ibid., pp. 74, 78, 106, 115, 124–25.

of non-practical education. University extension was in reality a means to "dispense erudition by mail-order." The relation of a Divinity School or a School of Commerce to a university were clear evidence of a president possessed of a "histrionic sensibility." To Veblen the Divinity School was simply a remnant of the declining old order of learning, while the School of Commerce represented the "suppression of learning by worldly wisdom." To this relentless critic the new configuration of higher education which Harper had worked to consolidate, was merely an "enterprise in assorted education."[21]

At the center of this destructive attempt to squeeze extra-economic learning into the bureaucratic organization of American business, Veblen placed the "captain of erudition." His criticisms became quite personal:

> One is constrained to believe that the academic executive who has been so thrown up as putative director of the pursuit of learning must go in for this annexation of vocational schools, for amateurish "summer sessions," for the appointment of schoolmasters instead of scholars on the academic staff, for the safe-keeping and propagation of genteel conventionalities at the cost of scholarship, for devout and polite ceremonial,—one is constrained to believe that such a university executive goes in for this policy of tawdry routine because he lacks ordinary intelligence or because he lacks ordinary courage.

When he looked at the academic executive, i.e. Harper, Veblen saw only "threadbare motives of unreflecting imitation and boyish make-believe."[22]

In a footnote Veblen did grant that Harper had an "inconspicuously brief" interval when his academic policy was subject to scholarly ideals.[23] The subsequent footnote, however, described the process of "scarcely interrupted decay" which followed that interval.[24] Finally two words summed up Harper in the eye of his critic—"ravenous megalomania." The "duties of the office," as it was shaped in America, precipitated the tragic outcome. Veblen went so far as to give a physical description of what happened to presidential incumbents. Like professional politicians, they were

> visibly affected with those characteristic pathological marks that come of what is conventionally called "high living"—late hours, unseasonable vigils, surfeit of victuals and drink, the fatigue of sedentary ennui. A flabby habit of body, hypertrophy of the abdomen, varicose veins, particularly of the facial tissues, a blear eye and a coloration suggestive of bile and apoplexy,—when this unwholesome bulk is duly wrapped in a conventionally decorous costume it is accepted rather as a mark of weight and responsibility and so serves to distinguish the pillars of urbane society.[25]

[21] Ibid., pp. 80, 82, 87–88, 94, 140–41, 150.
[22] Ibid., p. 177.
[23] Ibid., p. 194 n. 11.
[24] Ibid., p. 195 n. 12.
[25] Ibid., pp. 195, 197, 178 n. 4.

In Veblen's eyes the university president was an abomination. Claiming that he had made "all due endeavor to avoid the appearance of a study in total depravity," Veblen tried to solve the problems he had diagnosed. Solutions like removing higher learning from the university or creating isolated intellectual retreats were rejected. Only one remedy would save learning: "abolition of the academic executive and of the governing board" of businessmen. Veblen called for disassembly of the academic configuration which had been created by Harper and his presidential colleagues. He longed for "small scale units"—in essence a return to part of the American college idea. A nostalgia for better days and a naive trust that learning would do best if left to follow its own course combined to shape his response.[26]

While Herrick, Sinclair and Veblen each brought distinct perspectives to their criticism of Harper and his university, it is possible to find a common view among them. If only begrudgingly, they agreed that a scholarly ideal had been present in the early days of Harper's presidency. But the ensuing tragedy was that the pressures of building a going concern overcame his ideal or vision leaving a legacy of sham, in which only a heroic few pursued learning for its own sake. The common enemies were business, urbanization and a crass set of values which passed for culture to those who did not know any better. All three wished for the university to be a place where free and unfettered learning could occur. All mourned the fact that the university was a place where no such feat seemed likely.

## THE VEBLENESQUE LEGACY

Harper's critics seem to have had the last word. If any vestige of Harper's vision remains it is usually closer to that depicted by Veblen than that which Harper's own writings reveal. The astonishing fact about the fate of Harper's vision is the silence which follows the bitter outburst of criticism in the second and third decades of the twentieth century. No one rose to defend the vision that Harper had carried into his work at Chicago. No loyal school of disciples strove to perpetuate the ideas of their master. Harper's efforts seemed potent enough to create a flash of reaction, but then they receded into the background, only to be partially resurrected in occasional dissertations or histories of education.

The question that looms is, why the silence? Were the criticisms levelled by Herrick, Sinclair and Veblen so devastating that no rejoinder was possible? Or are there other factors which account for the fact that if any image of Harper survives, it is of the energetic entrepreneur who seemed to share too many traits with Veblen's caricature of the captain of erudition?

When one looks at the alternatives which Herrick, Sinclair and Veblen proposed it becomes clear that their visions did not succeed in higher

[26] Ibid., pp. 192, 199–202, 207.

education either. The Harvard ideal, the uprising of scholars who would overthrow the plutocracy's interlocking directorate, the decentralized free zones of idle curiosity, remain unfulfilled wishes. Some of the overwhelming character of their collective criticism dims when their personal motives and biases are considered. Herrick, the disenchanted ivy leaguer; Sinclair, the scourge of American capitalism; Veblen, the scholar who found no hospitality in the American educational world—all had an animus against Harper impelled by far more than a mere encounter with the deficiencies in his vision. Indeed, it may be claimed that they never grasped his vision and instead reacted only to its institutional shell rather than to its religious substance. One searches in vain, for example, for the slightest reference in their works to the biblical gestalt which shaped Harper's perspective. Instead, their criticisms were of Harper's personal style, or of selected educational innovations. Herrick, Sinclair and Veblen groped for some evidence of intellectual substance in the midst of all the academic invention in the era of university-building. The irony is that they reacted primarily to Harper's administrative achievements, while ignoring his ideas. That legacy of ignorance, which can be traced to the earliest of the three published versions of Harper's failure, Veblen's, still obscures the modern view of Harper.

To account for this paradoxical depiction of an intellectually barren president who in fact understood himself to be driven by the "highest" ideals requires both historical and biographical explanations. Through an examination of the context in which Harper disappeared from prominence, the Veblenesque legacy can become more understandable. At the same time there were biographical factors which contributed to the disappearance of Harper's vision and those too need to be examined.

## FROM VOLUNTARYISM TO PROFESSIONALISM

Sidney E. Mead and James Luther Adams have each argued that a characteristic feature of American religious life has been voluntaryism.[27] Adams defined the voluntary principle as "the freedom to form, or to belong to, voluntary associations."[28] From their colonial beginnings Americans sought social meaning through groups formed and abandoned. American denominationalism, as well as much of the nation's benevolence and social reform, can be embraced within this understanding of voluntaryism.

The voluntary principle met a serious challenge during the age of Harper's ascent to prominence. The return to America of a generation of

---

[27] Sidney E. Mead, *The Lively Experiment: The Shaping of Christianity in America* (New York: Harper & Row, Publishers, 1963), pp. 96, 113–15; James Luther Adams, "The Voluntary Principle in the Forming of American Religion," *The Religion of the Republic*, Elwyn A. Smith, ed. (Philadelphia: Fortress Press, 1971), pp. 217ff.
[28] Adams, "The Voluntary Principle," p. 218.

German-trained scholars who assumed new places within divisions of learning signalled the rise of a new social dynamic, professionalism, which altered the American social and educational terrain. Thomas L. Haskell, for example, traced this transition from voluntaryism to professionalism in American social science during the nineteenth century. He found that in its early days anyone with a concern for improving the quality of American life could join the American Social Science Association, a voluntary organization formed in 1865 by Franklin Benjamin Sanborn. By the time of the organization's demise in 1909, university-based professions had erected a new structure of social science which made Sanborn's creation obsolete. Academic disciplines like sociology, economics and history had developed their own new organizations, which were formed voluntarily, but with professional restrictions and control over membership.[29] Another scholar of professionalism, Paul H. Mattingly, discovered a similar transition in the history of public-school teaching. At one time earnest reformers like Henry Barnard and Horace Mann formed schools and educational organizations almost at will. By the end of the nineteenth century the voluntary network of teachers once controlled by benevolent gentlemen like Barnard and Mann had been supplanted by a profession with its own standards and systems of employment.[30]

The consequences of this transition from voluntaryism to professionalism—which could be seen in many other zones in American life beyond social science and public school teaching—have been labeled "the culture of professionalism" by Burton Bledstein. In a spirit reminiscent of Veblen, Bledstein charged that there was a hollowness in the dominant culture of America, which was mediated by the university. By focusing on the dynamic of professionalism Bledstein moved beyond Veblen and indicted a larger cultural reality of which businessmen were only a part.[31]

When Harper rose to prominence during the late nineteenth century, he paradoxically served both as exemplar of voluntaryism and carrier of the new style of professionalism. Like so many other American entrepreneurs of his era Harper created organizations whenever the opportunity arose. His Hebrew Institute, Religious Education Association, and Chautauqua efforts were all examples of how an individual created or altered institutions as needs dictated. The University of Chicago, like all other private American universities, began as a voluntary organization—people were invited to support it, to join its faculty, to come and study.

Harper never broke with the voluntary principle. There was room for

[29] Thomas L. Haskell, *The Emergence of Professional Social Science: The American Social Science Association and the Nineteenth-Century Crisis of Authority* (Urbana: University of Illinois Press, 1977), pp. 24, 97ff.
[30] Paul H. Mattingly, *The Classless Profession: American Schoolmen in the Nineteenth Century* (New York: New York University Press, 1975).
[31] Bledstein, *The Culture of Professionalism*.

everybody in his configuration of education. His journals regularly asked people to join this group or take that action. At the same time, however, Harper was one of the new breed, a professional. A Ph.D. and obvious linguistic competence allowed him to create a special preserve of learning and to preside over it. Harper seemed to value both dynamics. He encouraged "specialism" in his university departments, but felt no contradiction when he sought to make a congregation out of his institution's many subgroups. Harper appealed to his audiences in the voluntary spirit and frequently sought to change the wills of his listeners—to convert them to his image of education, or Bible, or America.

The university world which grew in part because of the effectiveness of the voluntary principle succumbed to the attractions of professionalism. Laurence Veysey signalled the importance of this change when he concluded the first phase of his history of the American University at the turn of the twentieth century. Veysey claimed that after the era of people like Harper, "the university tended to lose itself among individual disciplines."[32] Scholars came to universities like the one that Harper built for a variety of reasons, many of them professional. At his institution Harper catered to professional dreams by promising opportunities for research, advancement, facilities, and journals. In essence Harper's voluntary style of presidency, which recruited people to participate in the creation of what promised to be the ultimate organization for remedying America's ills, made possible the individual professional pursuits which scholars like Bledstein and Veysey have posited as the norm in American higher education. Voluntaryism did not disappear because of professionalism. It was domesticated and often forced out of the university by professionals who brought new standards and styles to their tasks.

## THE QUEST FOR THE GREAT COMMUNITY

A second characteristic transition of Harper's age was the shift from village to metropolitan ways of life. Jean Quandt in *From the Small Town to the Great Community* has argued that progressives of Harper's era carried smalltown images with them as they attempted to construct solutions to the problems posed by unsettling urban environments. Quandt noticed that important social thinkers like John Dewey, Jane Addams, William Allen White, and Josiah Royce (and I would add Harper and Veblen) shared remarkably similar life trajectories.

> Born between 1855 and 1868, raised in small towns from Vermont to California, they came of age in an increasingly urban and industrial society. Their response to the social landscape was shaped by the religious and intellectual traditions, old and new, which they appropriated; but it was also formed by the values of the face-to-face

[32] Veysey, *The Emergence of the American University*, p. 12.

communities from which they came. Their formulation of the problems of community in the years after 1890 clearly reflected their social
origins.[33]

Quandt's hypothesis provides a useful perspective for viewing Harper's
efforts and also helps account for the distance between his concerns and
those of later generations. In many ways Harper attempted to make the
University of Chicago into a larger version of New Concord. Acting like a
parish pastor on some occasions and a political boss on others, Harper seized
one device after another in efforts to forge a community in the midst of the
pluralism of his new creation. Students were invited to his office at graduation time for face to face conversations about their futures. President Harper
appeared in residences to minister to the concerns and anxieties of dislo-
cated students. His administrative style often mimicked general-store days
in New Concord. Not content to be a specialized administrator, Harper
involved himself in a variety of minuscule matters like settling disputes over
library fines and selecting choir music for public programs.[34]

One of Harper's most prominent failures reveals the depth of his
community aspirations. The University of Chicago was designed to include
its own Congregation, which would meet quarterly to allow all of the varied
divisions to experience their oneness and "make recommendations to the
governing bodies of the University." Pastors of local churches, administrators of affiliated institutions, faculty, all the university's Ph.D.s, and other
representative alumni were all to be involved in one great democratic
congregation or assembly of people connected to the university. Harper's
longtime colleague, Thomas W. Goodspeed, claimed, however, that the one
thing the Congregation lacked was an "important function for it to perform."
Lacking genuine authority and purpose, the Congregation faded from view
reducing its number of meetings from four to one per year in 1909, before it

---

[33] Quandt, *From the Small Town to the Great Community*, p. 3.

[34] Harper sent a general invitation to eighteen prospective graduates on January 24, 1896,
inviting them to a series of weekly Tuesday afternoon meetings (Personal Papers, Box 6,
Folder 21). Nellie E. Fuller received an invitation on February 2, 1905 which stated:
"President Harper desires to become acquainted with the students who will graduate this
quarter, and to this end, is asking them from time to time to call upon him at his office hour
11:00 to 12:00. In case it is convenient, it will be a favor if you will come in at this time
to-morrow" (Personal Papers, Box 7, Folder 18).

    Harper also intervened in a squabble between student Louis G. Whitehead and a
librarian. On March 5, 1895, the president informed Mr. Whitehead that "I have taken a
great deal of trouble, as you yourself will appreciate, in the matter of the library fine. I have
done this not only for your sake but for the sake of all the students." Harper could not resist
adding "you were delinquent" in a subsequent paragraph (Personal Papers, Box 2, Folder
9).

    In a letter to Mr. Lester B. Jones, June 4, 1902, Harper vetoed a hymn selected for the
spring convocation religious service: "The President does not like the hymn numbered 1.
He wants something better. He does not like the anthem, 'Hark, hark, my soul.' It is too old.
Get something new" (Personal Papers, Box 6, Folder 15).

finally slipped from view altogether. The coherence Harper had hoped to provide through this innovation never materialized.[35]

At the same time that he strove for community, Harper also concentrated on individuals, searching for ways to make the often cumbersome machinery of learning work for those who needed help. His correspondence reveals presidential involvement in a variety of individual situations ranging from disciplinary cases at the Morgan Park Academy to informal counselling for those searching for religious faith. In addition to his exhausting administrative tasks Harper wrote personal sympathy notes to those in the university community who experienced illness or bereavement. Through these and other personal investments he hoped to foster face-to-face relations with every member of his burgeoning university family. Thus, his depiction of the ideal professor as "older brother" was more than a rhetorical device; instead it pointed to the smalltown core of his expansive scholarly vision.[36]

The intimate community with its unacknowledged roots in Harper's smalltown origins, remained a tacit assumption about how things ought to be rather than a stated goal. Indeed, the quest for such a community did not compel others who had never experienced the way of life Harper thought he had left behind. As generations of teachers and students with ever more urbanized backgrounds came to his university, his various attempts to create one community out of the many worlds of higher education took on increasingly quaint appearance and receded from view.

### THE PROBLEM OF PROGRESS

Another barrier between Harper's climate of opinion and that of the late twentieth century is the tarnishing of American notions of progress and manifest destiny. Progress was self-evident for Harper. Both the new possibilities opened by rapid advances in technology and a personal history of almost unlimited achievement united in his experience to provide seemingly unassailable reasons for individuals like Harper to assume that life was moving ever upward. The religious development he discovered in his study of the Scriptures meshed congruently into a progressive picture of life which was supported by data from his own experience. After all, life had

---

[35] Goodspeed, *A History of The University of Chicago*, p. 395–6.

[36] Harper informed Rev. J. Meier, on May 29, 1896, that "your son is giving the faculty at Morgan Park a great deal of trouble." He did the delicate task of expressing the Academy faculty's desire "to remove him from the school" (Personal Papers, Box 2, Folder 26). On February 22, 1898, Lloyd W. Bowers, General Counsel, Chicago and Northwestern Railway Company, wrote Harper about his "craving" for "Christian confidence" and his need for sympathy following his spouse's death. Harper responded with an undated luncheon invitation in order to discuss Bowers' questions (Personal Papers, Box 4, Folders 2 and 3). Harper's description of the university professor as "older brother" is found in "The College Officer and the College Student," *The Trend in Higher Education*, p. 331.

moved rapidly upward from his smalltown origins to his university presidency. The rest of the world could take similar arduous but promising roads.

Already in Harper's era there were more than a few doubters who questioned assumptions of inevitable progress and America's special destiny. Upton Sinclair and others who shared similar perspectives were alarmed at what was happening to America and strove to turn the tide. But the idealistic age was to last until the crisis of Woodrow Wilson's presidency. Elected as the national exemplar of idealism, Wilson led America into a war to "make the world safe for democracy." His ill-fated proposal for a League of Nations was the last natural gasp of the American blend of special destiny and unchastened idealism. The rejection of his plan for a new order of international existence by both the European nations and his own people contributed to Wilson's personal breakdown and subsequent nationwide disillusionment. Americans revived notions of specialness and divinely mandated status at later points in the twentieth century, but they did so in the face of troubling national circumstances, not out of a self-evident sense that the nation and progress were natural partners.

Professionalism, the passing of the generation which made the transit from small town to great community, and the weakening of the idea of progress are major factors which separate Harper's world from ours. America's increasingly pluralist character and the irrevocable process of urbanization combine with those factors to form a social moraine between Harper and later generations. Although the chronological distance between him and present-day readers is not great, the social distance is immense.

## The Transformation of American Religion

More than social distance is involved, however, in the silence about Harper. American religion also underwent decisive transformation in the era of Harper and Wilson. In *Righteous Empire* Martin E. Marty described the religious transformation which began in the years following post-Civil War Reconstruction as a shift "from Evangelical Empire to Protestant Experience."[37] During Harper's era, religion in America was relocated. Harper came of age in a predominantly Protestant world, but his career contained many encounters with varieties of religious experience that served to relativize his own. Immigrants brought ethnic styles of Catholicism, Lutheranism, Judaism, and other more exotic varieties of Old World religions. New religions emerged on the American scene—products of revivalism, social dislocation, and compelling personal experiences.

No longer could Americans assume a common Protestant framework shared by all. The social variety of religious expression made it difficult for individuals to find common religious symbols to comprehend differences of

---

[37] Marty, *Righteous Empire*, pp. 131ff.

heredity, environment and experience. A public demeanor began to emerge which bracketed religious questions. "The ordeal of civility" was John Murray Cuddihy's aphorism for the personal turmoil which accompanied the emergence of this public civil style. As individuals sought to find public ways to relate to others who did not share common beliefs, they began to build private spheres where old beliefs could survive. New social and religious habits gradually emerged which made religion seem unrelated to most public areas of life. Cuddihy believed that modern humans came to be fragmented individuals, struggling to "pass" in public while clinging tenaciously to fundamental beliefs in private.[38]

The public consequences of this religious relocation can be seen in various attempts during the twentieth century of people like John Dewey to construct a "common faith" for democracy.[39] In its encounter with modernity America's religious life had been so transformed that by midcentury Will Herberg could describe the sociological contours of a religion of the American way of life which seemed to provide minimal social integration in the face of pluralism and fragmentation.[40] In the mid-1960s, little more than a decade after Herberg made his social diagnosis, historian Sidney Mead traced the development in America of an inclusive "theonomous cosmopolitanism," while sociologist Robert Bellah argued for both the existence of and need for a "civil religion."[41] Each of these attempts to discern a publicly acceptable common religion or faith for America were responses to the religious pluralism which had fractured the Protestant Empire of the nineteenth century.

Even denominations, once the intact subcultures which provided secure religious frameworks for adherents, experienced the effects of the new religious situation. Fundamentalism and modernism cut across traditionally secure denominational boundaries, with Protestants being divided over a variety of social and theological issues, just as were Catholics and Jews. The result was that religion had become a source of fragmentation rather than integration; every time it appeared in the public sphere it was fisiporous.

Harper's understanding of religion was quite different from that of subsequent generations. He strove to create a new public form of religion which provided empirically verifiable grounds upon which to construct a common faith. In response to his era's religious needs biblical criticism became the chosen intellectual solution for overcoming problems posed by

[38] John Murray Cuddihy, *The Ordeal of Civility: Freud, Marx, Levi-Strauss and the Jewish Struggle with Modernity* (New York: Dell Publishing Company, 1974).

[39] Dewey, *A Common Faith*.

[40] Will Herberg, *Protestant—Catholic—Jew: An Essay in American Religious Sociology* (Garden City, N.Y.: Anchor Books, 1960).

[41] Mead, *The Nation with the Soul of a Church*, (New York: Harper & Row, 1975), p. 76, and Bellah, "Civil Religion in America," *Beyond Belief: Essays on Religion in a Post-Traditional World* (New York: Harper & Row, 1970), pp. 168–89.

the various denominational traditions. The university, on the other hand, could lead all sorts of inquirers into a religious quest which would eventually discover a common ethos, grounded in the verifiable results of modern biblical scholarship. Harper thus can be seen as one of the early proponents of a new form of public religion which could respond to the new social and religious realities of his day.

Although concerned to support the public weal, Harper unwittingly aided in the relegation of religion to the private sphere. His reticence about his own conversion experience demonstrates how the distinction between public and private spheres of life was reshaping American religion. In early periods of American life conversion had been a community affair. However, when Harper and others like him began to move into a pluralistic public world that found claims based on conversion less than plausible, they frequently chose to keep those matters out of view.

But Harper also contributed to the privatization of religion in America in far more overt ways. Ironically, his very "drive toward publicness"[42] undermined his goal. Biblical criticism and the messianic university were, in his vision, means for providing integration for modern life. Instead Harper's integrators became disintegrators. Biblical criticism helped to create what Marty has called a "two-party system" within American Protestantism.[43] Along with revivalism, slavery, and the social gospel, such scholarship became another source of conflict rather than a means of uniting American religion. And the nation's universities soon became quintessential exemplars of fragmented learning and competing perspectives. On the university campuses of the land, religion, if it was given any space at all, found its private places.

Harper's efforts met a fate similar to that of other religious attempts to provide new solutions to the problems of the always perplexing American environment. Seeking to provide an alternative which could embrace or cut through the knotty problems of American diversity, Harper's public form of religion ended up nurturing one more subgroup—this time a scholarly elite of exegetes—which took its place among the myriad subcultures of America. His biblical movement, which had at first seemed so encompassing, constricted into a scholarly discipline.


## THE INVISIBLE VISION

If Harper's critics seemed to find little but ruin in his vision, and if the social and religious changes in America seem to place Harper on the opposite side of an insurmountable moraine from late twentieth-century

---

[42] The phrase is from David Tracy's, *The Analogical Imagination: Christian Theology and the Culture of Pluralism* (New York: Crossroad Press, 1981), p. 80.
[43] Marty, *Righteous Empire*, pp. 177ff.

readers, is anything possible but a nostalgic glance at the ruins? The answer is found by turning back to Harper for one last perusal.

Harper's vision, although it seems almost too public by late twentieth-century standards, was not clearly visible to people of his own age. His publishing career, with the exception of the commentary on Amos and Hosea, consisted of occasional pieces on selected topics. He never sought to construct what this book attempts—a comprehensive statement of what he was about. Admitting that he was not a systematic thinker, Harper parcelled out pieces of his vision in a variety of places. Unless his contemporaries read all of his journals, accompanied him to Chautauqua, and listened to the variety of talks he gave at the University of Chicago and around the nation, they could not have had a full picture of Harper's vision.

One possible explanation for Harper's reluctance to state his complete vision can be found in the cautious editorial policy he adopted when considering whether or not to discuss historical critical questions in his fledgling journal, The *Hebrew Student*. In 1882 he had decided that "make haste, slowly" would be his guiding principle. Six years later, he intentionally ignored the advice of many readers who encouraged him to consider controversial Pentateuchal questions on the pages of his publication, which by that time had become *The Old Testament Student*. Harper's reply was "the time has not yet come when even such a journal as *The Student* can take up and present such material with impunity."[44] Harper the scholar-editor clearly had a vision for biblical studies in the 1880s, but he deliberately chose a path of cautious discretion about introducing that vision in a complete form to the public.

Harper's death at age 50 interrupted a career that, at least in his own ✓ eyes, had many tasks left to accomplish. The new Religious Education Association, the yet to be realized national university, and plans for his own growing university all called for many more goals and efforts. Since Harper did not discuss his failure to state his total educational and religious vision in a complete and systematic way, perhaps it is reasonable to assume, given the sense of cautious timing present throughout his editorial career, that he did not state such a vision because in his estimation his audience was not yet ready for it.

When cancer closed in on him during his last year of life Harper tried to pull together some key fragments of his thought in both *The Trend* and his commentary on Amos and Hosea. But even those hurried attempts resulted only in a collection of his thoughts on higher education on one hand and a partial statement of his biblical perspective on the other. He died before his vision was fully stated. Moreover, those who worked with him seemed to grasp only the particular piece of his vision that affected them directly. Biblical colleagues welcomed his articles and commentary but seemed to

[44] See Chapter 3, p. 57.

know little of his larger vision for higher education and the nation. Educators, as Veblen and Herrick amply demonstrate, reacted to his innovations in their world but saw no connection between Harper the president and Harper the biblical scholar.

Harper seems never to have pressed his faculty to grapple with his full vision. In fact, colleagues felt free to participate in it selectively, appropriating only what meshed with their own wishes and dreams. Thus J.W. Moncrief assumed he was hired to teach at a "Baptist University" while his colleague William C. Hale chafed when he heard the term and was concerned that Chicago's non-religious character be maintained. Clarence Luther Herrick (no relation to Robert) saw in Harper's university the opportunity to do a Christian version of field-encompassing science. Charles Whitman, on the other hand, came to Chicago to devote a career to studying the evolution of pigeons. Each found aspects of Harper's vision to be compatible with basic private goals and beliefs; although many, like Veblen, thought they understood him, few if any of his colleagues seemed fully aware of what he was up to.[45]

Harper's style of leadership was an additional factor responsible for both the success he experienced and his subsequent disappearance from view. Harper built his critical reformation on an ability to interpret sacred texts of an ancient tradition in a new manner. The weight of the most recent scholarship and thousands of years of religious history buttressed his claim. But Harper also had about him a quality which, if not totally charismatic, was at least quasi-charismatic. Goodspeed's previously noted description of his first encounter with Harper revealed an unusual dimension in the young Harper which separated him from other bright young men.[46] There was an observable ability in him to compel others. Those who worked with him in tedious tasks of mastering ancient verb forms and editing journals sensed that they were doing far more—participating in a Hebrew movement. Rockefeller and the wealthy Chicagoans who sat on the University of Chicago's Board of Trustees were swayed by the force of Harper's persona, as were faculty who left secure teaching positions in other institutions to participate in Harper's grand vision.

A distinctive mixture of leadership qualities enabled Harper to succeed. His ability to salvage a religious tradition suffering under the weight of modernity attracted religious supporters. At the same time that he found a new way to invoke a traditional authority he helped people make the transit to life in a new university setting by the force of his own authority, the promises he made, the opportunities he offered. Harper's idiosyncratic

---

[45] J. W. Moncrief to William Rainey Harper, December 9, 1890, Personal Papers, Box 14, Folder 14; W.G. Hale to William Rainey Harper, May 2, 1892, Personal Papers, Box 13, Folder 38; Herrick and Whitman's perceptions are assessed in Blake, "The Concept and Development of Science at The University of Chicago, 1890–1905," pp. 118, 24.
[46] See Chapter 2, p. 37.

combination of these different styles of leadership allowed people to follow him without having to commit themselves to his entire vision. Students could be inspired by their Hebrew teacher without knowing where he stood on key issues of hermeneutics. Faculty could come to his university without an awareness that they were joining a messianic institution.

The multiform character of Harper's interest also served to undermine his vision. Interested in nearly every phase of university life, Harper seemed unable or unwilling to disentangle himself from routine administrative matters in order to consolidate and state his vision. The picture that emerges from his "red books" is of a president who continually sought to do everything. Daily lists of "things to do" often contained more than fifty items. Again and again Harper would map out his day, trying to broker all of his interests.[47] The pressure of so many competing concerns prevented systematic efforts at developing and nurturing a vision. Temperament and circumstances seemed to conspire to keep Harper's envisioning occasional rather than sustained and disciplined.

When Harper died in 1906 there was an immense outpouring of grief. Richard D. Harlan, President of Lake Forest College, affirmed Harper's visionary capacities by calling him "a seer among educators." Numerous other educators, pastors, students and scholars flooded the Harper household with glowing tributes to the man who had built their university or their picture of religious reality.[48] But although the encomia were overwhelming, no one arose to carry on the Harper vision. The presidential dynamo had failed to hand on his largest dreams to a school of prophets.


## THE CULTURED TRANSFORMER

The disappearance of Harper's vision can also be attributed to his unavoidable participation in social dynamics which mitigated against his purposes. Harper conceived of himself as a reformer, whose purpose was to clear away old interpretations of Scripture and old models of learning in order to usher in new, higher types. He sought to transform his culture in a manner which exemplified the pattern of Christian existence in society that H. Richard Niebuhr identified as the "Christ transforming culture" type.[49] Not so pessimistic about American life that he could consider either withdrawal from it or its destruction, Harper was a meliorist who sought to convert the culture to a biblical way of life.

[47] William Rainey Harper, "July 8 Monday Things to Do," *Red Book No. 6*, Personal Papers, p. 38, and *Red Book No. 2*, p. 94.
[48] Harlan to Mrs. William Rainey Harper, January 18, 1906, Personal Papers, Box 17, Folder 4. A wide variety of letters of sympathy on the occasion of Harper's death are collected in Box 17 of his Personal Papers.
[49] H. Richard Niebuhr, *Christ and Culture* (New York: Harper & Row, Publishers, 1951), pp. 190ff.

What he could not perceive about himself was that his behavior also resembled one of the other categories in Niebuhr's famous typology. Harper was "of the culture" he sought to transform.[50] As he built his university he furthered the development of academic disciplines, of professionalism, and of the fragmentation of knowledge. Despite hopes to the contrary, his efforts at reinterpreting the Scriptures exacerbated the fracturing process within American religion and weakened already shaky denominational traditions instead of creating a more learned Christian public. Heavy emphasis on publishing helped foster the explosion of knowledge which made coteries of experts increasingly necessary. Harper helped to bureaucratize learning and routinize its development in the process of trying to include all fields of knowledge within his university. His problem-centered approach to education furthered the individualizing of knowledge rather than enhancing the common discovery of it.

Harper's itinerant presidency presaged an age when university executives became important primarily for abilities at fundraising, public relations and administration. His sporadic attempts to state his vision took place within a context where the college president who synthesized all learning in a course called Moral Philosophy had become obsolete. One sign that the new organization of learning had arrived may be Harper's failure to pass on his vision. As Harper strove to carry on his biblical scholarship and to run his edifice of learning, he straddled two eras, strenuously advocating a Messianic ideal while simultaneously supporting developments which reshaped it. In short, vision of the type that motivated Harper was becoming a private matter in the public world of education.

### PLACING A PRESIDENT

A survey of the most vocal and, at times, shrill criticisms made of Harper, along with consideration of several factors which have raised the social and religious moraine between Harper and subsequent generations, helps account for his relegation to the back corridors of American history. Aware of the legacy of ignorance which cloaks his vision like a shroud, and mindful of the experiential distance between then and now, the historian finally attempts to place Harper within the limits and possibilities of his own particular period. Part of the reason for the enduring obscurity which surrounds Harper is a pervasive vagueness about his era. Turn-of-the-century America has remained a neglected historical era, almost guaranteeing fundamental misreadings of the period and its people.

One important attempt to penetrate the historical haze which surrounds Harper and his contemporaries is Laurence R. Veysey's *The Emergence of the American University*. This complex narrative about the formation of the

[50] Ibid., pp. 83ff.

American university is indispensable for understanding the plot of American intellectual and institutional history. In broad outline, Veysey's narrative tells the following story. American higher education prior to the Civil War was dominated by a "mental discipline" paradigm. This model of shaping a mind via the drudgery of recitation, translation and regurgitation became increasingly cumbersome in the rapidly changing environment of postbellum America. During the 1870s and 1880s a new institution, the university, appeared on the American horizon to challenge the prevailing collegiate style. It did not appear all at once, but rather was the product of a rich interplay of ideas and environment, beliefs and behavior. The decades of the 1870s and 1880s were marked by numerous attempts to restructure American education. A variety of scholars and visionaries contended for more or less distinct approaches which Veysey has classified in terms of basic commitments to utility, research or liberal culture.

At about the time that Harper became president of the University of Chicago, Veysey suggests, institutional constraints began to overwhelm these ideas about the university. Pressures of finances, diverse programs, complex bureaucratic imperatives, and the increasing burden of creating and sustaining a public image acceptable to a growing American clientele began to mold universities into amazingly similar shapes. Institutions as diverse as Yale—defender for some time of the old "mental discipline" model—and Johns Hopkins—archetype of the research paradigm—blurred into one common university type. By the end of the period which Veysey describes, universities had become distressingly alike, characterized by bureaucratic types of organization, serious gaps between student desires and faculty concerns, and administrators who had fundamentally different interests than those which first gave rise to the complex institutions under their care. Commitments as diverse as pure research, championship football, fraternity culture and professional careerism coexisted, for the most part peacefully, under the umbrella of institutions which were held together more by organizational linkages than by commitment to ideals or personalities.[51]

Veysey's instructive version of the story of the university provides a much needed historical perspective for viewing one of the central institutions in modern American life. His tracing of the complex and haphazard development of an entity which seemed to intrude abruptly into American life and then with equal suddenness come to a place of pre-eminence, corrects notions that the university was formed according to one blueprint, or that American education *had* to take the shape it did. Further, Veysey's placing of Harper within the larger plot of this complex story helps us to relocate him within his own context and to assess him on its terms rather than by standards imposed from later times.

Harper was, according to Veysey, part of the second act of the American

---

[51] Veysey, *The Emergence of the American University.*

university drama. Others, like Andrew Dickson White of Cornell, Charles Eliot of Harvard, Daniel Coit Gilman of Johns Hopkins, G. Stanley Hall of Clark or Woodrow Wilson of Princeton, were key representatives of contending ideas within the first phase of American university history. Harper, on the other hand (here once again the Veblenesque legacy!), was of significance because he represented, almost to the point of caricature, the new administrative tenor which came to supplant powerful ideas about education in the 1890s. He thus becomes for Veysey the great blender and reconciler of American higher education, holding together within the complex matrix of his institution the many diverse and contradictory components of the emergent modern organization of knowledge.[52]

Before challenging Veysey's overall portrait of Harper, it is important to note points of convergence between his description and the one developed on these pages. Thus Veysey's portrait calls attention to Harper's pronounced ability to gather people of competing interests and perspectives and fashion them into a faculty. Veysey's Harper presided adroitly over a burgeoning bureaucracy, seemed to relish creating new administrative structures, and gained distinction chiefly as an unparalleled fundraiser and enthusiastic promoter of his new university.

But once again Harper's vision, his biblical perspective and his evangelical commitment have been ignored. Instead, an incomplete portrait has been presented, which captures many of the facts about Harper the bureaucrat while omitting his alternative integrator to administration as the glue for the modern American configuration of learning. To counter such a portrait, a brief overview of the distinctive approaches and achievements of several representative university presidents of the era will provide points of comparison with the Harper vision developed in the preceding chapters. Such a comparison, building on Veysey's descriptions of Harper's colleagues, may allow Harper to take a new place in American religious and educational history. It may also suggest the need to tell the late nineteenth-century American religious story in ways that capture more than disintegration, retreat and impotence.

While many regard the founding of the Johns Hopkins University in 1876 as the opening page of the university story in America, Veysey carefully recalls its prehistory. Andrew Dickson White and Charles Eliot, for example, made serious earlier attempts to reform the "mental discipline" paradigm of collegiate education. White (1832–1918) came from affluent Episcopal New York origins along a circuitous, gentlemanly route to become the founding president of Cornell University in 1868. Along the way he escaped from the sectarian confines of Geneva College by going into hiding, where he remained until his parents consented to a change to Yale. After study in Paris and Berlin, work as attaché to the American delegation to St. Petersburg, and

---

[52] Ibid., pp. 367–80.

a tour of Italy, he began to teach history at the University of Michigan. His formative experience of dissatisfaction with American education and his subsequent exposure to the academic and cultural riches of Europe, provided raw materials for a dream of an institution that would surpass even Yale, his first haven from sectarian narrowness. At the University of Michigan, White began to outline his plans for a university for the state of New York. A brief stint as senator back in New York included service as Chairman of the New York Senate's Education Committee. White used both his senatorial clout (over the state's land allotment under the Morril Act of 1862) and a friendship with fellow senator Ezra Cornell, to secure a charter for his new university.[53]

Veysey suggests that three controlling ideas guided White as he shaped Cornell University: non-sectarianism in religion, freedom of choice among various courses of study, and equality of status among the various subjects of learning. But underneath these three "guiding ideas" Veysey found a fundamental commitment to the "idea of the university as a training ground for politically-oriented public service."

> White pictured . . . graduates pouring into the legislatures, staffing the newspapers, and penetrating the municipal and county boards of America. Corruption would come to an end; pure American ideals would prosper until one day they governed the entire world.

In short, White was a proponent of the ideal of utility. The university was to serve public well-being, not the interests of any smaller group or sect. Practical types of learning such as pharmacy and industrial studies were to have a place in the Cornell curriculum.[54]

Charles William Eliot (1834–1926) seemed to follow a streamlined trajectory from birth in a prominent Bostonian family to the presidency of Harvard in 1869. Rigorous preparatory education at Boston's Latin School and the Unitarianism of King's Chapel shaped Eliot for entry to Harvard College at age fifteen. Four years later he became tutor of mathematics, then assistant professor at his alma mater. The only major hitch in his Harvard rise came in 1863 when he failed to secure promotion and lost his position. Europe beckoned in 1865 and again in 1867, affording opportunity for a survey of continental educational models. An article summarizing his findings, entitled "The New Education: Its Organization," appeared in an 1869 issue of *The Atlantic Monthly*. Suddenly the Harvard Corporation rediscovered its interest in Eliot and elected him president of the College, although not without some objection. The twenty-second president of America's senior academic institution, Eliot was its third non-clergy president.[55]

[53] "Andrew Dickson White," *Dictionary of American Biography*, 20:88–93.
[54] White is discussed and quoted in Veysey, *The Emergence of the American University*, pp. 81–86.
[55] "Charles William Eliot," *Dictionary of American Biography*, 6:71–78.

In his 1869 Inaugural Address, Eliot called for an end to the imposed curriculum. The elective system remains as a monument to his presidency. Concerned to educate individuals for "real life," Eliot felt that teaching students responsible decision-making was essential. Thus, selecting courses of study became a lesson for living in a world saturated with the problem of choice. Eliot's forty-year presidential tenure during these years of higher-educational transition allowed him to participate in numerous reforms of professional and secondary education. It is instructive to recall, however, that he came into office with very little in the way of a concrete academic program except a desire to advance the elective system. The goal of his reform was to shape a new kind of student; Eliot's ideal student would not be molded in the rubber-stamp image of the mental discipline era, but equipped to serve in public life with abilities to decide responsibly. Veysey discerned a less obvious motive in Eliot's "rationalistic individualism": an "intelligent patrician's adjustment to a new threat from 'below.'" In his efforts to make Harvard "a voluntary cooperative association of highly individualistic persons," Eliot was also responding to new social realities which challenged the imagination of New England's elite.[56]

While both White and Eliot were committed to allowing choice and social utility to reshape higher education, they lacked commitment to research as the basic purpose of their universities. Although they distanced their institutions from the "mental discipline" paradigm, their concern remained with a particular type of student: the socially useful, competent citizen. Only after the sudden appearance of a new institution dedicated to research as its highest goal—the Johns Hopkins—did either White or Eliot begin to move their institutions to respond to the need for graduate studies. White and Eliot both supported Daniel Coit Gilman as the best person to lead the Balitmore institution. Yet in their recommendations supporting his candidacy neither mentioned research as the reason for their choice.[57]

Gilman (1831–1908) came from affluent Connecticut Congregational roots and followed a path to university-leadership similar to that of Andrew Dickson White. In fact, the two shared several of their years of preparation as classmates at Yale and fellow travelers in Europe. After returning to Yale from Europe, Gilman was given the opportunity to design the Sheffield Scientific School, which he served as librarian, secretary and professor of physical and political geography. After seventeen years at these diverse specialties, Gilman accepted the offer to become president of the University of California in 1872. A recalcitrant California legislature, however, and the seven million dollar estate of Johns Hopkins combined to lure him to Baltimore where he shaped an institution devoted to graduate study and the

---

[56] Veysey, *The Emergence of the American University*, pp. 87–94.
[57] Ibid., p. 95.

ideal of research.[58] He came to his new post intending to build a "faculty of medicine and a faculty of philosophy," not a scientific school or a college. In fact,

> the usual college machinery of classes, commencements, etc. may be dispensed with; that each head of a great department,—say of mathematics, or of Language or of Chemistry or of History, etc. shall be as far as possible free from the interference of other heads of departments, & shall determine what scholars he will receive & how he will teach them; that advanced special students be first provided for; that degrees be given when scholars are ready to be graduated, in one year or in ten years after their admission.

Veysey has suggested that the individual scholars hired by Gilman to staff his fledgling university may have actually developed the school's bias toward research and that Gilman's main function was to erect a facade which allowed them room to do their work. But Gilman's initial move—whether or not it was surpassed by his faculty—was to create an institution that redirected the goal of the American university away from concern with student character and toward his era's emergent concern for the discovery of new knowledge.[59]

The ideal of pure research received its most complete institutional articulation, and its largest setback, at Clark University. Another of the new schools made possible by a windfall of American philanthropy, Clark provided considerable evidence to support the claim that the only good philanthropist (aside from being wealthy) was the dead one. Jonas Clark initially promised the kind of institution which could have firmly enshrined the research paradigm in American education. Then he managed to sabotage his own institution by withholding promised funds when it began to live up to the research ideal.[60]

Clark's first president was Granville Stanley Hall (1844–1924). Another New Englander, Hall did not share affluent origins with White, Gilman or Eliot. The son of a farmer, Hall was graduated from Williams College with no special distinction. After toying with entering the ministry, and conversing with Henry Ward Beecher about his suitability for the vocation, Hall set out for Europe where he studied theology and philosophy. He returned to Union Seminary in New York where he completed his theological training. Initial teaching posts at Antioch College and Harvard University preceded reception of the Ph.D. from Harvard in 1878. Again he travelled to Germany, this time to study psychology, physiology and physics. After two years of continental drifting he was hired by Johns Hopkins to create a psychology laboratory, where he soon held forth as professor of psychology and peda-

[58] "Daniel Coit Gilman," *Dictionary of American Biography*, 7:299–303.
[59] Gilman is discussed and quoted in Veysey, *The Emergence of the American University*, pp. 159–65.
[60] Ibid., p. 166.

gogy and almost instantly became established as a leader in his field. In 1889 he left Hopkins in order to head Clark University, a school which would, in his estimation, surpass even Johns Hopkins in its commitment to research. It was to be an all-graduate institution.[61]

Some of Hall's exuberant language about the religion of research was mentioned in Chapter 1 as an example of his era's intoxication with new types of education.[62] For people like Hall scholarship simply became "the highest vocation." But because of constant problems posed by lack of funds, the school remained small and assumed characteristics of an intimate community. No attendance was taken, and no exams were given except the oral doctor's examination. Albeit on a small scale, professors and students were relatively free to pursue what they pleased: research.[63]

A third option for shaping basic university commitments and an alternative to the ideals of utility or research was liberal culture. Princeton University, according to Veysey, struggled to reshape its educational pattern under the power of this ideal during the presidency of Woodrow Wilson. Wilson (1856–1924), the son of a Presbyterian parson, came of age in the south. He studied at home under the tutelage of his father and then went off to the College of New Jersey where he quickly showed competence in areas of political science and law. An unsuccessful entry into the field of law was followed by a graduate program at Johns Hopkins, where Wilson earned his Ph.D. under the supervision of historian Herbert Baxter Adams. Teaching posts at Bryn Mawr College and Wesleyan University were followed by an appointment in 1890 at Princeton as professor of jurisprudence and political economy. Twelve years later he became Princeton's president.[64]

During his eight years as president there, Wilson made a number of attempts to reshape the school, moving it away from the mental discipline paradigm and toward the ideal which Veysey has identified as liberal culture. Distressed by the social divisiveness represented by elite student "eating clubs," Wilson banished such bastions of exclusiveness and sought to create a more inclusive social community organized around quadrangles, where students from a variety of backgrounds lived together in a more egalitarian manner. Although trained in the research ethos of Johns Hopkins, Wilson did not, however, become a proponent of the gospel of research.

Instead his institution became "not a place of special but of general education, not a place where a lad finds a profession, but a place *where he finds himself.*" To that end Wilson organized a "preceptorial system" of instruction which allowed small groups of students to experience an alter-

---

[61] "Granville Stanley Hall," *Dictionary of American Biography*, 8:127–30.
[62] See above, pp. 18f.
[63] Veysey, *The Emergence of the American University*, pp. 165–70.
[64] "Woodrow Wilson," *Dictionary of American Biography*, 20:352–68.

native form of cohesiveness—one based on academic interests rather than social distinction. To him the ideal college

> should be a community . . . a place of close, natural, intimate association, not only of the young men who are its pupils and novices in various lines of study but also of young men with older men . . . of teachers with pupils, outside the classroom as well as inside of it.

This university was to equip students with ideals of "conduct," "truthful comradeship," "loyalty," "co-operation," and a sense of "esprit de corps"— a feeling that they were part of a common culture sharing a common service. Sharing his colleague Arthur F. West's concern about "the provincialization of learning," Wilson opposed the fragmentation of knowledge. Seeking to awaken "the whole man," to join "the intellectual and spiritual life," Wilson wanted both his university and college to share in "a pervading sense of the unity and unbroken circle of learning."[65]

This broadly drawn sketch of several of Harper's presidential colleagues cannot do justice to the richness of the story of the emergence of the university, or to Veysey's magisterial telling of it. But a survey of some of the leading ideas and institutional achievements of even a few of the dominant educators of the era helps locate Harper within a much larger story than one focused solely upon his own institution or ideas. The astonishing fact about Harper is that indeed he did "blend and reconcile" so many of the ideas and institutional attempts of these various leaders. Like Hall, and to a lesser extent Gilman, Harper was committed to research. He knew from firsthand experience what riches could come from specialized study. Like Wilson, he was concerned about the dangers of specialization and sought comprehensiveness. Harper's efforts to create a community of learning in the midst of his diverse university had obvious parallels to Wilson's communitarian agenda. Harper shared Eliot's concern for individual student responsibility in choosing courses but he also sought to balance individualism with an insistence upon student exposure to certain essential areas of learning. Harper went beyond Eliot's hope that the university would equip students for public service with a more comprehensive expectation that the university should lift individual students, and through them the culture, to a higher life.

But, what Veysey's portrait misses is the integrator Harper used to hold together various academic ideals and institutional arrangements. Arguing that Harper represented "charisma without ideology,"[66] Veysey has suggested that the University of Chicago was held together by an administrative structure that initially took shape because of the force of Harper's enthusiasm. What the preceding chapters claim, on the other hand, is that Harper wove his variegated configuration of learning together with a biblical thread,

[65] Wilson is discussed and quoted in Veysey, *The Emergence of the American University*, pp. 200, 241–47.
[66] Ibid., p. 368.

that in essence he was offering an alternative to those of mental discipline, utility, research or liberal culture. His religious understanding of the institution he led was the pivotal integrator, at least for him. Thus his idea of the role of the modern university included the messianic vocation to suffer over the nation's great problems, thereby leading students, and through them the nation, to a fully developed life which would occur only when the students and the land had developed their full religious potential. Throughout his career as president, Harper sought to embody such a vision in his efforts to lead people to the Scriptures, and through them to the higher life. In a postscript to a letter written in 1895 to President J.M. Taylor of Vassar College, Harper revealed his sense of the order of his activities. "You understand that my special business in the world is stirring up people on the English Bible. The University of Chicago is entirely a second hand matter." As late in his life as February 11, 1905, Harper reminded a correspondent that "all my work is in a very fundamental sense missionary work."[67]

Recovery of Harper's fundamental biblical vision makes possible a reconsideration of his importance in American educational and religious history. Alongside of the image of the academic entrepreneur who naively furthered the institutionalization of learning can be placed the portrait of an individual who attempted to hold together two clashing Americas of the late nineteenth century. The village Protestantism of the older America, and the modern pluralism fostered by technology, bureaucracy, immigration and urbanization, met in his attempts to build a complex configuration of learning which furthered while transforming the religious and social values of a passing era. Attempting to evangelize America with a fresh interpretation of the Scriptures, Harper was a representative of both the new critical scholarship and the older evangelistic impulse of the Righteous Empire. In his attempts to make the Bible a source book for the religious development of all Americans, and in his efforts to promote the modern university as a messianic agency for the religion of democracy, Harper was carrying on the tradition of a Christian America, as well as participating in the twentieth-century search for an inclusive religion for all members of the American republic. Small town and city, Sunday school and seminar, vicarious suffering and administrative procedure, ancient tradition and modern knowledge all somehow coexisted within the framework of his life and career. The ironies of being a charismatic leader who furthered on an immense scale what Max Weber called "the routinization of charisma,"[68] a modernist who used tradition to support his efforts, and a traditionalist who welcomed modernity to salvage a tradition, make him an important symbol for the era

[67] William Rainey Harper to President J.M. Taylor, n.d., Personal Papers, Box 2, Folder 17; William Rainey Harper to Rev. C.D. Edwards, February 11, 1905, Personal Papers, Box 7, Folder 19.
[68] Max Weber, *On Charisma and Institution Building*, S.N. Eisenstadt, ed. (Chicago: University of Chicago Press, 1968), pp. 54ff.

during which America was fundamentally remade. The concerns that vexed him, the solutions he offered, the paradoxes and contradictions that were his, were also those of an age. The fact that his vision, although extraordinarily ambitious, could not hold together the various strands of American reality does not render that vision insignificant any more than it does the vision of a Wilson, an Eliot, a James, or a Dewey—who all strove, like Harper, to impose coherence and order on an environment which ultimately overcame their attempts.

Instead Harper emerges as a potential eponym for America's great time of transition.[69] His quest for coherence, meaning, order, knowledge and religious understanding is representative of his era's attempts to come to terms with modernity. At the same time, it is a sign of the ongoing American burden to find coherence and oneness in the midst of the fragmentation, pluralism, impersonalism and meaninglessness that were the unexpected results of America's new professional, technological and urban way of life.

[69] The notion of an individual serving as an eponym for an era was developed in William A. Clebsch, *American Religious Thought: A History* (Chicago: University of Chicago Press, 1973), p. 7.

# BIBLIOGRAPHY

## WORKS BY WILLIAM RAINEY HARPER

"The American Institute of Sacred Literature." *The Old and New Testament Student* 12 (June 1891):381–82.

"The American Institute of Sacred Literature." *The Biblical World* 4 (October 1894):306–8.

"American Institute of Sacred Literature: An Examination on the Gospel of Luke." *The Old and New Testament Student* 10 (January 1890):57–58.

"The American Institute of Sacred Literature: Announcements for the Year 1904–5." *The Biblical World* 24 (September 1904):228–30.

"American Institute of Sacred Literature: Training Courses for Sunday School Teachers Under the Direction of the Institute." *The Biblical World* 23 (June 1904):467.

*Amos and Hosea.* The International Critical Commentary on the Scriptures of the Old and New Testaments. Edited by Charles Augustus Briggs, Samuel Rolles Driver, and Alfred Plummer. New York: Charles Scribner's Sons, 1905.

"The Bible and the Common Schools." *The Biblical World* 20 (October 1902):243–47.

"Bible Study and Religious Interest. *The Biblical World* 17 (June 1901):403–6.

"Bible Study Versus Theology." *The Old and New Testament Student* 10 (February 1890):120–21.

"The College President." *The William Rainey Harper Memorial Conference.* Edited by Robert N. Montgomery. Chicago: University of Chicago Press, 1938. Pp. 24–34.

"Constructive Studies in the Literature of Worship in the Old Testament. Study I." *The Biblical World* 19 (February 1902):132–46.

"Constructive Studies in the Literature of Worship in the Old Testament. Study IV. Part I." *The Biblical World* 19 (June 1902):443–55.

"Constructive Studies in the Literature of Worship in the Old Testament. Study IV. Part II." *The Biblical World* 20 (July 1902):49–57.

"Constructive Studies in the Literature of Worship in the Old Testament. Study IV. Part III." *The Biblical World* 2 (August 1902):134–45.

"Constructive Studies in the Priestly Element in the Old Testament. Part I." *The Biblical World* 17 (January 1901):46–54.

"Constructive Studies in the Priestly Element in the Old Testament. Part II." *The Biblical World* 17 (January 1901):121–34.

"Constructive Studies in the Priestly Element in the Old Testament. Part III." *The Biblical World* 17 (March 1901):206–20.

"Constructive Studies in the Priestly Element in the Old Testament. Part IV." *The Biblical World* 17 (May 1901):366–81.

"Constructive Studies in the Priestly Element in the Old Testament. Part V." *The Biblical World* 17 (June 1901): 450–62.

"Constructive Studies in the Prophetic Element in the Old Testament." *The Biblical World* 23 (January 1904): 50–58.

"Constructive Studies in the Prophetic Element in the Old Testament: Study II." *The Biblical World* 23 (February 1904):132–41.

"Constructive Studies in the Prophetic Element in the Old Testament. Study III." *The Biblical World* 23 (March 1904):212–23.

"Constructive Studies in the Prophetic Element in the Old Testament. Study VI." *The Biblical World* 24 (October 1904):292–300.

"Constructive Studies in the Prophetic Element in the Old Testament. Study VII." *The Biblical World* 24 (November 1904):361–76.

"Constructive Studies in the Prophetic Element in the Old Testament. Study VIII." *The Biblical World* 24 (December 1904):448–61.

"Constructive Studies in the Prophetic Element in the Old Testament. Study IX." *The Biblical World* 25 (January 1905):52–61.

"The Council of Seventy." *The Biblical World* 13 (January 1899):47–48.

"The Council of Seventy." *The Biblical World* 13 (March 1899): 209–10.

"The Deluge in Other Literatures and History." *The Biblical World* 4 (August 1894):114–23.

"The Divine Element in the Early Stories of Genesis." *The Biblical World* 4 (November 1894):349–58.

"Editorial." *The Hebrew Student* 1 (April 1882):11.

"Editorial." *The Old Testament Student* 5 (April 1886):321–25.

"Editorial." *The Old Testament Student* 6 (September 1886):1–4.

"Editorial." *The Old Testament Student* 6 (October 1886):33–37.

"Editorial." *The Old Testament Student* 6 (December 1886): 97–100.

"Editorial." *The Old Testament Student* 6 (February 1887): 161–63.

"Editorial." *The Old Testament Student* 6 (March 1887): 193–95.

"Editorial." *The Old Testament Student* 6 (April 1887): 225–28.

"Editorial." *The Old Testament Student* 7 (September 1887): 1–4.

"Editorial." *The Old Testament Student* 7 (October 1887): 37–39.

"Editorial." *The Old Testament Student* 7 (March 1888):209–11.

"Editorial." *The Old Testament Student* 7 (June 1888):305–7.

"Editorial." *The Old Testament Student* 8 (October 1888):41–44.

"Editorial." *The Old Testament Student* 8 (October 1888):81–84.

"Editorial." *The Old and New Testament Student* 8 (January 1889):161–63.

"Editorial." *The Old Testament Student* 8 (February 1889):201–6.

"Editorial." *The Old Testament Student* 8 (April 1889):281–83.

"Editorial." *The Old and New Testament Student* 9 (August 1889): 65–70.

"Editorial." *The Old and New Testament Student* 9 (October 1889):193–97.

"Editorial." *The Old and New Testament Student* 10 (January 1890):1–6.

"Editorial." *The Old and New Testament Student* 10 (February 1890):65–72.

"Editorial." *The Old and New Testament Student* 10 (April 1890):193–99.

"Editorial." *The Old and New Testament Student* 10 (May 1890): 257–64.

"Editorial." *The Old and New Testament Student* 11 (September 1890):129–33.

"Editorial." *The Old and New Testament Student* 11 (November 1890):257–61.

"Editorial." *The Old and New Testament Student* 12 (January 1891):1–6.

"Editorial." *The Old and New Testament Student* 12 (March 1891): 129–34.

"Editorial." *The Old and New Testament Student* 12 (April 1891): 193–97.

"Editorial." *The Old and New Testament Student* 12 (June 1891): 321–26.

"Editorial." *The Old and New Testament Student* 13 (November 1891):257–63.

"Editorial." *The Old and New Testament Student* 13 (December 1891):321–28.

"Editorial." *The Old and New Testament Student* 14 (February 1892):65–70.

"Editorial." *The Old and New Testament Student* 15 (July/August 1892):1–5.
"Editorial." *The Old and New Testament Student* 16 (September/October 1892):89–93.
"Editorial." *The Biblical World* 1 (January 1893):1–4.
"Editorial." *The Biblical World* 1 (February 1893):83–87.
"Editorial." *The Biblical World* 1 (April 1893):243–47.
"Editorial." *The Biblical World* 1 (June 1893):403–7.
"Editorial." *The Biblical World* 2 (July 1893):1–6.
"Editorial." *The Biblical World* 2 (August 1893):81–86.
"Editorial." *The Biblical World* 2 (September 1892):161–66.
"Editorial." *The Biblical World* 2 (October 1893):241–46.
"Editorial." *The Biblical World* 2 (November 1893):321–25.
"Editorial." *The Biblical World* 2 (December 1893):401–6.
"Editorial." *The Biblical World* 3 (March 1894):161–65.
"Editorial." *The Biblical World* 3 (April 1894):241–46.
"Editorial." *The Biblical World* 3 (May 1894):321–25.
"Editorial." *The Biblical World* 3 (June 1894):401–5.
"Editorial." *The Biblical World* 4 (August 1894):81–86.
"Editorial." *The Biblical World* 4 (October 1894):241–43.
"Editorial." *The Biblical World* 4 (November 1894):321–25.
"Editorial." *The Biblical World* 4 (December 1894):401–6.
"Editorial." *The Biblical World* 5 (April 1895):241–47.
"Editorial." *The Biblical World* 5 (June 1895):401–9.
"Editorial." *The Biblical World* 6 (September 1895):161–67.
"Editorial." *The Biblical World* 9 (February 1897):81–86.
"Editorial." *The Biblical World* 9 (March 1897):161–66.
"Editorial." *The Biblical World* 9 (April 1897):241–47.
"Editorial." *The Biblical World* 9 (May 1897):321–28.
"Editorial." *The Biblical World* 10 (October 1897):241–44.
"Editorial." *The Biblical World* 10 (November 1897):321–26.
"Editorial." *The Biblical World* 11 (March 1898):145–50.
"Editorial." *The Biblical World* 11 (April 1898):225–28.
"Editorial." *The Biblical World* 11 (May 1898):289–93.
"Editorial." *The Biblical World* 12 (July 1898):1–4.
"Editorial." *The Biblical World* 12 (August 1898):65–70.
"Editorial." *The Biblical World* 12 (September 1898):145–52.
"Editorial." *The Biblical World* 12 (October 1898):225–29.
"Editorial." *The Biblical World* 13 (February 1899):65–68.
"Editorial." *The Biblical World* 13 (March 1899):145–49.
"Editorial." *The Biblical World* 14 (December 1899):387–89.
"Editorial." *The Biblical World* 16 (August 1900):83–86.
"Editorial." *The Biblical World* 16 (October 1900):243–47.
"Editorial." *The Biblical World* 17 (February 1901):83–86.
"Editorial." *The Biblical World* 17 (March 1901):163–66.
"Editorial." *The Biblical World* 18 (September 1901):163–66.
"Editorial." *The Biblical World* 19 (January 1902):3–8.
"Editorial." *The Biblical World* 19 (June 1902):403–9.
"Editorial." *The Biblical World* 20 (August 1902):83–88.
"Editorial." *The Biblical World* 22 (September 1903):163–66.
"Editorial." *The Biblical World* 23 (January 1904):3–6.
"Editorial." *The Biblical World* 24 (December 1904):403–11.
"Editorial." *The Biblical World* 25 (February 1905):83–87.

1. ELEMENTS OF HEBREW
2. INTRO. HEBREW METHOD AND MANUAL        } P. 34 & AJSL VOL 22

"Editorial." *The Biblical World* 25 (March 1905):163–68.

"Editorial." *The Biblical World* 25 (April 1905):243–48.

"Editorial Letter." *The Biblical World* 14 (August 1899): 83–86.

"Editorial Letter." *The Biblical World* 14 (September 1899): 147–48.

"Editorial Letter." *The Biblical World* 15 (May 1900):323–25.

"Editorial Notes." *The Hebrew Student* 1 (May 1882):11.

"Editorial Notes." *The Hebrew Student* 1 (June 1882):51.

"Editorial Notes." *The Old Testament Student* 4 (November 1884): 134–38.

"Editorial Notes." *The Old Testament Student* 4 (February 1885): 282–84.

"Editorial Notes." *The Old Testament Student* 5 (September 1885):37–41.

"Editorial Notes." *The Old Testament Student* 5 (December 1885):181–83.

"Editorial Notes: The Duty of the Theological Seminary in Reference to Bible-Study." *The Old Testament Student* 5 (January 1886):234–35.

"The First Hebrew Story of Creation." *The Biblical World* 3 (January 1894):6–16.

"The Fratricide: The Canaanite Civilization. Genesis IV." *The Biblical World* 3 (April 1894):264–74.

"A General Statement." *The Hebrew Student* 1 (May 1882):10.

"The Hebrew Stories of the Deluge. Genesis VI–IX." *The Biblical World* 4 (July 1894):20–31.

"The Human Element in the Early Stories of Genesis." *The Biblical World* 4 (October 1894):266–78.

"The Jews in Babylon." *The Biblical World* 14 (August 1899): 104–11.

"The Modern Spirit and the New Evangelism." *The Biblical World* 18 (December 1901):403–9.

"The Necessity of Biblical Training for Lay Workers." *The Biblical World* 16 (December 1900):403–6.

"The New Apologetic—A Forecast." *The Biblical World* 19 (June 1902):403–9.

"Notes and Opinions: Should the Bible be Taught as Literature in our Public Schools?" *The Biblical World* 20 (October 1902):303–5.

"Outline Topics in the History of Old Testament Prophecy: Study II." *The Biblical World* 7 (February 1896):120–29.

"Outline Topics in the History of Old Testament Prophecy: Study III." *The Biblical World* 7 (March 1896):199–206.

"Paradise and the First Sin: Genesis III." *The Biblical World* 3 (March 1894):176–88.

"The Parting of the Ways." *The Biblical World* 20 (July 1902):3–8.

"A Plan of Bible Study for Sunday Schools." *The Old and New Testament Student* 11 (October 1890):198–206.

"Popular Bible Study: Its Significance and Its Lessons." *The Biblical World* 18 (September 1901):163–66.

*The President's Report, July 1892–July 1902*. Chicago: University of Chicago Press, 1903.

"The Prophetic Element in the Old Testament as Related to Christianity." Unpublished lecture, Personal Papers of William Rainey Harper, Department of Special Collections, University of Chicago, Box 16, Folder 9.

"The Rational and the Rationalistic Higher Criticism." *Chautauqua Assembly Herald* 17 (August 4, 1892):2–3, 6–7.

"The Reality and the Simplicity of Jesus." *The Biblical World* 16 (August 1900):83–86.

*Religion and the Higher Life*. Chicago: University of Chicago Press, 1904.

"Religious Education in the Home." *The Biblical World* 21 (January 1903):3–6.

"Report of the Principal of Schools of the American Institute of Hebrew." *The Old Testament Student* 6 (February 1887): 178–87.

"Report of the Principal of Schools of the American Institute of Hebrew (1888)." *The Old Testament Student* 8 (February 1889):224–28.

"The Return of the Jews from Exile." *The Biblical World* 14 (September 1899):157–63.

"Some General Considerations Relating to Genesis I-XI." *The Biblical World* 4 (September 1894):184–201.

"The Sons of God and the Daughters of Men. Genesis VI." *The Biblical World* 3 (June 1894):440–48.

"The Study of the Bible by College-Students." *The Old Testament Student* 6 (March 1887):196–202.

"A Symposium: Shall the Analyzed Pentateuch Be Published in The Old Testament Student?" *The Old Testament Student* 7 (June 1888):312–19.

"Teacher Training." *The Biblical World* 24 (October 1904): 243–47.

"The Teaching Ministry." *The Biblical World* 15 (March 1900): 164–68.

"A Theory of the Divine and Human Elements in Genesis I-XI." *The Biblical World* 4 (December 1894):407–20.

*The Trend in Higher Education in America.* Chicago: University of Chicago Press, 1905.

"The University and Religious Education." *The Biblical World* 24 (November 1904):323–29.

*The University and Democracy.* Foreword by Morris Philipson. Chicago: University of Chicago Press, 1970.

"The Use of Common Sense in Interpretation." *The Old Testament Student* 5 (October 1885):87–90.

"Wellhausen's History of Israel." *The Old Testament Student* 5 (March 1886):318–19.

"Work and Workers." *The Biblical World* 11 (March 1898):210–214.

"Work and Workers." *The Biblical World* 13 (May 1899):351–54.

"The Work of Isaiah." *The Biblical World* 10 (July 1897):48–57.

"Yale Rationalism." *The Old and New Testament Student* 9 (July 1889):52–54.

Harper, William Rainey, Ballantine, W.G., Beecher, Willis J., and Burroughs, C.S. "Inductive Bible Studies." *The Old Testament Student* 7 (September 1887):21–33.

Harper, William Rainey and Goodspeed, George S. "The Gospel of John." Study I. *The Old and New Testament Student* 12 (January 1891):43–52.

### SECONDARY WORKS

Adams, James Luther. "The Voluntary Principle in the Forming of American Religion." *The Religion of the Republic.* Edited by Elwyn A. Smith. Philadelphia: Fortress Press, 1971. Pp. 217–46.

Ahlstrom, Sydney E. *A Religious History of the American People.* 2 vols. Garden City, N.Y.: Image Books, 1975.

Arnold, Charles Harvey. *Near the Edge of Battle: A Short History of the Divinity School and the "Chicago School of Theology." 1866–1966.* Chicago: The Divinity School Association, 1966.

Beck, Kenneth Nathaniel. "The American Institute of Sacred Literature: A Historical Analysis of An Adult Education Institution." Ph.D. dissertation, University of Chicago, 1968.

Bedell, George C., Sandon, Lee, Jr., and Wellborn, Charles T. *Religion in America.* New York: Macmillan Publishing Co., Inc., 1975.

Beecher, Henry Ward. "The Battle Set in Array." *God's New Israel: Religious*

AJSL "APRIL 1906"

*Interpretations of American Destiny.* Edited by Conrad Cherry. Englewood Cliffs, N.J.: Prentice-Hall, Inc. 1971. Pp. 162–176.

Beecher, W.T. "Sunday School Lessons for the Third Quarter, 1885." *The Old Testament Student* 4 (June 1885):445–54.

Bellah, Robert N. "Civil Religion in America." *Beyond Belief: Essays on Religion in a Post-Traditional World.* New York: Harper & Row, Publishers, 1970. Pp. 168–89.

Berger, Peter, Berger, Brigitte and Kellner, Hansfried. *The Homeless Mind: Modernization and Consciousness.* New York: Vintage Books, 1974.

Blake, Lincoln C. "The Concept and Development of Science at The University of Chicago 1890–1905." Ph.D. dissertation, University of Chicago, 1966.

Bledstein, Burton J. *The Culture of Professionalism: The Middle Class and the Development of Higher Education in America.* New York: W.W. Norton & Company, Inc., 1976.

Boorstin, Daniel J. *The Republic of Technology: Reflections on Our Future Community.* New York: Harper & Row, Publishers, 1978.

Brown, Ira V. "The Higher Criticism Comes to America, 1880–1900." *Journal of the Presbyterian Historical Society* 38 (December 1960):193–212.

Brown, Jerry Wayne. *The Rise of Biblical Criticism in America 1800–1870: The New England Scholars.* Middletown, Conn.: Wesleyan University Press, 1969.

Carter, Paul A. *The Spiritual Crisis of the Gilded Age.* DeKalb, Ill.: Northern Illinois University Press, 1971.

"Chautauqua Seventeenth Season (1890) Preliminary Announcement." *Chautauqua University and Chautauqua College of Liberal Arts: Circulars, Announcements, Specimen Lesson Sheets, Specimen Syllabuses, Letter Heads.* Vol. 1. 1884–1892. Chautauqua Archives, p. 47.

"Chautauqua Seventeenth Season (1890) Preliminary Announcement No. 2." *Chautauqua University and Chautauqua College of Liberal Arts: Circulars, Announcements, Specimen Lesson Sheets, Specimen Syllabuses, Letter Heads.* Vol. 1. 1884–1892. Chautauqua Archives, p. 64.

Clebsch, William A. *American Religious Thought: A History.* Chicago: University of Chicago Press, 1973.

*The Cosmopolitan World Atlas.* Chicago: Rand McNally & Co., 1978.

Crandall, C. Eugene. "The American Institute of Sacred Literature." *The Biblical World* 1 (January 1893): 36–39.

Cremin, Lawrence A. *Traditions of American Education.* New York: Basic Books, Inc., 1977.

Cuddihy, John Murray. *The Ordeal of Civility: Freud, Marx, Levi-Strauss and the Jewish Struggle with Modernity.* New York: Dell Publishing Company, 1974.

Curti, Merle. *The Social Ideas of American Educators.* Totowa, N.J.: Littlefield, Adams & Co., 1978.

Darwin, Charles. *The Autobiography.* Edited by Nora Barlow. London: Collins, 1958.

Delitzsch, Franz. "The New Criticism." *The Hebrew Student* 1 (May 1882):6–7.

Dewey, John. *A Common Faith.* New Haven: Yale University Press, 1934.

Diehl, Carl. *Americans and German Scholarship, 1770–1870.* New Haven: Yale University Press, 1978.

Dreyvesteyn, Kent. "The World's Parliament of Religions." Ph.D. dissertation, University of Chicago, 1976.

"Dr. Harper Banqueted." *Chautauqua Assembly Herald,* 20, no.4 (July 25, 1891):4.

DuBois, W.B. Burghardt. *The Souls of Black Folk.* Greenwich, Conn.: Fawcett Publications, Inc., 1961.

Engle, Gale W. "William Rainey Harper's Conceptions of the Structuring of the

Functions Performed by Educational Institutions." Ph.D. dissertation, Stanford University, 1954.

Erikson, Erik H. *Identity, Youth and Crisis*. New York: W.W. Norton & Company, Inc. 1968.

Farley, Edward. *Theologia: The Fragmentation and Unity of Theological Education*. Philadelphia: Fortress Press, 1983.

Faunce, W.H.P. "Expository Preaching, I." *The Biblical World* 11 (February 1898):81–90.

Funk, Robert. "The Watershed of the American Biblical Tradition: The Chicago School, First Phase, 1892–1920." Journal of Biblical Literature 95 (March 1976):4–22.

Gates, Frederick T. *Chapters of My Life*. New York: Free Press, 1977.

Gaustad, Edwin Scott. *Historical Atlas of Religion in America*. Rev. ed. New York: Harper & Row, Publishers, 1976.

Goodspeed, Thomas Wakefield. *A History of The University of Chicago: The First Quarter Century*. Chicago: University of Chicago Press, 1966.

————. *William Rainey Harper: First President of The University of Chicago*. Chicago: University of Chicago Press, 1928.

Gould, Joseph E. *The Chautauqua Movement: An Episode in the Continuing American Revolution*. Fredonia, N.Y.: State University of New York, 1961.

Hahn, Herbert F. *The Old Testament in Modern Research*. Expanded edition. Philadelphia: Fortress Press, 1966.

Handlin, Oscar and Handlin, Mary. *The Wealth of the American People*. New York: McGraw-Hill Book Company, 1975.

Handy, Robert T. *A Christian America: Protestant Hopes and Historical Realities*. New York: Oxford University Press, 1971.

Haskell, Thomas L. *The Emergence of Professional Social Science: The American Social Science Association and the Nineteenth-Century Crisis of Authority*. Urbana: University of Illinois Press, 1977.

Hayes, John H. "Wellhausen as a Historian of Israel." *Semeia* 25 (1982):37–60.

Herberg, Will. *Protestant—Catholic—Jew: An Essay in American Religious Sociology*. Garden City, N.Y. Anchor Books, 1960.

Herbst, Jurgen. *The German Historical School in American Scholarship: A Study in the Transfer of Culture*. Port Washington, N.Y.: Kennikat Press, 1965.

Herrick, Robert. *Chimes*. New York: The Macmillan Company, 1926.

Higham, John. "The Matrix of Specialization." *The Organization of Knowledge in Modern America*. Edited by Alexandra Oleson and John Voss. Baltimore: Johns Hopkins University, 1979. Pp. 3–18.

Hoffman, Lars. "William Rainey Harper and the Chicago Fellowship." Ph.D. dissertation, University of Iowa, 1978.

Hofstadter, Richard. *The Age of Reform*. New York: Vintage Books, 1955.

————. *Social Darwinism in American Thought*. Boston: Beacon Press, 1955.

Horowitz, Helen Lefkowitz. *Culture and the City: Cultural Philanthropy in Chicago from the 1880s to 1917*. Lexington: University Press of Kentucky, 1976.

Hudson, Winthrop S. *Religion in America*. 3d ed. New York: Charles Scribner's Sons, 1981.

Hurlbut, Jesse Lyman. *The Story of Chautauqua*. New York: G.P. Putnam's Sons, 1921.

Hutchinson, William R. *The Modernist Impulse in American Protestantism*. Cambridge: Harvard University Press, 1976.

Hynes, William J. *Shirley Jackson Case and the Chicago School: The Socio-Historical Method*. Chico, California: Scholars Press, 1981.

James, William. *The Varieties of Religious Experience: A Study in Human Nature.* New York: The New American Library of World Literature, 1958.

———. "The Will to Believe." *Pragmatism and Other Essays.* Introduced by Joseph L. Blau. New York: Washington Square Press, 1963. Pp. 193–213.

Jencks, Christopher and Riesman, David. *The Academic Revolution.* Chicago: University of Chicago Press, 1968.

Kansfield, Norman J. "Study the Most Approved Authors: The Role of the Seminary Library in Nineteenth-Century American Protestant Ministerial Education." Ph.D. dissertation, University of Chicago, 1981.

Kitagawa, Joseph M. "The History of Religions in America." *The History of Religions: Essays in Methodology.* Edited by Mircea Eliade and Joseph M. Kitagawa. Chicago: University of Chicago Press, 1959. Pp. 1–30.

Knight, Douglas A. "Wellhausen and the Interpretation of Israel's Literature." *Semeia* 25 (1982):21–36.

Kniker, Charles R. "New Attitudes and New Curricula: The Changing Role of the Bible in Protestant Education, 1880–1920." *The Bible in American Education: From Source Book to Textbook.* Edited by David L. Barr and Nicholas Piediscalzi. Philadelphia: Fortress Press, 1982. Pp. 121–42.

Malone, Dumas, ed. *Dictionary of American Biography.* New York: Charles Scribner's Sons, 1936.

Mann, Arthur. *La Guardia: A Fighter Against His Times, 1882–1933.* Chicago: University of Chicago Press, 1969.

Marty, Martin E. *Righteous Empire: The Protestant Experience in America.* New York: The Dial Press, 1970.

Mathews, Shailer. *New Faith for Old: An Autobiography.* New York: The Macmillan Company, 1936.

Mattingly, Paul H. *The Classless Profession: American Schoolmen in the Nineteenth Century.* New York: New York University Press, 1975.

May, Henry F. *The Enlightenment in America.* New York: Oxford University Press, 1976.

Mayer, Milton. *Young Man in a Hurry: The Story of William Rainey Harper, First President of The University of Chicago.* Chicago: University of Chicago Alumni Association, 1957.

McLoughlin, William G. *Revivals, Awakenings, and Reform.* Chicago: University of Chicago Press, 1978.

Mead, Sidney E. *The Lively Experiment: The Shaping of Christianity in America.* New York: Harper & Row, Publishers, 1963.

———. *The Nation With the Soul of a Church.* New York: Harper & Row Publishers, 1975.

Miller, Patrick E., Jr. "Wellhausen and The History of Israel's Religion." *Semeia* 25 (1982):61–74.

Mills, C. Wright. *Sociology and Pragmatism: The Higher Learning in America.* New York: Oxford University Press, 1966.

Morrison, Theodore. *Chautauqua: A Center for Education, Religion, and the Arts in America.* Chicago: University of Chicago Press, 1974.

Mueller-Vollmer, Kurt. "Introduction: Language, Mind, and Artifact: An Outline of Hermeneutic Theory Since the Enlightenment." *Texts of the German Tradition from the Enlightenment to the Present.* New York: Continuum, 1985. Pp. 1–53.

Niebuhr, H. Richard. *Christ and Culture.* New York: Harper & Row, Publishers, 1951.

———. *The Kingdom of God in America.* New York: Harper Torchbooks, 1959.

K. S. LATOURETTE

Olbricht, Thomas H. "Intellectual Ferment and Instruction in the Scriptures: The Bible in Higher Education." *The Bible in American Education: From Source Book to Textbook.* Edited by David L. Barr and Nicholas Piediscalzi. Philadelphia: Fortress Press, 1982. Pp. 97–120.

Poland, Lynn M. *Literary Criticism and Biblical Hermeneutics: A Critique of Formalist Approaches.* Chico, California: Scholars Press, 1985.

Porter, Lorle Ann and Wilson, Galen R. *A Sesquicentennial History, 1828–1928: New Concord and Norwich, Bloomfield, Rix Mills, Stations on the National Road.* Muskingum, Ohio: Muskingum College Archives, 1978.

Quandt, Jean B. *From the Small Town to the Great Community: The Social Thought of Progressive Intellectuals.* New Brunswick, N.J.: Rutgers University Press, 1970.

Ricoeur, Paul. *Essays on Biblical Interpretation.* Edited by Lewis S. Mudge. Philadelphia: Fortress Press, 1980.

Ricoeur, Paul. *Freud and Philosophy: An Essay on Interpretation.* Translated by Denis Savage. New Haven: Yale University Press, 1970.

Rogers, Max Gray. "Charles Augustus Briggs: Heresy at Union." *American Religious Heretics. Formal and Informal Trials.* Edited by George H. Shriver. Nashville: Abingdon Press, 1966. Pp. 85–147.

Rosenthal, Robert, ed. *One in Spirit.* Chicago: University of Chicago, 1973.

Rudolph, Frederick. *The American College and University.* New York: Vintage Books, 1962.

Schlesinger, Arthur Meyer, Sr. *A Critical Period in American Religion 1875–1900.* Philadelphia: Fortress Press, 1967.

——. *The Rise of the City, 1878–98.* New York: New Viewpoints, 1975.

Schmidt, Stephen A. *A History of the Religious Education Association.* Birmingham: Religious Publication Press, 1982.

Sharpe, Dores Robinson. *Walter Rauschenbusch.* New York: The Macmillan Company, 1942.

Shils, Edward. "The Order of Learning in the United States: The Ascendancy of the University." *The Organization of Knowledge in Modern America, 1860–1920.* Edited by Alexandra Oleson and John Voss. Baltimore: Johns Hopkins University, 1979. Pp. 19–47.

Sinclair, Upton. *The Goose-Step: A Study of American Education.* Rev. ed. Pasadena: Upton Sinclair, 1923.

Smend, Rudolph. "Julius Wellhausen and His *Prolegomena to the History of Israel.*" *Semeia* 25 (1982):1–20.

Stern, Rabbi I. "Beams From the Talmud." *The Hebrew Student* 1 (April 1882):14.

Storr, Richard J. *Harper's University: The Beginnings.* Chicago: University of Chicago Press, 1966.

Tracy, David. *The Analogical Imagination: Christian Theology and the Culture of Pluralism.* New York: Crossroad Press, 1981.

Turner, Frederick Jackson. "The Significance of the Frontier in American History." *The Frontier in American History.* New York: Holt, Rinehart and Winston, 1920. Pp. 1–38.

Turner, Victor and Turner, Edith. *Image and Pilgrimage in Christian Culture.* New York: Columbia University Press, 1978.

Turner, Victor. *The Ritual Process: Structure and Anti-Structure.* Ithaca: Cornell Paperbacks, 1969.

*The University of Chicago Official Bulletins.* The Department of Special Collections, The Joseph L. Regenstein Library, The University of Chicago, 1891–1892.

Veblen, Thorstein. *The Higher Learning in America: A Memorandum on the*

*Conduct of Universities by Business Men.* Introduction by Louis M. Hacker. New York: Sagamore Press, 1957.

Veysey, Laurence R. *The Emergence of the American University.* Chicago: University of Chicago Press, 1965.

Vincent, John H. "Chautauqua: A Popular University." *Chautauqua University and Chautauqua College of Liberal Arts: Circulars, Announcements, Specimen Syllabuses, Letter Heads.* Volume I. 1884–1892. Chautauqua Archives, p. 733.

———. *The Chautauqua Movement.* Boston: Chautauqua Press, 1886.

———. "The Chautauqua University." *Chautauqua University and Chautauqua College of Liberal Arts: Circulars, Announcements, Specimen Lesson Sheets, Specimen Syllabuses, Letter Heads.* Volume I. 1884–1892. Chautauqua Archives. p. 2.

Vincent, Leon H. *John Heyl Vincent: A Biographical Sketch.* New York: The Macmillan Company, 1925.

Wacker, Grant. "The Demise of Biblical Civilization." In *The Bible in America: Essays in Cultural History.* Edited by Nathan O. Hatch and Mark A. Noll. New York: Oxford University Press, 1982. Pp. 121–38.

Washington, Booker T. *Up From Slavery.* Introduction by Louis Lomax. New York: Dell Publishing Company, 1965.

Weber, Max. *On Charisma and Institution Building.* Edited by S.N. Eisenstadt. Chicago: University of Chicago Press, 1968.

Whitehead, Alfred North. *Religion in the Making.* New York: New American Library, 1974.

Wiebe, Robert H. *The Search for Order, 1877–1920.* New York: Hill and Wang, 1967.

Willett, Herbert Lockwood. "The Corridor of Years." Unpublished Autobiography, The Archives of *The Christian Century*, Chicago, Illinois, pp. 91–96.

———. "The International Sunday School Lessons." *The Biblical World* 14 (July 1895):58–72.

Williams, George Hunston. *Wilderness and Paradise in Christian Thought.* New York: Harper & Brothers, 1962.

P113